Nick Thorpe was born in 1970. An award-winning travel writer and journalist, he has contributed to the *Guardian, Scotsman, Sunday Times, Daily Telegraph* and BBC Radio 4, among others. He has travelled widely on assignments ranging from Russian presidential elections to the coca wars of Bolivia, for which he was shortlisted for the Martha Gellhorn Prize for Journalism in 2000. He has since won a Travelex Travel Writer's Award and the Foreign Press Association prize for Travel Story of the Year. *Eight Men and a Duck*, his first book, recounts a voyage to Easter Island by reed boat and was published by Little, Brown in 2002. He lives in Edinburgh with his wife Ali.

For more information, visit: www.nickthorpe.co.uk

Adrift in Caledonia

Boat-hitching for the Unenlightened

NICK THORPE

ABACUS

First published in Great Britain in March 2006 by Little, Brown
This paperback edition published in 2007 by Abacus

Typeset in Centaur by M Rules
Printed and bound in Great Britain by
Clays Ltd, St Ives plc

Abacus
An imprint of
Little, Brown Book Group
Brettenham House
Lancaster Place
London WC2E 7EN

A Member of the Hachette Livre Group of Companies

www.littlebrown.co.uk

In grateful memory of
Eric Thorpe and
Desmond McBride

Voyagers who knew the way

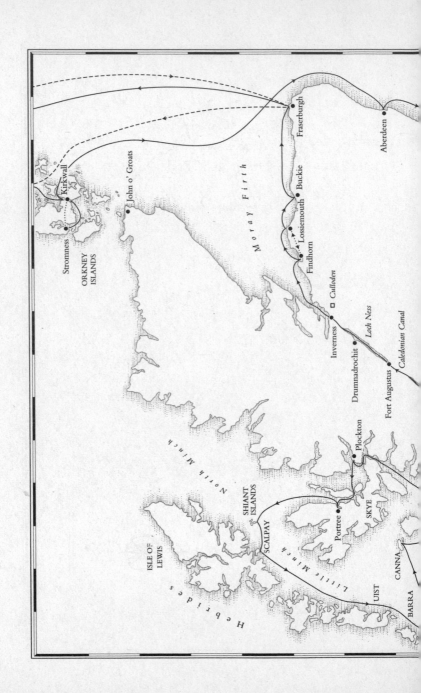

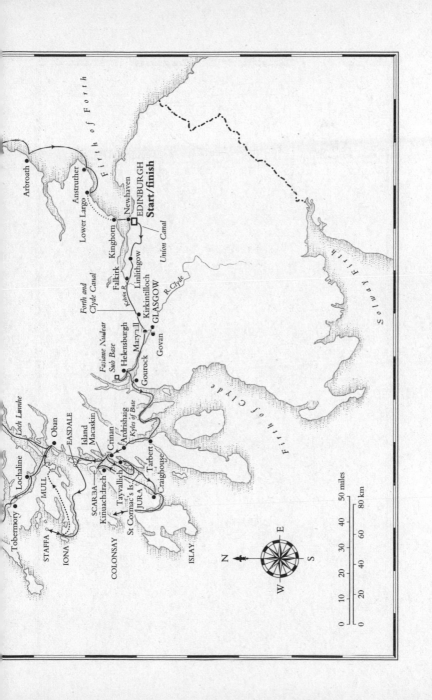

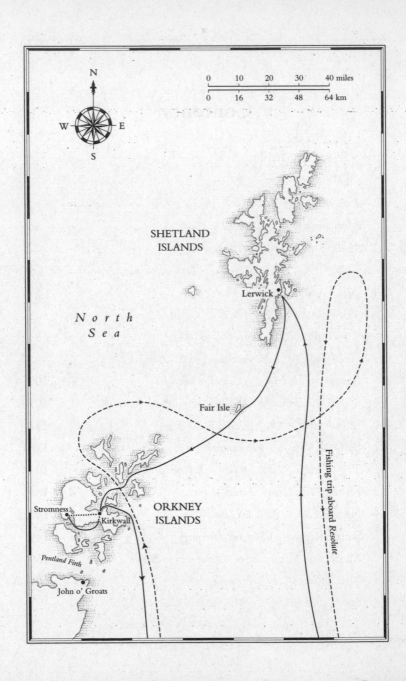

Contents

Water is sometimes sharp and sometimes strong, sometimes acid and sometimes bitter, sometimes sweet and sometimes thick or thin, sometimes it is seen bringing hurt or pestilence, sometimes health-giving, sometimes poisonous. It suffers change into as many natures as are the different places through which it passes. And as the mirror changes with the colour of its subject, so it alters with the nature of the place, becoming noisome, laxative, astringent, sulfurous, salty, incarnadined, mournful, raging, angry, red, yellow, green, black, blue, greasy, fat or slim . . .

In time and with water, everything changes.

LEONARDO DA VINCI

Everyone must believe in something. I believe I'll go canoeing.
HENRY DAVID THOREAU

Prologue

There was no doubt about it: the boat was sinking. Fat rivulets of tea-coloured canal water were creeping under the ribs of the old rowing tub, pooling silently along the hull. A footboard lifted and turned on the dark flood.

'Floating like an effing sieve!' muttered Bill Purves, kneeling up on the rowing bench to keep his kilt and shoes dry. 'There's 2 inches in here already.' Watching from the canal bank, five of us averted our eyes from his upturned tartan rump, and made polite, useless offers of assistance. The *Belle* was the first launch of the season at the Edinburgh Canal Society, and nobody could pretend things were going well.

'I've got a bit of submarine experience, if that's any help?' quipped Tony, a retired marine engineer in a flat cap. Bill ignored him and stood up precariously on the seat, his legs braced apart, wobbling slightly as he pondered the speed at which the water was creeping up below him. He seemed somehow wasted on a small rowing boat. With his Napoleonic nose and long ginger ponytail, his immaculate kilt and leather sporran, this Scottish septuagenarian would have been better suited to the poop deck of a doomed frigate, going down with bagpipes playing.

Admittedly the image was somewhat confused by his intriguing fondness for black tights, matched that day with an embroidered floral waistcoat, T-shirt and the kind of silver-buckled, square-heeled shoes normally associated with the Women's Institute. But his admirers prized such eccentricities. Bill was a *true original*, they had told me, a *real character*. More importantly for my own hidden purposes that day, he was a *fixer* – the one who knew everything there was to know about my escape route. 'He's basically *Mr Canal*,' my sources had told me. 'If he can't help you, nobody can.'

Mr Canal descended smoothly, as if in a lift, simultaneously punting himself back towards the bank with a single oar until the rising water lapped at the underside of the bench. Only then did he reach for an outstretched arm, stepping deftly ashore just as the *Belle* gave a final gurgle and came to rest on the bottom of the canal. 'We'll leave her submerged for a while to let the timbers swell,' he announced. 'Then we'll bail her and see what the damage is.'

The *Belle*, discovered half buried in a sand dune in Elie, was merely the latest in Bill's improbable flotilla of ramshackle boats. Looking at the scant inch of gunwale now visible above the surface, I couldn't help thinking there had been a good reason that she had been abandoned by her original owners. But what did I know? The Canal Society specialised in saving hopeless cases.

'Boats often do that to start with,' said Bill's wife, Sandra, from beneath a blue felt hat. 'When we first launched the *Kelvin*, she sank like a stone. And now look at her!' Out on the moorings lay an elegant round-bottomed wooden motor launch resplendent with brass fittings, a polished foredeck, bunting and a sun canopy. The *Kelvin* was the flagship of the Society, rescued from the scrap dealer for a bottle of whisky after being crushed by a fishing boat in Fisherrow harbour. Bill and his cohorts had painstakingly restored her and now ran Sunday afternoon pleasure trips in her, using an original Kelvin engine discovered in a cellar in Kuwait.

'Scandalous what people throw away,' said Bill cheerfully, swinging open the door to the white clapperboard boathouse set back on the bank. 'Watch your back, Derek, or you'll get a pole up your erse.'

The boathouse was the heart of Bill's shambolic empire. I had wondered for years what lay inside this mysterious building, as I crossed the road bridge above it on the way to the bus stop. Today, having paid my fiver as a fledgling member of the Society, I was ushered through a thicket of orphaned oars into a glorious guddle of nautical bric-a-brac. Picking my way past buckets of greased engine components, and an old display rail hung with lopsided lifejackets, I could make out the words 'bailers and scrubbers' chalked on a cupboard. Further inside, wedged between a shopping trolley full of traffic cones and a ship's funnel being used as a waste bin, an elderly lady made tea on a Calor Gas stove, her white hair flaring from a capacious cagoule. Above her, behind her, around her, were boats. Wooden boats, fibreglass boats, inflatable boats, boats with holes in them, hanging from the ceiling, rescued from the scrapheap, propped against the wall, one of them with a Saltire wedged in its bilges.

'Bill, I was wondering if I could pick your brains about something . . .' I had paid my membership dues, helped launch a boat and been ushered into the inner sanctum. Now it was time to come clean.

Bill stopped in his tracks and turned around. 'Pick my brains?' he repeated. 'My wife tells me the only brains I have are in my sporran along with my money and my ecstasy — and I'm not talking about drugs. So good luck to you!'

He cackled like a Dickensian degenerate, while I laughed nervously. Sandra rolled her eyes.

'Just kiddin', young man.' He slapped me on the shoulder. 'So whit is it exactly ye want to know?'

'The thing is, I've got this plan – a sort of boat trip. I'm hoping to leave from here.'

He squinted at me. 'Sounds interestin'. Where are ye goin'?' I was aware of the silence of the other Canal Society members behind me.

'Quite a long way, potentially. Hopefully right round Scotland.'

Bill's eyebrows shot up.

'That'll take you a wee while. What kind of a boat d'ye have?'

'Well that's the problem,' I said. 'I don't.'

The canal was an enchanted, elusive place. It began in a run-down goods yard behind a brewery, crept unobtrusively along the backs of tenements, a parallel universe with hidden portals.

Over the years I had grown to treasure its skewed timeframe, a slowed-down world which winked coyly through the trees every time I looked out of my kitchen window. I would head for the towpath whenever I needed to clear my head, following its ribbon of mirrored sky out of the city, watching the houses retreating politely up the lengthening gardens of suburbia, past wide playing fields and out into a lush corridor of hawthorn bushes, dark pools clotted with scribbles of weed.

It was perfectly flat, laid along the 73-metre contour line at the very end of Britain's canal-building boom, its impressive embankments and aqueducts demonstrating exactly how railway engineers would soon make it obsolete. It was hard to believe it had carried 127,000 passengers a year in its brief nineteenth-century heyday. Nowadays you could walk the whole 2-mile stretch without meeting more than a family of moorhens, before you hit the abrupt wall of a concrete culvert where some myopic sixties planner had dumped a housing estate on top of it. I preferred to turn round before that, walking back towards the distant mirage of Edinburgh Castle as if recrossing a vast drawbridge. In time you tended to forget that the drawbridge had once led somewhere.

Then, one Sunday afternoon, everything changed. I was strolling along the towpath with my wife, Ali, when, rounding the last corner for the first time in years, we discovered the wall had gone. Instead, the water shimmered into the distance under a newly built bridge. I stopped in mid-sentence and stared. The sensation was not unlike opening a familiar cupboard and finding a corridor or a valley or a pine forest. We wandered a little way under the bridge, then turned back like sheep nervous of a hole in a familiar fence. Until that moment, the canal had been primarily a *place*, a long thin sliver of solitude topped and tailed by concrete. Suddenly it was a *route*, a trajectory, going somewhere. But where? Just how far could one go?

There had been talk for years of a scheme to rejoin the old canals. Like most Edinburgh folk, I had adopted a believe-it-when-I-see-it approach, losing touch altogether when I went off to South America in 1999. Now, web-surfing to catch up, I learned that 'the Millennium Link' had been finalised in my absence. The chopped-up pieces of canal had been joined back together, a broken link restored across the slender waist of Scotland. Poring over my map, I experienced a sort of horizontal vertigo. Starting from my own doorstep, it was now possible to climb in a boat, travel west to Falkirk where the Union Canal joined the larger Forth and Clyde Canal, and continue all the way to Glasgow and the Clyde. But why stop there? The beginnings of an adventure shimmered like a mirage. Kneeling over a map on the floor of the lounge, I traced a possible route along the Clyde estuary as it widened and twisted out towards open sea. Once out among the islands of the west coast, you could head north, through the Caledonian Canal and the Great Glen, and up into the wild seas around the Northern Isles, before looping down the east coast back to Edinburgh again – one big, leisurely, circular odyssey, possible entirely by boat for the first time in a generation. It was irresistible.

It had been nearly ten years since I had wedged my worldly possessions into the back of a Mini Metro and driven up from London to begin a job on Edinburgh's evening newspaper. In that time I had met and married Ali and made some good friends. But none of it could quite disguise a lingering restlessness, an existential itch to understand what it all *meant*. Spirituality is a slippery word these days, embracing everything from monasticism to wind chimes, but I've never been able to resist a little tinkering under the bonnet of the soul. No longer convinced by the religious absolutes of my childhood, I nevertheless hankered after something to replace them, a workable credo with which to engage life.

In the meantime, I had the sense that I was not so much immersed in my adoptive country as floating on the surface of it. Relations weren't always easy between the Scots and their southern neighbours. 'Your country consists of two things, stone and water,' sniffed Dr Johnson, after being storm bound, rained on and thrown around in boats during his 1773 tour of the Western Isles with his almost supernaturally tolerant Scottish friend James Boswell. Indeed, water of one sort or another was still often the commonest thing which sprang to mind for those south of the border. Visitors seemed to imagine a sodden outpost lashed by horizontal rain – though this was mainly a rumour invented by the Scots to keep the English away.

But there was no doubt that water meant something different

up here. Scots were more familiar with the stuff. You only had to
look at a map to understand why. Nobody in this sea-scoured
nation was ever more than 45 miles from tidal waters. Many were
much closer, as the misshapen wedge of Britain tapered and frag-
mented into 6000 miles of scalloped coastline north of the
border, cross-hatched with rivers, lochs and canals. Scotland's
major cities – Edinburgh, Glasgow, Aberdeen, Dundee,
Inverness – were all ports, and her traditional industries – fishing,
oil, shipbuilding – were linked, for better or worse, to the bound-
less blue. Growing up in England, school history had taught me
that the sea was a defensive barrier, policed by the navy to ensure
that Britannia continued to rule the waves. To the explorers,
traders and emigrants of Scotland, however, it was predominantly
a connection to the world – and crucially one which didn't involve
kowtowing to Big Brother over the land border. Water was freedom and possibility.

I got my own first salty whiff of its latent potential in early
2000 when, during our travels in South America, I had pushed off
into the Pacific on a large bundle of reeds. There were eight of us
aboard the *Viracocha*, a 60-foot replica of a pre-Inca reed vessel,
which had begun slowly to sink from the moment she hit the
water. In retrospect it was not my most rational moment: our
makeshift crew included a journalist, a jewellery salesman and a
tree surgeon but conspicuously lacked a navigator as we set our
home-made sails for Easter Island, more than 2500 miles away. Yet
among our mixed motivations for pushing on with the trip –
curiosity, a couple of mid-life crises and the fact that we hadn't yet
worked out how to turn the boat round – was a desire to test a
nobler, overarching thesis. The Norwegian explorer Thor
Heyerdahl, whose 1947 *Kon-Tiki* raft expedition inspired our
voyage, had always argued that the ocean should be seen not as a

barrier between places, but as a means of connection. If modern-day amateurs on simple craft could join the dots – as we ultimately did – surely it was possible that many earlier navigators did too? This sense of possibility and connection now intrigued me afresh as I looked at the canal on my doorstep.

It was like an optical puzzle I remembered from childhood, in which a shape on a card can either be a solid candlestick or the space between two faces. Depending how you looked at it, the little strip of water outside my house could likewise be two different things. For commuters and town planners, it was there to be traversed or filled in. But if you took a quick walk down under the bridge, it magically became something else – a water route leading right round Scotland.

I wondered idly whether this quantum shift in perspective might also work on life's knottier questions: why were we here? What did I want to do when I grew up? What was the purpose of suffering? Would consumerism eventually eat itself? Would I ever truly *belong* in Scotland? Could men learn to multi task? Did God exist? And if so – *whose* God . . .? The more I thought about it, the more I suspected that a trip around the watery margins of my adopted country might change the way I saw almost anything. It would be a kind of nautical sabbatical, a time to work out exactly what I believed, consolidate how to live in the world. With growing certainty, I knew I had to do it.

There was just one, rather large, logistical problem.

'Hauld on in the bow!' yelled Bill, gunning the antiquated engine of the *Kelvin* to its chuffing maximum. 'We're gonnae do a wee experiment!' It was my second week at the Canal Society and we were on our way back to the boathouse. While carefully ignoring all the anvil-like hints I had dropped in connection with my trip,

Bill seemed to have taken it upon himself to train me as a crew member, which I took as a good sign. 'Now watch this!' He jammed the throttle back into neutral and then momentarily into reverse. The boat wallowed to a halt, and with a slow whoosh our modest bow wave overtook us, assembling itself into a broad and even hump which moved steadily westwards without us.

'That,' said Bill, 'is a major scientific phenomenon. John Scott Russell discovered it by accident and called it the wave of translation.' Bill's mind was, like his boathouse, stuffed full of intriguing and surprising artefacts. Russell, a young Scottish scientist, had been walking along the canal bank in 1834 when a horse-drawn boat stopped suddenly nearby, creating an unusually even-looking wave which the intrigued scientist had followed on horseback. The wave continued for nearly two miles 'without change of form or diminution of speed' before he lost it and gave up the chase. He had chanced on a kind of perpetual motion. Proclaiming it the happiest day of his life, he went off to build an experimental wave tank in his own garden. It would be the 1960s before fellow scientists began to take it seriously enough to discover its huge relevance to 'soliton' wave theory and modern fibre optics – but to Russell there was already something of deep significance about this 'singular and beautiful' phenomenon.

I could see why Bill was so taken with the discovery, though my own interest was a little less scientific. I loved the idea of this perpetual wave, rolling unobtrusively along at its own speed, across the country, mile after mile, without losing strength. As ours disappeared slowly round a bend in the canal, a taut band of sky crossing the dark reflection of a tree, I imagined cows near Falkirk looking up absently at its passing in a few hours' time; a man on a barge somewhere smudging his watercolour as it nudged underneath him; a dozing fisherman getting a cold, wet shock over the top of his wellies . . . but most of all I thought of my own journey and where it could take me. In the slop and hiss of that lonely wave I heard the sound of distant ocean.

Since the first shock of possibility, my plan had similarly taken on its own shape. I had told my friends, bought some maps, dredged a channel through my cluttered life. It was going to happen — and soon. It became obvious fairly early on that a boat suitable for navigating a 5-foot-deep canal would almost by definition *not* be suitable for traversing the mountainous swells of, say, the Pentland Firth. It was also obvious that six weeks aboard a reed boat had not rendered me sufficiently competent to circumnavigate Scotland's often treacherous coasts on my own, even if I wanted to, which I didn't particularly. What I had learned on the Pacific, however, was that water connected people as well as places — I felt sure I had got to know my fellow crew members much better by working alongside them, sharing the journey, than by, say, quizzing them over a pint. And if one aim of this voyage was to meet folk on their own territory, why not meet them on their own boats? I would hitchhike by water, all the way round Scotland.

Ali was gently pragmatic. 'I'd love this to work out for you,' she had said. 'But what makes you think folk are going to invite a complete stranger on to their boat just because he happens to want a lift somewhere? What's in it for them?'

She had a point. I definitely have a tendency to romanticise things. I was envisaging myself cheerily thumbing lifts from the end of rustic piers against a backdrop of Scottish mountains, for example, when I might as easily end up slitting haddock on some Russian factory boat. But I refused to be put off. The Scots are famously hospitable, and in any case I was quite happy to work for my passage, or chip in for petrol and lodging. Any vessel would do . . . rowing boat, oil tanker, fishing trawler, luxury yacht. If anyone resented my free ride, I'd willingly scrub the decks, pump the bilges or (more optimistically) shake the cocktails. I might even try captaining my own rented vessel from time to time. It was going to be about connections rather than barriers, about friendship rather than fear. I would overcome my English reticence by appealing to the best nature of my fellow countrymen. Really, how difficult could it be?

Looking around my local stretch of canal, I began to weigh up my options for that all-important first ride. It didn't take me long to rule out the rowers, scything up and down like hyperactive pond skaters – I wanted to mess about in boats in the great tradition of Ratty and Mole, not tear around like Toad. More alluringly bohemian were a pair of colourful narrowboats puffing wood smoke from their tin-hatted chimneys like Romany caravans. *Zazou* was a floating bistro run by a couple of jazz lovers who could simultaneously toss a salad and a mooring line. But delightful as it would have been to set off to the amiable tootling of Louis Armstrong while tucking into a steak, Pete and his wife only ever went a mile up and down the canal. I had no more luck with the other narrowboat, whose owner, an engineer called Ian, was worried about losing his berth after his drunken bongo playing had provoked official complaints from the neighbours. There were a few kayakers too, and a local anarchist with a bright green mohican who occasionally chugged up and down in a black boat shaped like a coffin. I considered asking him for a ride, but decided the symbolism was unhelpful.

With a week to go before my intended departure date, Bill was still my best hope. I decided it was time to bite the bullet and asked him straight out if he'd take me to the Clyde. 'Not a bloody chance,' he responded. 'I'm off on holiday tomorrow – won't be back for two weeks.' He and Sandra were driving down to an English canal to spend some time on their 'Caraboat' – presumably some kind of towable hybrid – and attend a vintage car rally. I wished them a happy holiday and slunk away, seized suddenly by self-doubt.

Ali kept a tactful and supportive silence as I scoured the canal for a back-up plan. For days none presented itself. I was just beginning to wonder if I should abandon the whole fantasy when one afternoon, walking back from town along the towpath, I noticed a new boat moored on my side of the canal. It was a wee fibreglass cabin cruiser, off-white in colour, a little scratched and chipped, its bright red button-down awning mottled by green mould. A friendly black and white dog appeared in the opening. As I patted her I was startled to discover there was someone watching me from the dim interior. He wore a black bomber jacket, jeans and Docs, and held a smouldering roll-up between his finger and thumb, with its live end cupped inside his palm. His frown, framed with stubble and short brown hair, made me wonder if he was contemplating smashing my middle-class face in.

'Nice dog,' I said, nervously.

'Aye. Border collie cross.' His voice was deep but gentle. He grinned briefly and ruffled the dog's mop. 'Bought her as a pup. Best tenner I ever spent.'

Craig was new on this part of the canal, usually moored his boat further east. She was serving as his home just now, but he said he was hoping to do her up and offer trips on her one day. I saw an opening and took it. 'Well, if you need a punter for a trial run, just let me know.'

He didn't blink or change his expression, just nodded slightly. 'Where exactly do you want to go?'

'Well . . . eventually all the way round Scotland.' He watched me as I told him about my quest. I think I saw a glint of amusement in his eyes. He pondered in silence.

'I could take you as far as Linlithgow,' he said, finally. 'And my dad's got a canal boat he might lend you from there . . .'

And that was how it began. A simple, unexpected connection, like the wave thrown up by something heavier splashing to a halt. After all my fruitless pushing, something gently set in motion. I hurried home, grinning.

I

Momentum

Edinburgh to Linlithgow

It was five to nine on a morning of brittle May sunshine when I kissed Ali goodbye, shouldered my rucksack and nosed outside into the slipstream of office workers. They flowed around me, heads down, following the pavement, shutting out the world as if this were just another ordinary day. I was momentarily tempted to nip in and buy a paper from Naz the newsagent, just so that I could say breezily: 'Right, that's me off to circumnavigate Scotland for a few months, then . . .' Instead, I hugged the secret and flowed with the current of commuters as far as the bridge, then eddied off down the embankment. Craig was waiting with the engine running, sucking on a roll-up and cradling a mug of tea.

'All ready?' he said, staring at my luggage.

It had been hard to know what to pack for such an unpredictable trip. All I knew for sure was that I would encounter a lot of water – some of it fresh, much of it salty. This hadn't given the outdoor pursuits shop assistant much to go on, but he'd done his best. My rucksack, equipped with an optional dry bag that could be rolled down over it, was my landlubber's approximation of a survival kit. Inside, in addition to dry clothes, a fleece jacket, a sleeping bag and miscellaneous books and bits of gadgetry, I had a complete set of all-weather waterproofs, deck shoes, spectacle retainers, sea-sickness tablets, a self-inflating life jacket and a safety harness. Faced with the Union Canal's 5 feet of placid water, this looked a bit over the top.

'Shall I stow this below?' I asked, trying to cover my embarrassment. Stow was one of those nautical words you had to use to persuade people you knew all about boats.

'Aye, whatever,' said Craig, untying the rear mooring line. Climbing aboard behind me, he pushed off gently and then eased himself into his captain's chair, below which Kaos the dog lay with her ears inquisitively cocked. Gunning his engine, the captain pushed up on the throttle, nudged the little ship's wheel and inserted a tape into the stereo. 'The epic journey begins,' he said with a deadpan expression, as a familiar tune whistled from the speakers. It was the theme from *The Good, the Bad and the Ugly*.

Behind us a familiar scene was drifting away: the blank profiles of lorry drivers queuing over the bridge, the canal barges in the shadow of overhanging trees, the *Kelvin*, the boathouse . . . and the *Belle*, now miraculously floating on a new mooring. Ahead of us lay a streak of rippled sky, a water road leading towards the smell of the sea and the scattered islands of the west coast. Something in me loosened and dropped away.

'So what's the master plan, then?' said Craig, presently.

The master plan had not progressed much since I first spread my map on the lounge floor; it was still a rather crumpled clockwise circle around Scotland, cutting first across the central belt to the Clyde estuary, then through the Western Isles and up the Caledonian Canal to Inverness. After continuing somehow to the Northern Isles of Orkney and Shetland, I would return to

Edinburgh via Aberdeen and the east coast. I had left the itinerary as open ended as possible with three exceptions: the first was a working ten-day passage around the Outer Hebrides as a crew member of a square-rigged sailing ship.

But that was still a month away. More imminently, I had heard from a friend that a group of men were re-enacting the sixth century voyage of St Columba from Ireland to the isle of Iona in a canvas curragh. This seemed too irresistibly bizarre to ignore. After one inquisitive e-mail, the organiser agreed to let me join the last part of the voyage if (a) I could get to the Kintyre peninsula within three weeks, and (b) I was willing to dress in a monk's robe and sing hymns while rowing. *Python*esque as this sounded, I drew a certain inspiration from the original Celtic seafaring friars. Known as *peregrini*, they had a spiritual practice of pushing themselves out on to the waves on skin boats with no particular destination in mind, believing that their Creator would guide them safely to their 'place of resurrection' – a sort of nautical version of going off travelling to 'find yourself'. I hoped it might work for me.

But even more alluring than either a tall ship or a curragh – and the reason I had been so keen not to delay my departure any longer – was the prospect of a rare opportunity to revisit a tiny west coast island with family friends. This was a childhood holiday haunt, and the very thought of it opened chasms of nostalgic longing in me for a time when I knew what I believed. I didn't tell Craig all of this – just that if I was going to meet my friends before they went home, I needed to reach Glasgow and get through the Clyde estuary in slightly less than two weeks. Even here, the specifics were sketchy. Craig would get me to Linlithgow, and his father's narrowboat to Falkirk – but beyond that I had no idea how I would do it.

'If you fancy a cuppa, help yourself,' said Craig now, watching the water ahead. 'I'll have one too if you're on your feet.' It was a sparse but homely little craft, and I embraced my role as tea boy enthusiastically. Ducking through a low doorway, I found myself in a cabin illuminated by curtainless windows. I lit the hob and looked around as the kettle sputtered and lisped its way towards boiling. Behind me was a little blackened wood-burning stove, its chimney disappearing through a rough-cut hole in the ceiling. Towards the front of the cabin stood a large honey-coloured wooden trunk. It was centred symmetrically below a tasselled blue lampshade, giving it a shrine-like quality. Craig's name was stencilled on to the polished lid, but there was no hint of what might be inside.

The kettle whistled and I searched around for mugs. I found them dangling from a wall-mounted set of stag's antlers, which also served as a coat hook, tool rack, toilet roll dispenser and display unit for what looked like an antique sword, complete with ornamental sheath. 'German cavalry,' said Craig, craning his neck briefly through the doorway. 'I sleep with it by my bed, in case anyone tries to come on board. But mainly it's for clearing nettles from the bank.' Craig's sleeping quarters were in a smaller aft cabin, barricaded by a small blue wardrobe. It occurred to me that I knew almost nothing about my enigmatic host. Not even the name of his boat.

'*Armorica*,' said Craig, rotating in his captain's chair. 'Dunno what it means, but I think it's a very pretty name. And it's bad luck to change a boat's name.' I thought it a strange, resonant hybrid, full of New World yearning: *America* crossed with *amor*, perhaps – or was it *armour*?*

Outside the engine noise was reverberating oddly. I poked my head through the awning and found we had reached the narrow

*Later I discovered it was an ancient name for Brittany.

channel of the Slateford aqueduct, soaring across the city suburbs. From far below came the electronic beeping of a reversing forklift truck in a goods yard, a pinprick in the soothing static of passing traffic. Both noises faded as the bushes surrounded us on the far side of the aqueduct, like clouds enveloping an ascending airliner. I settled back for a five-hour flight.

We were approaching the limits of the old, severed canal, heading towards Wester Hailes, a peripheral housing estate somewhat ominously heralded by carved wooden statues of Burke and Hare. Edinburgh's most famous serial killers had started their career as canal-digging navvies before branching into supplying corpses for medical dissection. I kept a wary eye on all possible places of ambush as we wound our way into a canyon of high-rise flats adorned with CCTV cameras. Tempting as it must have been to throw stones at Chardonnay-quaffing boatpeople drifting by, I suspected any kid with half a brain would probably have thought twice about targeting Craig. With a bomber jacket and stump of cigarette protruding from his lips, he had the same expression of grim imperturbability Clint Eastwood might have worn if Dirty Harry had for some reason chosen to travel in a little red and white cabin cruiser.

Today we encountered no trouble at all — just a couple of young mums pushing prams along the towpath, both of whom returned my wave with a giggle, and a vagrant who limped into view like a biblical prophet, his eyes scorched pinholes. His clothes were shiny with dirt, and he carried two plastic bags like sacks of ballast, as if the next gust of wind might blow him away. Craig stared at him for a long time. I got the impression he recognised him.

'I know most of the junkies and down and outs of Edinburgh,' he confirmed after a long pause. 'I spent some time on the streets myself, selling the *Big Issue*. These guys who wander about picking up dog ends – they've got nothing to look forward to, no hope . . . once people get to that place, do they ever pick themselves up again?' He gazed at the water. 'If my dad hadn't come up with the money for this boat I don't know where I'd be.'

Surprising as I found this revelation, Craig's gruff working-class exterior was equally misleading. He had attended one of Edinburgh's most prestigious private schools, I gathered, even gleaned his musical skills from the Queen's Trumpeter. He had gone briefly to art college, before taking a boat-building course on the Suffolk coast. It hadn't really worked out. Steady employment had been scarce, and he'd drifted in and out of jobs, living on a fishing boat for a while, then travelling abroad as a crewman. Coming home to Scotland only seemed to compound a growing sense of failure. He found himself sleeping on friends' floors, then in a lock-up garage, before his stint on the streets. For reasons he couldn't quite nail down, the leaky vessel of his life was slowly sinking.

Armorica was where his luck had changed. 'This boat is what I've been holding out for,' he said, flipping his cigarette stub out through the awning. He had found her mouldering in an English boatyard, picked her up for a good price with a loan from his dad, brought her north on the back of a lorry. 'She's my home, but once I've done her up, she's also going to earn me a living. She's the missing link.'

We were almost through Wester Hailes now, the canyon of high-rises widening towards a horizon of outrageous yellow. Fields of rapeseed swelled and undulated across the gentle West Lothian landscape, sending back the sweet, rank smell of bitch-on-heat. A swan sat on a nest of latticed twigs, with three or four freshly hatched grey cygnets huddled around her, the dried yolk still on their heads. Further on, two adult birds were copulating in a magnificent ballet of flapping, splashing wings.

'Beautiful creatures,' breathed Craig, grinning for the first time in a while. 'Unlike ducks. When ducks do it, there are about five males and they hold the female under water. It's not a pretty sight, believe me.'

On the right-hand bank a woman in a tracksuit steadily overtook us, doing one of those clenched American power-walking exercises which give the impression of someone who has recently sat down on something pointed. Crossing the Scott Russell aqueduct only emphasised our slowness, as we looked down on eight lanes of speeding traffic. These cars would cover the 40 miles to Glasgow in less than an hour. Right now I'd be happy to do it in less than a week.

Soon the traffic was a distant sigh, occasionally punctuated by the rattle of the Glasgow to Edinburgh train as it sliced through the fields below us. I was beginning to enjoy this pace. I peered south to the Pentland Hills, mottled with cloud shadows, then watched a plane rise effortlessly against the silver streak of the Firth of Forth. Kaos the dog trotted happily along the towpath at our side, her tail forming a perky question mark above the clumps of wild rhubarb. A milestone drifted by.

'This is the speed humans are meant to travel,' said Craig, yawning contentedly. 'Everything else goes too fast.'

The last of Britain's canals was not originally built for dawdlers. The fact that we now saw it primarily as a leisurely backwater was only because it had ultimately failed in its original purpose as a freight and passenger route, conceived for its speed and efficiency in much the same manner as a modern motorway.

The Scots had been slower than the rest of Britain to adopt the canal system, mainly because their biggest cities were already coastal or estuarine ports. But by the nineteenth century the tax on the ship-borne coal trade made it too expensive to bring coal around the coast, and local supplies were controlled by a price-fixing cartel of mine owners and carters infamous for their short measures. Most galling of all, Glasgow had pushed ahead with the opening of the Forth and Clyde Canal in 1790, which meant that Edinburgh folk were treated to the spectacle of their arch business rivals prospering on cheap fuel while east coasters shivered in their tenements, too far from the Forth end of the canal at Grangemouth to benefit. It was high time Edinburgh had its own link.

After various wrangles over routes, and the intervention of the Napoleonic Wars, Hugh Baird proposed a branch canal linking with the Forth and Clyde at Falkirk, which Thomas Telford helpfully backed as 'the most perfect inland navigation between Edinburgh and Glasgow'. Getting it through Parliament was a formality, and in March 1818 the proprietors hurled the first sod into the air to the cheering of vast crowds. The normally torturous inter-city journey by stagecoach, they boasted, would be replaced by a smooth and comfortable boat ride taking as little as nine hours.

Naturally there were those who found the whole idea of the 'Mathematical River' – so-called because of its long-distance adherence to the 73-metre contour line – an appalling example of modern vandalism. William Forbes, one of the most vociferous Nimbys, forced navvies to tunnel 696 yards under his Callender Park estate to avoid spoiling the scenery. The project consequently overran by more than four years, during which time it was common to see flaming torches lining the banks as work went on through the night. The newspapers and Jeremiahs had more or less lost interest when, in May 1822, a boat loaded with flagstones drifted into Edinburgh from Denny Quarry, and revealed almost by accident that the Union Canal – 31.5 miles long, 5 feet deep and 37 feet wide – was finally complete.

The early boat operators pandered to the romanticism of the age, naming their Dutch-style passenger launches after characters in the latest Walter Scott novels – *Di Vernon, Flora MacIvor* among them – and offering honeymoon suites on overnight voyages. But it became increasingly obvious that the whole enterprise would stand or fall on its speed. Obsolescence was already looming impolitely in the background like a drunk at a tea party. Even as the Irish navvies hacked their last few feet of tunnel, a new breed of engineer was learning exactly how such immaculate levelling techniques might be adapted for railway building. Nobody could afford to ignore the competition.

With admirable determination the operators shaved every possible minute from the journey time. One ingenious innovation was the Pop Inn, a canal-side pub with a door at each end, allowing a thirsty horse handler to down a pint as he walked through and rejoin his charge at the other exit without having to stop the boat. Even this liquid drive-through was a bit leisurely for the lighter, faster passenger boats, towed at a gallop and given suitably adrenalin-charged names like *Velocity* and *Rapid*. By 1835 they had slashed the journey between Edinburgh and Glasgow to just over seven hours, though departure times had to be staggered after complaints about collisions and injuries to passengers. Neighbours who had grown accustomed to an afternoon constitutional along the towpath were greeted with notices informing them that fast-moving horses now made it unsafe to walk there at all. Small boys in uniform galloped ahead shouting warnings, while sinister sickle-like attachments on the bow slashed the towropes of any boat careless or ponderous enough to get in the way.

None of it did any good in the long run. In the relentless

pursuit of speed, water was never going to be a match for rails. In 1865, already haemorrhaging passengers, the canal was bought by the North British Railway board itself, which downgraded it to a coal route. Before long even that function had ceased, and in 1935 it was closed to commercial traffic, progressively choked with weed and severed by road building. Canals had been overtaken by railways, just as railways would eventually be overtaken by motorways. Speed always prevailed.

I wondered if the Victorians had sensed the way things were going. Did any of the passengers glimpse the future as their boats juddered off the bank and another poor sod had his towrope slashed? Or did they just hang on and congratulate themselves grimly on a few more hours saved?

A century and a half later it was harder to claim the same ignorance about the effects of our speed obsession. Doctors were treating an epidemic of anxiety and depression, helping passengers cope with the next looming bend in the psychic towpath. But few of us dared slow the horses. Because if anything was more frightening than the speed, it was what might happen if you stopped. I had seen it in Craig's eyes when he had recognised the homeless man. The terror of invisibility in a world that registered only movement.

I thought about this as we glided silently through the village of Ratho, past empty boats whose owners were too busy to use them. Little spearlike brown leaves pulled themselves timidly below the surface as our gentle wave first lowered then raised the water level, whispering in the reeds at our passing, slopping gently on slimy Victorian stones.

Later, going below to make another round of tea, I noticed the honey coloured trunk again. 'That's my toolbox, from the boat-building course,' shouted Craig above the engine noise. 'We had to start by making our own tools. Take a look if you want.' I lifted the lid carefully. Inside I found a mallet with a lovingly sanded handle, a little plane with a curved blade, chisels, bevels, clamps, and other things I couldn't identify. Symbols of a productive life, laid out like religious relics. It seemed wrong to touch them. I closed the lid.

'Now that I've got my tools on board I can get to where other boats are, doing repairs, wee jobs – run it as a business,' said Craig, perhaps sensing my thoughts. 'Better that it earns money for itself and I can put money into it. It's always been a dream of mine . . .'

It was a sacred mystery, this momentum we all sought. A life neither hurried nor stalled. I thought about the wave of translation – how, once unleashed and untangled from the crude lurch and heave of the barge, it neither grew nor shrank. There was a dignity to it, which Craig had discovered, and which I craved for myself – the dignity of a body which has found its natural velocity.

It was mid-afternoon when we rounded a corner, went through a narrow stone bridge and pulled alongside a cobbled wharf in the pretty canal basin of Linlithgow. Ahead of us, moored nose to tail with a few other craft, was a red and green narrowboat.

'That's Thistledown,' said Craig, nodding towards her. 'My dad's boat. Your next ride.' I was already a fan of Craig's dad. He had helped his son buy his floating home, and now, without ever having met me, was apparently prepared to let me take advantage of a quiet week for bookings to skipper his canal boat to Falkirk. I was delighted and slightly apprehensive.

She was shorter than I had expected, less fussy and ornamented than English narrowboats, her tiller rising like a steel cobra from the surface of her unadorned rear. 'Pretty self-explanatory, is she?' I asked.

By way of an answer Craig slid back the hatch, opened the double doors, and turned a key in an instrument panel just inside. There was a cough, a rumble and the *ak-ak-ak* of a diesel engine. 'Don't get too worried about that rumbling,' he said, throttling forward in neutral. 'Just keep the revs up. There should always be water coming out of that pipe – it's cooling the engine.' He took me for a brief practice run, nosing out into the bottle-green stillness of the canal, pushing the tiller round in time to swing the long thin torpedo shape around bends.

'Just try and avoid the weed,' he said, as we returned to the landing stage. 'And the banks, obviously.'

And with that, he turned and went back to his boat, his dog, his toolbox and his dream.

2

Thistledown

Linlithgow to Falkirk

I had a few hours to kill before Ali came to join me, so I stowed my gear, locked up *Thistledown* and strolled across to Linlithgow's high street. It was a quaint, historic little place, its cobbled lanes emptied each morning by the commuter trains to Edinburgh or Glasgow. I startled the elderly ladies in Cameron's Traditional Tea and Coffee Shop by being younger than sixty, and ate my tuna roll in silence. Then I walked quickly back towards the canal, pausing by the windswept loch and the ancient kirk, whose tower had a curious hairstyle of angular metallic spikes.

Linlithgow hadn't always been this deserted. The palace perched above the loch was for many years Scotland's main royal seat, birthplace of the ill-fated Mary Queen of Scots in 1542. It had only been allowed to become a neglected second home by James VI when he took on the dual title of James I of England after the death of Elizabeth I in 1603, and flitted off to live out the rest of his reign in London, much to the dismay of his Scottish subjects. Four centuries later it was an empty, roofless shell, its windows framing only bruised sky and fists of gravity-defying grass which shook furiously in the breeze.

Back at the canal basin, I found the aft deck of *Thistledown* wedged solid with parents angling their camcorders at a party of schoolchildren paddling around in open canoes. I left them to their filming and sat down on a bench on the towpath, beside an elderly man in a baseball cap.

'Of course, it was the canoe people who really started it all,' said the man, presently waving at the squealing kids with his walking stick. 'Messing about in boats, I mean. They were the ones who really started using the canal again.'

Mel Gray had lived in a house on the opposite bank of the canal ever since he'd married in 1952. He was now eighty-three. He had once been a judge, but his great passion had always been for the weed-clogged strip of water at the end of his garden. His eyes lit up when I told him I was planning to travel all the way to Glasgow. 'Then you must see our museum before you go,' he said, easing himself slowly to his feet and fishing a key out of his pocket. 'It used to be a stable for the horses.' Inside the little stone building set back along the quay the walls were hung with sepia photographs: rowing boats, the perfect 'O' of a mirrored bridge; industrial backwaters with little boys in white collars; an enormous icicle descending from an aqueduct; and moustached men in waist-coats and peak caps, carrying shovels.

'They're navvies,' said Mel, pointing at a group of workmen on an empty canal bed. 'The only help they got was one wheelbarrow per group. They spent a whole day puddling the clay, marching up and down, like this.' He gave a comic little display, his walking stick raised before him, to demonstrate how the canal base had been stomped watertight with clay.

Like the Ulstermen Burke and Hare, most navvies had been outsiders, much to the consternation of worried villagers. In November 1818, the army only narrowly averted a riot between

Highlanders and Irishmen after a brawl escalated into a crowd of three hundred navvies brandishing cudgels and pickaxes. These days the local population was peppered with their descendants and their hard-drinking reputation had mellowed to 'local colour'. I found this encouraging: outsiders usually managed to become insiders in the end.

Mel rummaged in a drawer and handed me a yellow booklet. 'Perhaps this will help you on your trip,' he smiled. 'It's what the first travellers used. Now, if you'll excuse me, I always like to be home in time for the six o clock news . . .'

Outside, the canoeists were loading up their trailer. I went aboard *Thistledown*, filled a kettle at the sink and sat down to look at Mel's leaflet. *A Companion for Canal Passengers betwixt Edinburgh and Glasgow* had first been printed in 1823, only a year after the canal had opened. I flicked through the guide to Linlithgow:

> The first glance of this place raises the expectation of the passen-
> ger; but as he gradually advances, and sees the majestic ruins of the
> palace, and the venerable Gothic church . . . and the fine green
> mount on which they stand, together with the placid lake which
> embosoms it, his heart is animated with a rapturous pleasure,
> which is softly blended with melancholy.

There was no clue as to the identity of the author, but I imagined a sort of ringmaster cum-museum curator, with waxed moustache, tartan trews and a Walter Scott novel tucked inside his jacket. I named him Torquil: a cultivated and frilly-shirted soul of height-ened sensibilities, gesturing expansively to hushed Victorians in the kind of leisurely barge which would later have its towrope cut for timewasting.

Thistledown's instruction manual was refreshingly blunt by contrast, a home-concocted affair littered with capital letters and obviously written in the full knowledge of the levels of idiocy of which holiday makers were capable.

REMEMBER – IF WARNING LIGHTS COME ON OR
THE ALARM BUZZER SOUNDS, PULL INTO THE SIDE
AND STOP THE ENGINE IMMEDIATELY.

I went nervously through the starting procedure a few times, then rummaged about in search of something called a 'weed hatch' until a mischievous yell of 'Ahoy there, Cap'n' signalled Ali's arrival.

The evening was poised and luminous as we nosed out into the channel between banks of lush grass and reeds. The tiller moved as slowly as an old oak door, worn smooth by many summers of use. We took it in turns to steer, scuffing the bank on a couple of corners until we got used to the counterintuitive business of pushing left to go right. 'Good thing you don't have to pass a driving test for these things,' said Ali. 'I wouldn't fancy the three-point turn.' At 45 feet the boat was longer than the canal was wide.

We chugged on for a couple of hours, silenced by engine noise, facing forward with the tiller in the small of the back as Craig had demonstrated earlier. The lonely countryside darkened and then dropped away as we crossed the high arches of the Avon aqueduct. We stopped in the middle of this wonder to watch the sun set, looking down the valley over hedgerows and quiet cows and a railway bridge to where the Forth estuary glimmered faintly in the last rays. According to Torquil, the nineteenth-century tour guide, the correct appreciation of this view 'must raise sensations of pleasure in every feeling heart'.

My heart, contrary as ever, was a bit more of a mixed bag. Exhilarated as I was by the momentum of my first day's travel, I felt something close to melancholy at the thought of a final twenty-four hours with Ali before heading on alone – a kind of emotional vertigo. Far away, silhouetted on the horizon, Grangemouth Oil Refinery burned with perpetual orange fire, like the flaming towers of Mordor.

God knows what Torquil would have made of that.

'Any idea why the fridge is purring?' said Ali.

It was eight o'clock the following morning and there was no mistaking it. Above the sound of rain on the roof like flung pebbles, the little fridge was making an intermittent noise like a cat trying to charm its way into bed with us.

I opened my eyes enough to focus on a little red warning light flashing on and off a foot from my head. 'Search me.' Last night we'd been hugely impressed by all the boat's cunning space-saving ruses – a slot-in dining table which converted into part of the double bed, a bit of backrest which became the mattress. Today, staring blearily at the dirty dishes on the bedside table, I felt that the kitchen had some boundary issues to confront. It should at least have knocked before entering.

The advantage of this squashed-together houseboat was that, with a simple flick of the curtain, you had a view from your bed. This was useful, as I had only the vaguest idea where we were, having eventually come to a halt against the remains of an old landing stage under cover of darkness. Looking out this morning, we were greeted by a huddle of startled-looking rabbits and a frisky white horse eyeing us from a field. A swan cruised past, proprietorially. As far as I could tell, we were satisfactorily in the middle of nowhere. The rain stopped and I wandered out on to the aft deck, watched the reeds dancing in a light wind. We sat around reading papers and drinking coffee for a while, trying to ignore the fridge. Finally, I gave in and consulted the instruction manual. It turned out that the thing was hungry – for power. In order to keep the electrics charged up, the engine had to be running for five hours a day, and yesterday we had barely managed two.

'Right, time to get under way,' I said, feeling suddenly invigorated by the excuse to do something. Following the daily start-up procedure, I cranked open the rear hatch, checked the engine oil and gave a couple of turns to the prop shaft greaser. I could get into this nautical malarkey. There was an almost Zen-like discipline to it. *You have to keep moving to recharge your batteries.* It rang symbolically true, somehow. The momentum of the perpetual wave.

Ali was less enthusiastic. 'What's the hurry?' she said, peering out from under the duvet. 'Can't we just chill out here for the morning?' Ali, it was true, did not need to keep moving to recharge her batteries. She tapped into pools of relaxation wherever she was anchored, while I, eternal cliché of the restless male, sniffed the horizon. It was a sore point just now, this wandering impulse.

Ali's job as a youth counsellor would not permit her to join me for more than a few days during the whole trip, even if she had wanted to, which she didn't, not really. After our year away in South America, she had lost the yen for travel, devoting herself instead to the web of friendships she had built up since coming to Edinburgh from Northern Ireland eighteen years before. Meanwhile, I was as itchy-footed as ever. These differing impulses weren't necessarily problems in themselves. We had been married six years, and our experience so far had been that freeing each other to follow personal projects ultimately strengthened our relationship. Ali, for example, had allowed me to board the slowly sinking raft for four months in the Pacific, while on our return I had supported her decision to leave paid work for a year to train in counselling. But this time it seemed a much harder sacrifice for Ali, crucially because she had lost her dad to an aneurysm earlier in the year. Although she had not asked me to cancel the trip, I knew it was taking all her emotional energy to allow me to be away from home at all at a time when she was grieving.

We steered carefully around such issues as we navigated onwards together, through tree-lined corridors and fields where cows slurped water at the canal edge. We needed to push on if we were to reach Falkirk before 5 p.m. and avoid being stranded on the wrong side of the canal's only locks. As the morning wore on, the trees and fields grew sparser, and the urban landscape began to intrude. I noticed more junk in the water – milk crates, punctured footballs and, of course, shopping trolleys, which apparently migrate to canals for breeding purposes. *You are now entering the twilight zone,* announced a graffito beneath a bridge. We drifted along the barbed wire fence of Polmont Young Offenders' Institution, a deserted looking place studded with CCTV cameras and exuding the institutional smell of cooked mince. The fence dropped away and opened on to muddy industrial land where workmen in luminous jerkins slouched around a snack caravan parked by a vast heap of old car tyres. A little further on we passed a site for travellers, shunted to the fringes of the wasteland like scrap metal.

Somewhere inside me a shutter was coming down. What was it about the urban landscape which bred this alienation? Was it fear? Indifference? Even 'home' in Edinburgh, sitting on a bus or walking through a shopping centre, it was possible to feel cut off from fellow urbanites by a sort of membrane. You had to keep remembering to push through it. Perhaps that was why I was making the trip: a compulsive individualist learning to connect with other people – over and over again.

'Had a good think?' said Ali, peering at me over her novel with
a friendly grin. 'How about some grub?' I took the hint and unfur-
rowed my brow. Sometimes I got the impression Ali found the
tortured male psyche darkly amusing. I steered us gently into the
bank, throttled back, jumped off with the mooring rope, jumped
back aboard, put the gas on and opened a tin of tomato soup.
Whoever said men can't multitask?

The afternoon scrolled past in a blur of aqueous green until the
banks began to deepen, absorbing our engine noise with walls of
spongy moss. High above us, a carved face leered eastwards from
the stonework of a bridge, only to turn to a rictus of woe on the
west side as the canal funnelled us towards the Falkirk tunnel.
Torquil the tour guide was doing his best to whip us into a gothic
froth:

> When they see the wide chasm, and the distant light, glimmering
> through the lonely dark arch of nearly half a mile in length, they
> are struck with feelings of awe; and, as they proceed through it,
> and see the damp roof above their heads, – feel the chill rarefied
> air – and hear every sound re-echoing through the gloomy cavern –
> their feelings are wound to the highest pitch.

I aimed the bow at the dark hole in the rock and switched on the
headlight as we were enveloped by engine noise. It was certainly
dank, and the limestone loomed in surprising fungal shapes. But
the most alarming thing about it was glancing at my watch as we
emerged. Ten past four, and a mile still to go.

With the jumbled grey roofs of Falkirk spread below us, I
opened the throttle and upped the pace to the speed limit, a somewhat underwhelming 4 mph. At times like this, the clip-clopping
pace of canal travel didn't seem quite so idyllic. I was beginning to

lose patience when all of a sudden there was an electronic beeping. Ali burst out through the door. 'You're overheating!'

I froze momentarily like a driver caught in a speed camera, remembering all those capital letters in the instruction manual. Then I reached over and turned off the ignition. The engine died with a shudder, and we spent what seemed like several minutes drifting towards the bank, where Ali leapt ashore with a rope.

'Bugger.' There was silence and an odd smell. I lifted the engine hatch gingerly. A cloud of grey smoke hung around the engine.

'Now what?'

I knew nothing at all about engines. We were tantalisingly close to our target – probably just round the next bend – so I hopped ashore again, put the bowline over my shoulder and started to pull. Ali frowned for a moment from the tiller, then burst out laughing.

'Giddy-up!'

'Very funny.'

I have to hand it to horses – it was bloody hard work. I managed about 100 yards of grunting and straining before I gave up and jumped back aboard. Craig's mobile wasn't responding, but the instruction book yielded a number for his Uncle Ron. His tone suggested he wasn't particularly surprised to hear from us.

'Maybe you've got some weed in the water intake,' he suggested.

'Ah,' I said, peering over the side. 'Is that easy to fix?'

There was a short silence. 'Tell you what,' said Ron. 'If you're not too far from the lock, why not just start her up again, keep her low and drive her the last bit? Just be ready to stop if there's no water coming out of the engine cooling pipe.'

The next ten minutes of the journey ticked past like a detonator waiting to be defused by 007. We watched the clock, watched the water in the pipe, watched the speedometer, trying not to overheat, trying not to miss the lock deadline. Finally, at 4.55 p.m., we rounded a bend and saw two men standing by a lockhouse. We waved urgently. They didn't wave back.

'Cutting it fine, are we?' said the man who took our bowline. He looked like Billy Connolly, only without the grin. He sealed the great wooden doors shut behind us, and soon the boat began to sink down a concrete wall studded with tiny water snails.

'Sorry — our engine overheated,' said Ali, craning her neck up. 'Beautiful canal, though.'

'Aye, if you like that sort of thing,' grunted Billy. 'You wouldn't catch me on it. I don't like boats much.'

This seemed to me to be something of a disadvantage in a lock-keeper.

'Not really,' said Billy, as the bottom gates opened in front of us. 'I usually work The Wheel.'

The Falkirk Wheel was the centrepiece of the restored Millennium Link and pride of Scotland's canal workers. The promotional blurb described it as 'the world's first and only rotating boatlift' — but that really only deepened the suspense. Motoring out of the lower lock, we rounded a bend and entered the last tunnel. It turned out to be a wormhole through time: having spent the day idling past meadows and farms like leisurely Victorians, we emerged from the tunnel to find ourselves navigating in space.

'What exactly *is* that?' said Ali. We were drifting through vast concrete hoops along a channel which emerged from the hillside and appeared to end hundreds of feet in midair. From where we were standing, it was hard to see what was going to happen next.

'Don't forget to stop,' shouted a boatman from British Waterways, taking our mooring line as I backthrust the engine. We came to a halt alongside a blue pleasure boat in a metal trough of water in the sky. None of it made much sense until, after some hydraulic hisses and clunks, during which two metal barriers arose from the water behind us, our entire boat's length of canal began to move sideways and downwards like the gondola of a Ferris wheel. We giggled incredulously as an identical section came slowly up past us, balanced on the far side of a vast axle.

The tourists in their glass-sided sightseeing boat peered mutely outwards at this astonishing feat of engineering as we all floated down through the damp air towards a broad basin. In a single elegant move it was doing the work of the eleven locks that had once connected the canals of Edinburgh and Glasgow, gently scooping boats from the Union down to the level of the Forth and Clyde more than 100 feet below.

'The two gondolas are so well balanced that it only takes the same power as eight toasters to run it,' boasted a man in a British Waterways polo shirt, clearly enjoying our reaction as we whirred quietly to a halt. *Thistledown* was a somewhat less finely balance machine by comparison, but even she seemed to have stopped belching black smoke. We motored out carefully over the now lowered end section of the gondola and tied up in the basin.

Our last night aboard *Thistledown* was a strange, sad goodbye. We cooked a meal and tried to shut out the giant structure now looming still and sinister above us. The wind howled around the concrete supports and rippled the water into fractured diamonds. We buoyed ourselves up with alcohol and reminiscences about the day, but I didn't know when I would next see Ali – indeed, I didn't know much at all beyond that evening – and this gnawed at both of us. The sheer provisionality of the trip had seemed a wonderful gamble on paper, but suddenly it felt about as sensible as hacking off a limb to see what it felt like.

'Something will turn up,' she said, stoically. 'You'll see.'

Later, I put on my rain gear and took a brief walk. I had thought we were alone, but I was wrong. On the other side of the basin a control tower overlooked the locks which met the Forth and Clyde Canal at right angles. Inside was a lone security guard called Vince, one of those rare beings for whom solitude does not seem to be a problem. He greeted me cheerily enough and listened with interest to my plan. Then he pointed to a big green boat moored at a landing stage. 'I think they've gone tae Falkirk fae the night,' he said, observing that there were no lights on. 'But ye might catch 'em in the morning. I hear they're on their way tae Glasgae.'

3

Kirkintilloch by Crowbar

The Forth and Clyde Canal

The *Zeepaard* was an elegant craft: 60 feet of glossy green curves, with a varnished mast folded along the roof of a glass wheelhouse. I kept glancing over as I locked up *Thistledown*, but there was no sign of life on board so I left my rucksack behind a wall and walked Ali to her taxi. It was a ludicrously difficult goodbye, both of us choked and tearful and me feeling like Judas and wanting to get it over. As soon as the taxi turned the corner I hurried back to the quay in search of another world in which to lose myself. I was in luck. The glass-sided wheelhouse took up much of the deck, and showcased a scene of idyllic domesticity as four people sat chattering soundlessly around a healthy spread of fruit and cafetières, like a TV advertisement for breakfast cereal. I stood dorkishly on the landing stage until one of them caught my eye. It was now or never. *Be confident, be friendly, and not too pushy.* I knew from Vince that this was the only guaranteed westbound vessel that day.

'Beautiful boat you've got there,' I said, as a silver-haired gentleman emerged on to the aft deck. A bit of gentle flattery never did any harm.

'Thank you! Her name's *Zeepaard*.' He had a kindly but powerful face, his American voice gravelly and disconcertingly like that of Top Cat. 'She's a ninety-two-year-old lady – but we rather like old ladies. Come aboard and have a look if you like. My name's Don.'

Don's wife Abbie emerged from inside the wheelhouse and gave a warm hello, her eyes smiley and wise. *God bless Americans* – always ready to connect. 'Do you know what *Zeepaard* means?' she said. 'It means sea horse. She's a Dutch barge.'

Behind her I glimpsed a red Persian carpet, bookcases, lace curtains and baskets of flowers hung from brass rods. They had found their sea horse languishing in a boatyard in Holland and had spent large chunks of the past twenty-three years renovating or navigating her on 40,000 miles' worth of holidays around Europe's coasts and canal systems. Down in the galley, their daughter Tracey and her husband Carl, a tanned, outdoorsy couple, were clearing away breakfast and stocking a vast American refrigerator. On this vacation the four of them had crossed the English Channel, followed the coast north and entered the Forth and Clyde Canal from the North Sea the previous day.

In return I told them a few of my own nautical experiences, and remembered to mention Ali, which I calculated would make me seem less like a rootless drifter. Finally, I asked if they had heard of any boats heading towards Glasgow that day – trying not to sound as if I was dropping a huge hint, which of course I was.

Don, being a good American, cut to the chase. 'Well, you're welcome to come along with us today if you like,' he said, looking at his watch. 'We leave in half an hour, and it could be an interesting ride. A lot of people have told us we'll never get through on a boat as big as this. But I'm taking that as a challenge.'

Abjectly grateful, I retrieved my rucksack from its tactful hiding place behind a wall and climbed aboard, being careful to remove my boots before treading on the Persian rug. It was certainly a different experience to *Thistledown*. In a recent upgrade Don had added bow thrusters and a tiny joystick, which now moved the door-sized rudder, adorned with its Dutch scroll and meticulous paintwork, in hydraulic shudders. Standing on the aft deck as he accelerated away from the landing stage to the regulation 4 mph, I watched whole beds of waterlilies disappear in our bow wave.

Don was not too worried. After all, the Forth and Clyde had been built for bigger boats than this, transoceanic traders and fishing boats, whose sails could once be seen drifting incongruously across cornfields. The only problem, he said, was that someone had since invented motorway bridges, which now reduced the maximum headroom in some cases to around 3 metres.

'And how high is *Zeepaard*?'

'With the masts down? Exactly 3.14 metres.'

It seemed to me that there was something wrong with the maths here. But Don said the men from British Waterways had measured all the gaps with lasers the previous day and were convinced they could get the *Zeepaard* through. Indeed, they seemed to relish the challenge as much as Don. They were waiting for us at the next lock, along with lunchtime drinkers from a canalside pub, a proud little cluster of men in blue boiler suits who took photographs of what was evidently a kind of trophy boat – the biggest to come through the canal in modern times.

Their smiles clouded slightly, however, as we edged towards the footbridge. 'Whoa!' yelled Carl, suddenly from outside the cabin. 'Back up!' Don backthrust to a halt and rushed out to observe what Carl had thankfully spotted – that even with the masts folded flat against the roof, we were about to lose the foghorn, radar dish and navigation lights. All protruded above the lowest timbers by several inches.

'I thought we'd already been through the lowest bridge, yester-day,' said Abbie, frowning, as we all congregated on deck. A row of spectators grinned down at us from the parapet of the footbridge and shouted bits of advice like: 'That'll never go through, pal.' The pub, I noticed, was called somewhat optimistically A Passage to India. At this rate we'd be lucky to make it to Kirkintilloch.

The canal men looked sheepish, but Don was not about to be publicly beaten. Seeing the way things were going, he handed out spanners and screwdrivers, and we began to take the boat to pieces. 'Will removing the chimney affect the engine?' wondered Carl aloud. I unbolted the foghorn and confessed I didn't know. He shrugged and yanked the chimney out anyway.

On the second attempt the bow glided through with centi-metres to spare, until the mast socket met the bridge with a quiet crunch of timber. 'Whoa!' said a drinker, belatedly. Now we were wedged fast. 'This is ridiculous,' muttered Don, coming out on deck to inspect the underside of the footbridge. 'Don't tell me we're going to have to dismantle the whole cabin.' I didn't doubt he was prepared to do it to complete his challenge. A couple of men in British Waterways outfits were scratching their heads. The dis-tance was tantalisingly small – about 14 millimetres.

I had a glimmer of an idea: 'Has anyone got a crowbar?' Carl narrowed his eyes, assuming I was joking. 'All you've got to do is force the boat to float a centimetre lower in the water, and you'll be able to fit under.' Carl thought for a moment, and disappeared with two of the workmen. He returned with a crowbar. 'Okay, a little power,' shouted Tracey to Don, getting the idea as Carl and I levered away at the end of it. And inch by painstaking inch, we shoehorned that boat through, until we popped out the other side to a round of applause and a small crowbar-shaped dent in the mast. 'Glad we brought you along!' said Don, making my day.

It was a victory for the men from British Waterways too, as they squeezed us into the lock. 'It was the motorway which really killed this canal,' said William, a quiet, friendly worker, as the boat rose slowly in the lock. 'Until then it was all lifting bridges.' He had worked here since he was a child, riding the fishing boats free in return for help at the lock gates. The voyage of the *Zeepaard* was for him a matter of personal honour. 'The next bridge is the real test,' he shouted, speeding ahead of us down the towpath on a quad bike.

Luckily William and his fellow workers had an ingenious ace up their sleeve to squeeze us under the M80 at Castlecarry. It was the lowest bridge, at exactly 3 metres clearance, and yet we glided harmlessly beneath it with several inches to spare. I only worked out how when I noticed that the sides of the canal seemed noticeably muddier than before. Unable to raise the bridges, they had lowered the water level. More than a million gallons had drained away through open sluices overnight. 'We're lucky in Scotland,' said William. 'We've got plenty of water to spare.'

This fact reinforced itself during the afternoon in the form of a thickening drizzle on the wheelhouse windows. 'Is the weather always like this in Scotland?' said Abbie, rustling up a potato salad from the fridge. The canal stretched ahead of us as broad and blank as a rain-slicked motorway.

'Not at all – though it does tend to get wetter towards the west coast.'

Abbie looked miserable. 'Really?'

It was their first time in Scotland, and I noticed their Stars and Stripes ensign was rolled up inside the cabin. Don insisted he had removed it after it broke off in a tight-fitting lock, rather than as a precaution against anti-American feeling.

'George Bush may be the asshole of the world right now,' he said, eating lunch while Carl took the helm. 'But on a person-to-person basis we've found that any problems disappear. People here are very friendly.' He looked at me mischievously. 'Anyway, I'd heard it was the English who got a rough ride in Scotland, not the Americans.'

There was no getting away from my Englishness. I was not by any definition a Scot, even by the ingenious ancestor-hunting which allowed New Zealanders to captain Scottish rugby teams. I had no forgotten great-granny from Auchtermuchty to bundle me through the genealogical mettle detector. While Ali was Ulster Scots by descent, the furthest north I could trace my lineage was Yorkshire, and even that could never really compensate for growing up in Surbiton – home of *The Good Life*, heart of the affluent Tory-voting south, and generally not the first place that would spring to mind for twinning with, say, Clydebank.

Given the devastating economic and psychological effect of eighteen years of Thatcherism on a country which had consistently voted against the Iron Lady, it was perhaps surprising that in ten years in Scotland I had personally never experienced overt anti-English racism. Yet it couldn't take away an underlying tension. Occasionally, standing in a shop queue of bantering Scots, I'd find the conversation icing over into clipped, terse sentences when I reached the till. I could never decide if that was because of my English accent, or because I lacked the natural Scottish talent for banter.

Robert Louis Stevenson had put it down to a fundamental personality difference he had noted between the Scots and English travellers:

'A Scotchman is vain, interested in himself and others, eager for sympathy, setting forth his thoughts and experience in the best light. The egoism of the Englishman is self-contained. He does not seek to proselytise. He takes no interest in Scotland or the Scotch, and, what is the unkindest cut of all, he does not care to justify his indifference.'

Despite its obvious generalisation, this seemed to me to shed useful light on the problem. I was anything but indifferent to the Scots, but I could see how my southern English reticence, the desire not to offend or disturb, could be misconstrued as aloofness in a country where banter and engagement were the rule. Self-containment and politeness alone would win you few friends in a nation which, historically at least, was communitarian.

In that sense, Scots and Americans had a lot in common – both of them impatient with the English tendency to beat around the bush. Life was too short to apologise for 'bothering' your fellow humans – wasn't that just part of living on the same planet? That was partly why I had decided to make this voyage, I explained to my new hosts – to learn to stop tiptoeing around the edges, and throw myself in.

Don nodded understandingly at this, but still seemed baffled by the ferocity of the ancient enmity which, for example, required any good sporting Scot to support whoever was playing *against* England. 'It's the same wherever you go in the world,' he sighed. 'In France they were appalled we were going to Spain. In Spain they told us not to bother with Naples. The people in Holland told us not to bother with Belgium. Everywhere we go, people are appalled that we want to visit their neighbours. But we've loved them all.'

The rain had passed and the boat chuntered on through lush fields. Kirkintilloch rose on the horizon, a huddle of church steeples glimpsed over treetops. After the delays of the morning, William and his men had advised Don to moor up here for the night and head for Glasgow the following day. Abbie offered me a

berth in a spare cabin, which I gratefully accepted. As soon as we
were moored, I washed up the lunch things by way of a thank you
and then wandered off on my own to give the family a little private
space together. It was possible this was just English reticence which
would be interpreted as aloofness, but I hoped not.

Apart from its historical status as Scotland's first inland port,
'Kirky' was famous for the number of churches it seemed to have
acquired over the centuries. It seemed an odd sort of boast – as
if the endless splintering of congregations was somehow evidence of holiness rather than the inability to find common
ground. I wandered down the steeple-barbed high street and
opted for an exhibition about Kirky's other main speciality: the
classic red British telephone box. These national treasures had
been manufactured in their thousands at the local Lion Foundry
until, in 1984, BT's decision to replace them with anodyne glass
cubicles had sealed the fate of the town's last surviving industry.
Sitting on a park bench to phone home, I used my mobile by way
of protest.

Back at the *Zeepaard* local people had been dropping by all afternoon, drawn to the shiny new boat in town. Don's conversational
partners had so far ranged from schoolgirls demanding a tour of
his living room to a man determined to convince him that the only
hope for the country was the reintroduction of dancehalls. I wondered if Don had ever regretted opting for glass walls.

Abbie put a more positive spin on it. 'This boat is really one big
focal point of conversation,' she said, as we sat down to dinner that
night. 'It makes it easy to make friends.'

It had certainly worked for me. We sat around for hours that
night talking about the day's events, and sharing stories of voyages
we had made. Carl, I learned, was trying to write a novel and sub-
sidising himself through carpentry, while Tracey was a therapist

and dancer who doted on her dogs. Don had made his money through farming and had gone to school with Donald Rumsfeld 'twenty years before he betrayed everything'. It was great to be with liberal Americans – all the positivity but none of the crusading agenda. I had fallen on my feet. Don's coughing broke into the conversation. He sounded like a cat with a fur ball – a remnant, I discovered, of a battle against throat cancer.

'It's a little hard to eat sometimes,' he croaked presently.

'It's *very* hard to eat,' added Abbie, handing him a glass of water.

Abbie and Don had been married since the fifties, and had that seamless way of easing the conversation for each other. I sensed their shared pain and remembered I was trespassing on family territory here. Still, Don's story fascinated me. 'Do you feel like travelling has given you a different perspective on life?' I asked carefully.

Tracey butted in gently. 'Speaking as his daughter, I'd say that it's the other way round. It's seeing life differently that made him travel in the first place.'

Her dad made no attempt to add anything, and she smiled at him, patting his hand.

The next morning I awoke to muttered curses. Someone had untied one of the mooring lines in the middle the night. 'Can you believe it?' said Don, staring at the limp rope on the jetty. 'If the other one hadn't been tied on better, I bet they'd have taken that off too. First time that's happened in twenty-three years. *Thanks very much . . .'*

Things only got worse when we cast off ourselves, soon after 9 a.m. Packing my bag in the guest cabin, I heard a thud from below my feet, and the engine cut out with a grinding shudder. I could hear only the rippling of water along the hull.

'Holy shit,' shouted Don, as I rushed up to the wheelhouse. He tried the engine again, it turned over and thudded once more. 'Get ropes to those boats!' he shouted, as we drifted onwards under our own momentum. Carl and Tracey managed to slow us down by grabbing the rail of a moored yacht and then tying us to the pontoon. The towpath was deserted. Four of us peered over the stern, but it was impossible to see anything in the murky water.

'I guess someone's going to need to go in there,' said Don. He left a small pause in which nobody volunteered, then disappeared to his cabin. Moments later he emerged wearing a windsurfing wetsuit, some old jeans and a pair of wellies, like a children's game of Consequences jumbling the legs and bodies of a diver, farmer and cowboy. Grabbing a snorkel and mask from a locker, he clambered over the stern and down a series of metal rungs fitted to the side of the rudder. I watched as his balding head disappeared among the reeds and bobbing drinks cans. For a moment he was invisible but for the tip of his snorkel.

'We got a big ball of wire round the prop,' he shouted up a few minutes later. 'We're going to need some boltcutters.'

Abbie, standing peering over at him, let out a long sigh. 'When we get home people always think we've had such a relaxing vacation,' she said, hands on hip. 'They have no idea.'

Scottish hospitality soon kicked in. A man out painting a boat brought the boltcutters and a nautical gift book 'to try and make up for the trouble you're having'. Carl thanked him and passed the boltcutters down to Don, who tried without success to sever the wire around the propeller.

'If we were in the middle of nowhere, I'd just have to stand under there and snip through them one by one,' he lamented, crawling back up, shivering. 'At fifty I'd have done it, at sixty I'd

have done it . . . at seventy I figure I'm going to wait for the pro-
fessionals.'

Donald was *seventy?* I felt suddenly ashamed and threw myself
into the crisis, helping Carl secure the boat to a tree on the far side
of the towpath while Don called British Waterways to alert them
to the problem.

Rummaging around among the reeds, Carl discovered a 4-foot
long, intricately carved wooden fork of the kind found in Hawaii.
'Well, what do you know?' he said, with a quizzical grin. 'Conclusive
proof that the Polynesians migrated as far as Kirkintilloch.'

It was, we all agreed, the most improbable thing ever pulled out
of a canal – though not without some good competition. 'I've
thought of naming my boat the *Magnet*,' said the boat painter. 'Last
thing I had round the prop was a 28-foot piece of carpet, 3 feet
wide. And before that, a Keep Left sign.'

'In the Netherlands we ran over a large television set,' offered
Carl. 'The cable snagged on the prop, and it floated round after us.'

Abbie looked wistful: 'And the diver who freed us last time
brought up an old, old demitasse cup with a pretty little china pattern.'

Just as Abbie was setting out some lunch, a van pulled up on the
towpath. Three men from British Waterways climbed out, promised to phone some divers, and then climbed back into the van to
read the *Daily Record*.

'Or even just *one* diver would probably be fine,' said Don, a little
nervously.

It was long past noon when a couple of pumped-up SUVs
pulled up behind the van and disgorged no fewer than *four*
industrial diving experts. 'We can't do it with one man,' explained
the Divemaster, who wore a white open-necked shirt, a rug of
chest hair and a well-attended tan. 'We've got the whole team

here — very strict rules — a minimum of four men is the regula-
tions.'

Don looked a little pale. 'But it's only a metre deep!'

A diver already peeling his trousers off peered out cheekily
from behind the van. 'Guess we'll have to lie down then!' Laden
with tanks and with the word 'Otter' inexplicably stamped on his
insulated rubber forehead, he slopped down the bank on the end
of a long piece of rope which Divemaster paid out through his
hands.

Don lay on the stern and watched the bubbles emerging from
beneath the boat, until Otter surfaced with the prognosis. 'It's a
mattress — but it doesn't look too comfy!' he quipped. 'Can you
hand me the boltcutters?'

For the next two hours we waited and watched, like anxious relatives in the operating theatre waiting room. Otter bubbled
occasionally into view to demand a different implement — any
small pliers? Wirecutters? — then retreated into the murk again.
The rope holder held the rope, while the emergency assistance
diver stood around in his diving gear. Divemaster answered mobile
phone calls and occasionally wrote things on a clipboard.

'It's happened to us all,' sympathised the skipper of a passing
barge for disabled day-trippers, handing us a box of biscuits as
consolation. 'We picked up a single duvet the other day . . .'

A rumble of thunder sounded overhead and we gratefully
retired inside to escape the light shower. Eventually, Otter attached
a rope to whatever he'd found beneath the surface, and suggested
that the SUV pulled the other end. With a revving and rending, up
came two chunks of coiled springs, ragged shreds of old bedding
and a nest of rusty wire.

Otter beamed like a proud midwife. '*That* was your problem!'

*

It was 3.15 when we finally got under way again. Don was determined to make it as far through the canal as possible that night, so
I offered to take a shift at the helm, a nerve-wracking process
which involved giving predictive countertwitches of the joystick
long before the big boat began to turn, to avoid a kind of slalom.
We listened nervously for any further impediment on the bottom,
but heard only occasional clanks. Once a car tyre surfaced briefly
in our wake and sank again.

The landscape had been getting gradually more urban. We
passed fields, pylons, a grey heron hunched in a watermeadow;
occasional high-rises over treetops; a burned-out joyrider's car with
its nose in the reeds; and assorted children's balls, bobbing by the
banks. Finally we rounded a corner and found ourselves at the top
of a staircase of locks. Maryhill was a 'notorious' council estate
where other boatmen had warned us to be alert, but we found only
a sadly deserted looking place, a derelict lock-keeper's cottage and
façades of boarded-up windows scrawled with graffiti.

The view, on the other hand, was stunning. No matter that it
had taken me the best part of a working week to do a journey
which normally took an hour. As the men from British Waterways
squeezed us from one lock to another, we were finally gazing down
at Scotland's largest city, her circuit-board tracery of streets, houses
and gasometers basking in the evening sun.

4

The Riverman

On the Clyde

In truth, I'd always been a bit intimidated by Glasgow. I could trace it back to my first glimpse of its menacing industrial skyline through a rain-beaded car window at the age of eight. We were driving up for a family holiday on a little west coast island, our first visit to a country I had been told was wild and green and full of mountains. So it had been confusing, waking sleepily in the early hours of a grey dawn in the back of the family Peugeot, to find we were lost among the blank walls of warehouses, and cranes so vast they seemed to prop up the low, bruised sky. My parents were whispering urgently over a map, trying to find their way back to a flyover somewhere. I shivered and hid under a blanket. The memory stuck.

I felt an after-tremor of that childhood anxiety now, winding down a flight of steps, looking over its industrial sprawl of six hundred thousand people. After a final night aboard the *Zeepaard*, moored at the Kelvin aqueduct, I had waved Don and family off on their onward trip to the sea lock at Bowling, opting for an alternative route through Glasgow to explore my lingering trepidation. According to my map, I could descend to join the Kelvin from the

point where it flowed under the aqueduct, and follow it right down
through the city until it joined the Clyde, where presumably I'd be
able to pick up a boat going out towards the sea. I could see her in
the distance now, that greasy brown icon of Glasgow's fortune and
decline, her surface dulled like cooling gravy.

The Kelvin, meanwhile, was barely deep enough to accommodate a shopping trolley, let alone a boat, so I walked along its
banks, following it through shallow pools and cool leafy dells, and
examined my preconceptions about Scotland's largest city. In the
traditional cat-and-dog antipathy between Edinburgh and
Glasgow, there was no doubt that Edinburgh was the cat: aloof,
individualistic and slightly up itself. But while doggy, friendly
Glasgow prided itself on its in-your-face eagerness to help, I wasn't
totally convinced it wouldn't turn on you and take your arm off. It
had never quite shaken off the associations of a criminal under-
world, in which rival gangs of 'big men' fought bitter turf wars,
chibbed each other with Stanley knives and dropped body parts off
piers.

I felt a long way from all that now. I met nobody except a
designer jogger and a slightly startled fisherman as I wound
beneath Victorian bridges from which the disembodied sounds of
traffic and chatter drifted barely to the periphery of consciousness.
After days floating along a man-made ditch, it was wonderful to
see water at play again, burbling, chuckling, tumbling over itself.
Once polluted by mills and chemical works, this leafy post-
industrial idyll made at least some sense of the Gaelic meaning of
Glasgow: 'dear green place'.

By the time I got into Kelvingrove Park, however, the urban
membrane was hardening. I saw it in the bloodshot eyes of a
benchful of drunks, yelling at passers-by; in the suspicious faces of
mothers guarding the kiddies' playground from this lone male with

a grubby looking rucksack. The river veered round past the grand Victorian buildings of Glasgow University and across a main road before taking on the appearance of a flood drain. Then it slithered off under a low bridge, where I lost it.

I was skirting through a backstreet in the hope of rejoining it when I caught a strain of music echoing faintly off buildings. It was a high, piccolo-shrill refrain, chirpily upbeat, like Steve McQueen's defiant little signature anthem in *The Great Escape*. On impulse, I followed it past a newsagent and the delicious morning smells of a bakery, until the refrain grew ominous with the rattle of snare drums. With sinking heart, I realised what it was.

I reached the main road at the same time as the Orange parade. Young men with pimply faces and dark uniforms played piccolos, flutes and drums behind a banner bearing the legend 'West End Loyalists'. Their sashes, white gloves and pompomed berets gave them a pseudo-military air. Behind them marched a phalanx of older men with grey suits and oily comb-overs, while women with pushchairs trailed along the pavement with other men in shell suits or Glasgow Rangers FC shirts. Everybody wore an expression of grim determination, staring straight ahead as if defying anyone to stop them.

I'd seen many parades like this on assignment in Northern Ireland. Falling into step beside a suited man, I asked what the occasion was. 'This,' he said, thrusting his chin out proudly, 'is a commemoration of the siege of Londonderry.'

It is almost impossible to understand Glasgow without touching on its tangled relationship with Ireland. The thousands of itinerant navvies who had dug the canals represented only a fraction of the quarter of a million Irish-born immigrants who had poured into Scotland by the mid-nineteenth century. In this urban hub they came mainly from Ulster, barely 20 miles off the west coast. By 1831, one in six of Glasgow's two hundred thousand population were Irish, whole neighbourhoods of them fuelling the city's industrial expansion in textiles, shipbuilding and mining. The Irish Potato Famine of 1845–7 only increased the flood of destitute families seeking work. Most were Catholic, but a significant quarter were Protestant, the direct descendants of Presbyterian Scots who had settled in Ulster in the seventeenth century. Perhaps inevitably, the tribal hatreds of Ulster began to manifest themselves here in the soot-blackened side streets.

Glasgow had, thankfully, never seen the all-out violence of the Province, but in times of economic hardship the immigrant Catholics made a convenient scapegoat. In the 1920s post-war depression the Church of Scotland threw a thin cloak of respectability around the whole festering mess with an incendiary report titled *The Menace of the Irish Race to Our Scottish Nationality*, railing against a papist conspiracy and calling for enforced deportation. At less desperate times, it was left to the Irish to persecute each other. Nowadays the Loyal Orange Lodges were as active as ever, organising the majority of a staggering 741 sectarian marches planned for the Strathclyde region in 2003 alone.

'So is this a religious parade or a political one?' I asked the marcher. It seemed odd to me that men whose links with their homeland were tenuous at best should still be playing Punch and Judy over ancient battles. The man grimaced with irritation, showing a single tooth embedded in his upper jaw. 'It's non-sectarian, non-political,' he said, as if reading from a PR manual.

'But if the whole point of the siege of Londonderry was that it defeated the Catholics, surely it must seem a bit like a victory parade to them?'

The man glared at me and straightened his sash. 'Not at all,' he insisted, doggedly. 'We'd *never* exclude Catholics — in fact, any Catholic that wants to join us today is welcome.'

This seemed a bit like claiming that any woman was welcome to join a stag party at a lap-dancing club. I shrugged and watched them trail into the distance. The most heartening thing about it was that, apart from a couple of disgruntled drivers, nobody was taking a blind bit of notice.

By now I had lost the Kelvin altogether, and decided to head straight for the Clyde. I boarded a tour bus going in that direction. On the open-top deck a name-badged guide called Shona was trying to coax some reaction from the blank faces of a group of Japanese tourists.

'. . . I'm sure somebody will have heard of Charles Rennie Mackintosh?' she was saying into a microphone. 'A very famous architect born in Glasgow? Anybody? No?'

I sat down and nodded supportively to her as she ran through her script: Glasgow's cultural icons, Glasgow's patron saint, Glasgow's breathtaking architecture, Glasgow's shipbuilding past, Glasgow's post-industrial restoration . . . None of it managed to distract her audience even temporarily from the serious business of keeping their camcorders wedged in their eye sockets. But Shona wouldn't give up. 'And now, of course, we've got a new industry,' she said. 'Shopping.'

'Shopping?' murmured somebody. Suddenly the Japanese tourists were paying attention.

'Shopping is very important to this city,' she said, as we passed the boxy edifice of Glasgow Caledonian University. 'There's someone in that building who is being paid a lot of money to be the *Professor of Retail Therapy*.' She lowered her voice into a theatrical aside: 'Now, why didn't *I* get the job? I know a lot about retail therapy: you take your wee plastic card along, exchange it for lots of clothes, and most importantly, go home and smile at your husband . . .'

The delighted tittering from the sixth row persuaded Shona that she had at last hit her mark with the one thing that made Glasgow indistinguishable from any other Western city. As I got off the bus in the city centre, she was struggling stoically through a familiar advertorial: 'And on Buchanan Street you'll find all the designer brands you'd expect from a premier shopping destination: Calvin Klein, Yves St Laurent . . .' I waded through the crowds of shoppers, craving a glimpse of water.

The Riverman lived in the only house on Glasgow Green, overlooking the Clyde from behind a little picket fence. He had a day job as art teacher at a local secondary school, but from time to time he would disappear dramatically from his classes to take up duties that were much more pressing. He went by many names – Riverman, Lifeboat Man, even plain George Parsonage – but for as long as anybody could remember, he was the one you called when the Clyde was threatening to take another life. A kind of people's superhero. If you happened to fall off the quayside, capsize your canoe, or even threw yourself off a bridge, your greatest – perhaps only – hope would be the urgent slap and creak of his oars. For the Riverman favoured an unglamorous form of transport which had nevertheless proved its worth over the years: an old rowing boat, into which hundreds of sodden Glaswegians had been dragged to safety.

Today his little lifeboat station was obscured by a white catering marquee pitched next to the footpath. Wandering inside, I found a bewilderingly eclectic cast of characters: a brown-robed friar, a policeman, a tracksuited rower, a clergyman, a coastguard, a gaggle of large-bosomed matrons and an assortment of dignitaries wearing gold chains. None looked much like a super-hero. Intrigued, I tucked my rucksack behind a table of vol-au-vents and joined the drinks queue. I had just missed the formal dedication of a new safety boat, said a businessman, who was himself one of the Riverman's early success stories.

'I shouldn't have been out at all,' confided Jan de Vries, munch-ing sheepishly on a sausage roll. 'It had been raining and the river was in spate. It all happened very quickly.' His sculling boat had capsized suddenly in the swollen current, dragging him downriver towards the tidal weir where the water thundered down over a steel barrier. Luckily the lifeboat man had seen it happen from the window of his cottage, and within seconds there had been shouts from the bank and two men had ploughed across the current towards him in a rowing boat. 'They threw me a line and told me to leave the boat and hang on.' He did, and was hauled to safety only feet from the weir. His sculling boat was not so fortunate, and was sucked over and smashed to pieces before their eyes. Jan shook his head wonderingly. 'If George and his father hadn't been around, there's a very good chance I wouldn't be here now.'

Much had changed since then. Ben Parsonage had died in 1979, handing George his little house and historic title of president and sole officer of the Glasgow Humane Society. And the half-drowned student had gone on to become managing director of an engineering firm. But thirty years on from his narrow escape, Jan still felt the debt, and worked voluntarily as a fundraiser for the man who had saved him. I wondered how many others here were in the same position. I strolled down to the river's edge, where the dark water flowed languidly downstream towards the riveted weir that had so nearly claimed Jan's life. The new boat, a white fibre-glass affair named *Ben Parsonage*, sat at the top of a launch ramp. The boatyard was deserted apart from a Catholic priest swapping pleasantries over its shiny outboard motor with a man in a monk's robes — and somebody I took to be the caretaker, lingering by the boathouse.

'Thought I'd better get it blessed by both a Catholic and a Protestant, just to be on the safe side,' growled the latter at my shoulder. 'You can get strung up for things like that round here.' I turned to face a squat, muscular man, wearing a slightly worn three-piece suit with shiny gold buttons. He grinned at me from a ruddy, rugged face framed with silvery hair, and extended his hand. 'George Parsonage.'

He took my hand with a firm, dry grasp and shook it. A safe grip. Strong rower's fingers. 'Nice boat,' I said, after introducing myself.

'Aye,' sighed George, nodding. 'But between you and me she'll never beat the original *Bennie*.' He beckoned me down the ramp to a sleek old wooden rowing boat, the same one his father had used before him. 'That's the fastest boat you can row in a river and still get a man over the gunwale.'

I blinked at him. 'Faster than an outboard?'

'*Better* than an outboard, for a number of reasons. If you're in a rowing boat you'll hear people shouting from the bank, telling you what's going on — you won't hear that over an engine.' He took a sip of champagne. '*And* if you're picking up someone using an engine you can end up capsizing another boat with your wash. *And* outboard motors are notoriously finicky. Whereas your arms will always work in an emergency.' He grinned and flexed his muscles.

Strathclyde Police had developed an improbable but time-tested relationship with George over the years, part-funding his job and dealing with tricky health and safety issues, while largely letting him get on with the task in the way he knew best. When a call came in, often in the middle of the night, a patrol car towing his rowing boat on a trailer would rush him to the place the victim had entered the water. Where there was no obvious launch point, George – always adrenalin-charged by this stage – would heave the *Bennie* over walls or even railings and clamber in as best he could. Rowing furiously out into the stream, he would strain his eyes for a glimpse of breaking surface water, listening for shouts or cries in the darkness. The first half-hour was crucial. After that, the temperature of the water probably meant he was looking for a dead body. He'd saved nearly 1500 people from the river in his life – but recovered almost 400 corpses.

'It's a love-hate relationship, this job,' he admitted, as we sat looking out over the water. 'There's nothing to beat the adrenalin when you save a life, but equally there's nothing like the depression that comes in when someone drowns, when you deal with the parents. It makes you so determined to prevent the next accident.'

Sometimes corpses floated or washed ashore. But often he would search for weeks at a time, trawling up and down with his grappling iron, waiting for the river to release her burden. He knew every back eddy, every obstruction; he had an instinct for how the river responded in different kinds of weather, a hunch as to where things got stuck in holes on the bottom. Frequently he had pulled out bodies right under the noses of the police divers, snagging something with his grappling iron after the official search had been called off. Then he would tow the remains slowly back upstream, keeping them beneath the boat for propriety's sake until he could find the shelter of a bridge or jetty to bring his burden aboard less publicly. If he was quick or lucky, it would still be recognisably human, and in one piece.

'You never really get used to it,' sighed George. 'But if it was somebody I knew, I'd want the body back too. It's closure, much better than never finding it. But believe me, I'd do anything to be redundant.'

George's job was itself a historical anomaly. Humane societies had once existed all over the world, an enlightenment reaction to religious censure of attempted suicides. 'Before that you were thought of as a felon if you tried to take your own life,' said George. 'And if you tried to rescue a suicide you could be arrested as accessory after the fact! But it was the time of the French Revolution, equality, fraternity and so on, and people thought this was a bad law.' Many societies, like Edinburgh's, had simply offered equipment and rewards for public rescues, and many had gradually handed over to conventional emergency services. But Glasgow had had a full-time officer at the ready on the Green since 1794 and wasn't about to retire him now.

'My father never wanted me to do this job,' said George. As a child he was asked to wait in the boathouse at certain times, unsettled by strong smells and lowered voices from outside as his mother comforted relatives who came to identify their dead. Yet his rowing skills outstripped most policemen's, and it was only a matter of time before George joined his father on their first joint recovery. One summer's day at the age of fifteen he helped drag the body of a young boy from the river after an accident on a home-made raft. It marked a turning point. Father and son became an inseparable team. The horrible scenes they witnessed together over the years seemed only to strengthen the bond.

The day Ben Parsonage died had started like any other. The pair had woken early in the morning of 1 October 1979. 'We'd been out on the river the day before,' said George, shaking his head. 'I was chatting to him, he was sitting on the side of his bed then he went to stand up – and collapsed.' George had tried and failed to resuscitate his father. It was a heart attack. 'My father died on the job. He never went abroad, never knew what it was like to have a holiday. I was stunned.'

Amid the shock and funeral arrangements of that day, a question hovered in George's mind: who would now guard the river? He wondered guiltily if now was the time to leave all this pain behind and devote himself to his art. But that afternoon the phone rang. 'It was Strathclyde Police G division CID saying there'd been an incident at Carylon Place and they wanted father to make a search of the river. They obviously didn't know Dad had died. I just said "Certainly, sir" – and went out and did the search myself. There was no way out. It was as though I was destined.'

He broke off and looked at something over my shoulder. On the far river bank a man in a Rangers shirt was moving unsteadily around a concrete bunker above the water's edge. George fished a mobile phone from his breast pocket and dialled a police contact. 'Aye, George here, at the river – I'm watching a guy here, definitely up to something in that wee workman's shelter opposite me. I've been watching dealing and injecting going on there for two or three weeks, and this guy is out of his box. You might want to send someone along . . . or he's going to end up in the water.'

George rang off and kept watching the man, who sat and rocked on his haunches, clutching his forearm with the other hand. A police car pulled up slowly on the footpath opposite, and two officers made their way gently down the bank. After a brief exchange one of the officers went into the concrete bunker and brought out another man, who was staggering even more than the first. The policemen searched them and found nothing, then let them go. They wandered off along the bank, holding each other up.

'I get very angry with the likes of that man,' said George, shaking his head. 'He could cause someone else to lose their life trying to rescue him. It's so flaming selfish. I tell that to every junkie I pull out of the water. I ask him if he's willing to see someone else die for his addiction!'

A young man in wraparound shades and an Irish coastguard jumper arrived from the marquee to tell George someone was looking for him. Mark Gash was an occasional volunteer with his older friend while studying in Glasgow. 'Nasty job,' I said. 'But it must have its compensations, all that gratitude?'

Mark looked unconvinced. 'To be honest, even the people that are rescued are embarrassed, they want to forget about it — we almost never hear from them again.' It was not uncommon for George to be cursed or assaulted by drunks or drug abusers as he tried to save their lives. People threw things in rivers when they didn't want them found: murder weapons, drugs stashes, torsos, body parts. There were gang fights, murders, people tied up and thrown off bridges wrapped in carpets or shod with concrete. When George inevitably retrieved them, not everyone was pleased. A few years ago, someone had dropped a paving slab on his head from a bridge as he passed beneath, fracturing his skull.

We stood in silence with Mark for a moment, watching the current stipple and eddy around a mooring post. 'When does George get time off?' I asked.

Mark shrugged. 'He doesn't, not really. It's a problem, because everybody is relying on him. There's nobody with that much knowledge.' He pointed out into the middle of the river. 'See that crisp packet out there? George would be able to tell you exactly where it will be in an hour.'

'But you can always be wrong,' cautioned George, reappearing behind us with a rueful grin and a half-glass of champagne. 'There was a man supposedly jumped off the Erskine Bridge last week but the police said they'd found him in Port Glasgow. I said that's impossible. But then the postmortem came through last week and the injuries were consistent with a fall from 200 feet, which certainly makes it sound like the Erskine Bridge.' He took a sip of champagne. 'So it looks like I was wrong.'

Most Glaswegians saw their river through a haze of grateful nostalgia. *Oh the River Clyde, the wonderful Clyde*, ran an old chorus, *The name of it thrills me and fills me with pride*. *Clyd* actually meant sheltered or warm – as fishermen in dugouts had first discovered four thousand years ago – and the original medieval city had grown up at a place so shallow that horses could wade across at low tide. Once dredged for commerce and cluttered with shipyards, it had made Glasgow the second city in the Empire, while hundreds of residents boarded steamers every Sunday for recreational outings 'doon the watter'. But George understood what most Glaswegians had forgotten about the river. You could trammel it between concrete quays, use it as a burnished backdrop for new housing, but you could never really domesticate it. The water now sucking at our landing stage had sluiced only hours ago from the Lanarkshire hills 100 miles away. By tomorrow it would be mingled with Atlantic salt, perhaps cloud vapour. There was none of Russell's orderly momentum here, no perpetual wave. Here, water reclaimed its true nature: that of turbulent anarchy, an energy whose only constant was change.

'You're never too old to learn from the river, always throwing up something new,' said George. 'She can be a good friend, but also a very cruel mistress.'

It was hard to imagine a more authoritative guide to the Clyde than the Riverman himself. I enquired casually whether George was planning any routine patrols downstream in the next couple of days, and told him briefly about my ongoing journey. He cocked his head and looked at me curiously, as if weighing me up. 'I'm not ruling it out,' he said with a half smile. 'How about a wee ride in the *Bennie* just for now, if you fancy it?'

The rowing boat pitched worryingly as I got aboard, followed by Mark. George untied us, pushed us off and stepped aboard in one seamless movement, gauging the balance of a boat perfectly. It was a balmy summer afternoon, ideal for messing about on the river, and George seemed to relax for the first time that day as he adopted the rowing pose and pulled us upstream, under an elegant iron suspension bridge.

'You know George was a champion rower?' said Mark.

'Still am,' grinned George. 'Scottish Open Champion in fixed-seat boats.' He also held the world record for Loch Ness in a rowing skiff. 'Two hours, 43 minutes, 34.1 seconds.' It was good to see him unwind a little, though he looked around him all the time, commentating on his daily patrol, how he always looked out for dangerous ladders, or retrieved lifebelts or balls that had been thrown into the river . . .

'Yeah, there were lots of balls in the Forth and Clyde Canal . . .' I recalled cheerfully – and then stopped. George was staring at me.

'And what did you do about them?' he asked, his oars poised mid-stroke.

I flushed. '*Do*? . . .' I trailed off.

George began to row slowly. 'No offence, but how would you feel if you read in the newspaper today that a child had drowned trying to get one of those footballs?'

I opened my mouth and closed it again. Mark was studying the floorboards. 'I'll tell you a story: there was a rowing eight going up the river not far from here, and a wee boy shouted to the rowers to pass the ball back to him on the bank, but they didn't. Half an hour later a policeman called them as they came back in the other direction, and asked them to help retrieve another object from the water: the body of the wee boy, who had drowned trying to reach his ball. They never went near the water again – that still haunts them, I'll bet. Just stop and think, that's all it takes.'

'When did that happen?' I stammered, eventually.

George frowned at me. 'I forget the date now – sometime in the fifties.'

We continued in near silence, the oars creaking in unison. A shadow had passed over the afternoon, the sunlight blotted out by the spectral vision of bones and bloated faces.

'Luckily kids are more interested in playing computers a lot just now, not many of them are poking around in canals,' he said, trying half-heartedly to lighten the atmosphere. 'But the pendulum will swing back, and God help us when it does!'

A klaxon sounded from the boathouse. George stiffened and turned the boat round, speeding the pace back to the shore to answer the phone in case it was an emergency (it wasn't). Clambering out of the rowing boat, I felt both guilty and annoyed by his lecture. Surely something was wrong when you got to the stage of hoping that kids would remain square-eyed sofa fodder rather than risk the physical danger of going outside?

Mark, struggling to change the subject, asked cheerily if I had seen George's sculptures. 'You know his real job is an art teacher?' he said, showing me into a makeshift gallery next to the boathouse. There were gondolas, motorbikes, flowers, galleons, fiddlers, all made from wire and bolts and welded scrap dragged from the bottom of the river. But dominating the small room was a near-lifesize metal representation of a sculler standing on end in such a way that it resembled a crucifix. Looking closer, I noticed that the sculler's hands were not gripping the oars, but were *nailed* to them.

If ever a man was in need of a holiday, it was George. I collared him outside, still troubled. 'It must be hard to see it like this when you're pulling them out of the water, but don't you ever think that kids taking risks is just one of those facts of life . . .'

George looked at me down his nose. 'You mean, is it worth me flogging myself to save six lives a year when there are thousands dying in wars?'

I hadn't quite meant that, no. But I found there was no acceptable way to frame the question. What I really meant was: isn't there a place where your responsibility ends and others' begins? Isn't there a place where life saving becomes life denying? I felt ashamed of the question, and dropped it.

Sitting in the office of George's little brick house, sipping tea a few minutes later, I peered around me at the trappings of a hero: a framed picture of George receiving his MBE from the Queen, the Mountbatten Medal for the best rescue in the Commonwealth, a number of policemen's helmets given as tributes and now balanced on the banister. There was a photograph of a younger George with his father, manhandling a grubby pink blanket bundled up with string, from which protruded a greyish human foot. It wasn't the sort of work that traditional superheroes did – this eternal battle with death, trawling the river for living flesh or gruesome relics. George had the hero's sense of destiny, but he carried it like a boulder.

'It's far too consuming for anyone three hundred and sixty-five days a year,' he admitted now. 'You can't put a frying pan on in case the doorbell goes, daren't have a bath unless there's someone else in the house. I never dared even make a commitment to meet a girlfriend because I might not turn up.'

In the end, he had met his future wife only when she did the one thing guaranteed to attract his full attention: 'I rescued her when her boat capsized!' Stephanie was a competitive rower, one of the few women who could rival him at the oars. She was also a born adventurer, which had a certain exoticism to a man who had spent his entire life on the same stretch of river. They had married ten years ago, and had two children together. 'She's been all over the place,' boasted George. 'Got kidnapped in Borneo, and a Papua New Guinean chief tried to buy her hand in marriage with a herd of pigs . . .'

'He should have offered more pigs!' said a voice in the hall. The front door clunked shut and in walked Stephanie, wearing a tired smile. She was a decade or so younger than George, with a rower's shoulders, frizzy red hair tied back in a ponytail and a summer-print dress. She kissed him, nodded at me and Mark, then frowned suddenly. 'Did you collect Matthew?'

'Oh, Christ!' said George, cringing out through the door. 'I forgot!'

There was an awkward and volatile pause, following the bang of the front door, in which Stephanie looked as if she was trying very hard not to swear.

'Must be hard being married to a superhero,' I joked. She gave a long sigh, not smiling. I offered to make her a cup of tea.

'Frankly, I have to function as a single parent,' she said presently, sinking into a chair and taking a sip. 'To me this house is a prison. I'm hoping very much that someone will sort it out.' Stephanie was a doctor at the local hospital, her salary keeping their heads financially above water. She had scored a minor victory in inducing George to take a week's holiday in Greece, but her ultimate aim was to help him find a way to ditch the job altogether.

'But who's going to take it on? Strathclyde Police won't recognise anyone he trains up because they're not qualified. He's the person who holds all the information on the River Clyde, the flood risks, the currents, where a body will go if it goes in at a certain point.

I've seen George do some incredible rescues, and some really stupid things. He's gone over the top of the weir, under the weir in a boat to save people's lives ... How do you allow yourself to have a normal life after that?'

I thought of George's sculpture of the crucified sculler, the inner agony it implied. Stephanie nodded slowly.

'Yes, and it's not just the feeling you get at the end of a sculling race. It's also that he believes his destiny is here, and that he can't wriggle out of it. He's a complicated man. He's an artist, that's where his talent is, and he did try his hardest to get out, have a life, but he never managed it. He would have to give up so much to have another life. I think the guilt would override it.' She sipped her tea sadly. 'He's still trapped. He's still the Lifeboat Man.'

George came back with their two children, who scampered upstairs. He gave Stephanie a contrite kiss, and she smiled forgivingly at him. It was a day for celebrating his considerable achievements, and they weren't about to ruin it with an argument.

'One thing I'm sure of — our children aren't going to find themselves in this same situation,' said George suddenly, just as his father had done before him. 'They're going to have a normal life.'

It was past 5 p.m. and time to be going. Just as I made my excuses, however, the peace was broken by an electronic trilling. The change in George was remarkable. He sprang to his feet, wide-eyed and rigid, and foraged desperately under the papers on his desk. 'Where's the bloody phone?!' he said. 'You know what that means, tonight of all nights . . .'

But Stephanie had found the source of the trilling: it was an alarm clock she had brought from the hospital, a gift from a pharmaceuticals firm. She held it up in front of George, and his relief fell across the room like warm rain.

I never did push George for that lift. It seemed a frivolous and unnecessary thing to expect from a man who lived his whole life on a state of high alert. As I wandered back through the park the afternoon was melting into a honey-coloured haze and people were lying on the grassy riverbank, chatting, laughing, pointing at swans. But all I could think of was how easily they might slip and fall in and drown and decompose and add to the intolerable burden of corpses on a man who had already spent too many years dredging for pain. I admired him tremendously, but I have never met a man so trapped in his life.

After so many years of saving others, who was going to save George?

5

The Buoyancy of the Human Soul

Glasgow to Helensburgh

I was pining for a seaside resort. An old-fashioned Victorian one, with a promenade and fish and chip shops and a warm salt wind off the sea. It was what Glaswegians once did to blow away the city blues: swarms of them boarded steamers at the Broomielaw Quay, and escaped 'doon the watter' to the summer resorts of Gourock or Helensburgh, trailing scarves of funnel smog behind them.

That was the age before continental package holidays, of course. Today the Broomielaw loomed empty and desolate, and the man I met walking his dog couldn't understand why I didn't just get a bus to Helensburgh like anybody else. 'Naebody uses the river any more,' he said. 'Them days are over.' Stubbornly, I walked on to the place where the Kelvin joined the Clyde, and looked across to the home of Glasgow's other great nautical tradition.

There was a time when Govan led the world in shipbuilding. At peak of production its string of yards were the epicentre of a *Clyde-built* boom which produced half the new ships on the planet. Looking across at its weed-infested wharves and tatty council housing today, it was hard to imagine. There was no longer even a ferry that could take me to the beleaguered south bank community. Long a symbol of urban deprivation, Govan's best-known resident was a fictional TV character, Rab C. Nesbitt, a string-vested welfare junkie with a tragicomic line in armchair philosophy.

Yet I had also heard intriguing rumours about a different breed of Govanite. While only a couple of yards were still open on the Clyde, with ever dwindling orders, someone had recently begun to produce *wooden* boats again: replicas of the ancient Highland galleys which plied the Western Isles; little rowing boats like the yoals used northwards in Shetland or Orkney.

Perhaps I could get a lift to the seaside with a group of urban Vikings?

'D'ye wannae know how ah got ma respect when I wis young?' said the man at the other side of the pub table, staring at me from pouched eyes. 'Running up tae random folk in the street and crackin' em round the head wi' a bottle!'

It was a quiet Monday evening at the Brechin Bar in Govan, and things weren't going quite as I had expected. After an afternoon of enquiries my best hope seemed to be Jamie Prentice, one-time hoodlum and reformed junkie who was passionate about rowing boats.

'I've been on heroin since I was nine, right?' said Jamie, rolling a cigarette. 'I was out on the streets when I was thirteen. Twelve years ago I stabbed my friend twenty times. I was drunk for fifteen weeks . . .' I nodded carefully, wrestling with the truly mental arithmetic. 'But I cannae live like that any mair. I've changed, man! Even my social workers cannae believe how much I've changed! Now, when I think aboot aw the stuff I done when I was a stupit wee boy, it hurts me. Cos I'm sensitive, man . . .'

He looked at me imploringly from under his baseball cap, his downy upper lip scrunching into a scowl through force of habit. In paranoid middle-class minds, people like Jamie spent their evenings hotwiring cars, shooting up in stairwells or sharpening their blades for the weekend scuffles outside the nightclubs. But this pale twenty-six-year-old seemed genuinely softened by something. He had ditched the heroin in favour of methadone, ditched the blades in favour of a guitar, and, perhaps most surprisingly, ditched fast cars in favour of a sedate form of river transport.

'It was destiny, man!' he said, his eyes wide. 'One day I just happens to walk into this shop. I thought it was selling furniture. I walked in and said: "Whit's happenin' here?" Turns out these guys build *boats*, for fuck's sake! It's shit hot craftsmanship! An' now *I'm* gonnae learn tae build a boat! Something I can be proud of!'

I had walked into the same 'shop' that morning, in a side street near to Govan tube station. Emblazoned 'Galgael' and festooned with fishing nets and carved wooden eagles and sea chests, it wasn't really a shop in the normal sense, explained its proprietor, a bear of a man with a long grey beard and an impressive mane of dreadlocks. Colin Macleod saw it more as a recruitment centre for his workshops, where people like Jamie were learning how to refloat their lives amid the tang of fresh-cut timber and linseed oil.

'The motto for Govan is *Nothing Without Labour*,' said Colin now, his dreadlocks swinging back and forth across his broad shoulders as he thumped the pub table for emphasis. 'We're trying to bring that work ethic back, restore that pride in craftsmanship, so Jamie here is a fuckin' inspiration to us all – know whit I'm saying?'

I had never met anyone quite like Colin. He threw out energy and ideas like a welding torch, always sparring and prodding for reaction — *know whit I'm saying?* — his eyes blazing with frustrated passion for his hometown and his river. As soon as I had mentioned I was looking for a lift, he had promised to help. The Brechin Bar would once have been crowded at this time of day, he told me. Raucous with half-deaf riveters, welders and joiners from the big shipyards lining the river banks: John Brown, Harland and Woolf, Elder & Co ... He listed them like the names on a war memorial. Shipbuilders still ruled the town when Colin's grandparents had come down from the Hebridean island of Lewis in the 1930s, like thousands of other crofters hoping to profit in the busy smog of Glasgow's industrialisation. But by the time he was old enough to benefit, orders had already haemorrhaged elsewhere. As the shipyards closed and the once-proud town slid into mass unemployment and drug addiction, Colin found his Hebridean heritage was all he had left.

Roaming the abandoned docks in his youth he had learned to carve ornate Celtic knotwork or mythical creatures into the old stone quays alongside the usual expletives and declarations of love. As his skill had grown, he'd taught himself to carve slabs and chairs and eagles. And boats. If they couldn't make vast steel ships like the *QE2* any more, the youth of Govan would learn to make little wooden ones. A forestry expert by training, he had begged storm-damaged timbers from friendly park wardens and grants from relevant bodies, and slowly an improbable nautical academy had taken shape. That afternoon, at an industrial unit squeezed between lockups and paintshops at the edge of the water, I had watched young lads standing alongside older men — skilled craftsmen thrown on the scrapheap when the yards closed — learning the patient art of priming wood with linseed oil, bending it to frame a shape.

'We're trying to open up a way for old people to come back and share their stories,' said Colin now, wiping beer off his beard. 'Up in the islands, if you've finished your career, you mend nets, you pass on your wisdom.' There were furniture and metal workshops, too, which it was hoped would spawn saleable products, but the big idea was that the young apprentices would row or sail the boats they had built. The Clyde, almost forgotten behind the derelict waterfront warehouses, would quicken the lifeblood of the community once again. We had already collared a couple of willing recruits to help get me downriver the following day, but we needed four or five. Before the night was up, I was hoping one of them might be Jamie.

We finished our drinks and wandered back to Jamie's flat, where he'd promised Colin a rendition of a new song he'd been writing. In the dusky remnants of a summer's evening, Govan had a melancholy air, its once-proud civic centre empty of people, the blackened stone buildings interspersed with the steel shutters of charity shops. We passed a statue on a plinth, a town hall, a library and a couple of conspicuously deserted tanning parlours. 'You might have noticed,' muttered Colin, 'that most Govan folk are milkbottle white.' The river, dark and mute, exhaled silently behind the buildings.

The door to Jamie's flat was meshed with scorched steel – somebody had recently tied to wrench it off and set it on fire. Jamie unlocked it warily, looking over his shoulder. Inside, the flat was meticulously neat, furnished with a sofa and beanbags, the obligatory silver television. On the wall was a framed Victorian print of a child blowing bubbles. Jamie made us mugs of strong tea and brought out his guitar.

'The thing aboot singing, right, man, is that if you sing tae a burd, ye'll get a shag,' he explained. 'It's been a while, I can tell ye . . .' He fiddled with an electric guitar tuner, twiddling the pegs experimentally.

'C'moan, man, it disnae need to be perfect,' said Colin.

Jamie frowned, shuffled a pile of handwritten sheets, chose one, then suddenly threw back his head and thrummed a chord. He sang in a throaty, Dylanesque way, closing his eyes except when he needed to check his fingers on the fretboard.

> *Like a bird for the first time*
> *Spreads its wings and flies away*
> *Everything that it sees will*
> *Fade away, will fade, I say.*

It was heartfelt and soulful – if a little frayed. We clapped extravagantly and Jamie opened his eyes.

'If I could be off methadone my voice would be a lot better,' he mumbled, smiling. 'Methadone closes your vocal cords, you cannae breathe properly. I know what my voice sounds like when I'm drug free and I'm positive and I've got the butterflies in my stomach and I'm happy . . .' He shrugged sadly. 'But all you can do is try.' His arm fell slack on his lap, revealing old needle marks on the white flesh. Suddenly I could see why his new boatbuilding hobby was so important.

'It's all behind you, man!' said Colin, sensing a sudden dip in confidence. 'You've been through a few things, but you've resurfaced. We'll get you off the methadone at some point. In the meantime, I can see you with your wee guitar, being an inspiration for these younger guys!'

He put down his mug and we got up to go. 'And while we're at it, how's aboot a wee row tomorrow? Nick here is needing to get doon river . . .'

Jamie looked from Colin to me, uncertainly.

'Whit time?'

'Nine?' I winced apologetically.

He held out a hand of friendship. 'Sorted.'

Colin seemed charged with new energy as we strolled back through Elder Park, gesticulating under great oaks and spangled skies. 'When I look at Jamie's life and what he's been through, Nick, I feel *hope*. I remember why I do what I do. Cos I believe in the *buoyancy of the human soul*.' He spoke it like an article of faith, and perhaps it was. 'You can push somebody down, down and down, but eventually they'll come up like a bubble. D'ye know what I'm sayin'?'

I did. I felt it too, this buoyancy. I thought of my defensive fears at the beginning of the evening — *junkie, ned, hoodlum* — and how inadequate the labels were if you bothered to look beyond them. How fear stunted potential. How cities bred fear. Colin had built the Galgael Trust on the philosophy that everybody belonged. 'Listen, *Galgael* actually means "strange or foreign gaels",' he said, as we climbed the stairs to his flat. 'It was the name given to the Norse incomers who became part of the Scottish melting pot, along with the Picts, Angles, Scots and Irish. If you look back in history, you can see how all this rich and diverse cultural input has made Scotland such an interesting place to be. The Celtic way has always been that you bring things to the table, and you're treated as an equal.'

I could have hugged the man. Being English, however, I simply grinned and told him how much I liked his vision. We lapsed slowly into silence, sipping whisky and contemplating the miles of orange sodium lights from the window. 'Well then, *Slainte Mhath*, boy,' said Colin, clinking my glass in a Gaelic toast:

Good health. 'We've got some serious rowing to do tomorrow.'

I bedded down on the lounge floor and fell asleep to the sound of sirens. But when I dreamed, it was of sea birds keening over empty shores.

'C'moan lads, gie it some welly!' bellowed Colin from behind his dreadlocks. 'We've got tae beat the tide!' It was a shorter-than-average longboat which laboured on past the deserted quays of derelict shipyards the following day. There were four of us paired on two benches, our oars flailing like the legs of a drowning beetle.

My lift downriver had begun later than I had hoped. Jamie had backed out after oversleeping, and a number of other likely rowing apprentices were apparently halfway along the Forth and Clyde Canal on their way back from a festival. Colin, not wanting to delay any longer, had rustled up three reserves to make up our crew of five, and we had launched the *Arthurlie* through a dilapidated boatshed.

'This boat is a carrier of dreams and aspirations,' he proclaimed, standing over us as we rowed slowly past the dark verticals of abandoned docks. 'Our average apprentice is not only building a boat, he's picking up skills and teamwork along the way: three months building the boat, then three months sailing her in the Hebrides. A rite of passage, a connection with your heritage . . .'

We were apparently rowing not so much a boat as a symbol. Even the best symbols needed to stay afloat, however, and a disconcerting trickling sound from beneath the floorboards was putting that in doubt. When an inch of water had risen around our feet, the man at the tiller had a sudden revelation. 'Colin, did you remember to put the bung back in the bottom of the boat before we launched her?' Three of us paused as the urgent implications of the question sank in.

Colin's brow furrowed momentarily. Then his eyes widened. 'Right boys!' he yelled. 'Row for the shore!' We pulled like madmen, the water rising steadily. Of the thoughts that raced through my head in those crucial minutes, the nightmare of drowning seemed curiously muted alongside the far more terrifying prospect of being dragged out alive by a furious George Parsonage. His thunderous expression of disappointment haunted me all the way to the disused wharf, where three of us scrambled up an iron ladder. Colin groped around valiantly under the floorboards in search of the small drainage hole which needed corking, then bailed robustly with a cut-off bottle for several minutes before using his own hat.

'Problem solved, lads!' he chuckled apologetically, as we climbed back aboard. 'I'd lose my head if it wasn't screwed on!'

But the tide had turned and we were still less than a mile from Govan. We would not be going to Helensburgh that day – at least not in a rowing boat. Instead we turned, raised a mast and canvas sail and switched to plan B – a call on a friend of Colin's on the north side of the river who had a powerboat.

I felt sorry to be leaving this band of optimists, but it was time to speed things up a little. Clambering onto a pier with my rucksack, I thanked them and watched the sail blossom defiantly against the grey docklands. 'Go well, Nick!' bellowed Colin from the helm. I waved them back off to Govan, thinking of the buoyancy of the human soul.

Gregor Connelly met me at the top of the steps. An affable, outdoor type, he ran a business as a powerboat trainer and wildlife tour guide, which allowed him to race around impressively in his sleek twin-engined rib. He quickly warmed to the idea of an evening spin down to Helensburgh.

'The most amazing thing about the Clyde today is the absence of boats,' he said, kitting me out with waterproofs, gloves and goggles. 'In the early seventies we would have had to book a time to make this journey – the ships were moored six deep along the banks.' Now the waterline was almost bare – a few half-built defence contract ships tied up at the BAE Systems yard, disused wharfs caked with slime and vast piles of scrap bound for Russia.

'Hold on,' yelled Gregor as we aquaplaned forward, sitting one behind the other astride a long black central saddle pleasingly reminiscent of a Raleigh Chopper. A startled heron flapped across the water ahead of us.

We roared past the empty slip where the *QE2* was once launched, and on beneath the darkening silhouette of the Erskine Bridge. Soon we were among hills and wooded slopes, the waters ahead brushed with a light mist drifting in from the sea. It was strange, after travelling so slowly for the past two weeks, to feel the thrust of a powerful engine. A vast blanket of cloud was drawing towards us from the west, gashed with sunset.

At Dumbarton Rock I took a turn at the wheel, keeping red buoys on the right, green on the left, my flexed legs absorbing the shudder of wavelets against the hull, an idiot grin on my face. It was getting dark, and there was a new smell in the air: the salty tang of the sea. Ahead of us the right-hand bank was receding into a vast estuarine darkness, speckled with lights which disappeared one by one behind the black silhouette of a capsized cargo ship. We navigated towards Helensburgh using the red neon of a fish and chip shop, and growled to a halt at the end of a long dark pier. I had barely thanked him and unloaded my stuff before Gregor was away again into the darkness.

A small, shrill bird, flew angrily around me – *Peewit! Peewit!* – as I walked towards Helensburgh's *terra firma* with an exultant shiver. A genuine seaside town. At the head of the pier, a gaggle of girls were sitting on some railings eating chips. They fell silent at my approach.

'Hello,' I said, awkwardly. They stared at me, their greasy fingers hovering like insects over the open petals of their chip supper. As I walked on past, exhausted, through the door of a convenient seafront guesthouse, I heard them giggle explosively.

'Where the hell did *he* come frae?'

6

The Red Button

Faslane Naval Base

Light rain clouds smudged the mountains out across the Firth of Clyde. The flat silvery expanse promised better things ahead, like the damp tarmac of an airport runway. I had slept deeply, and even padding 4 feet from the bed to the window felt an uphill struggle. In fact it *was* an uphill struggle: the entire floor sagged away from the walls on a noticeable gradient.

'Aye, she's an auld hoose, right enough,' agreed Anne, the landlady of the Imperial Hotel, shovelling up a cholesterol-boosting fry-up – sausage, bacon, fried bread, beans, black pudding and glistening fried egg – in a dingy back room bar. 'More than a hundred years auld, they say, but dinnae ask me any history.' I liked Anne. She had a faded but resilient beauty, a husky smoker's voice and the kind of earthy sadness that had probably earned her more than her share of lost souls spilling their personal tragedies over her counter.

This morning she left her three late risers to eat at separate tables, staring through coils of cigarette smoke at the television screen bolted to the wall. 'Are you a snob?' asked a chat-show host, facing the camera, in front of a studio audience bristling like a boxing crowd. 'Do you think you're better than other people?' He turned to goad a woman with a posh accent who had been foolish enough to admit she wasn't enjoying living on a council estate.

Helensburgh had a better-than-average claim to be the birthplace of television, having once been the home of John Logie Baird, whose experiments first revealed the potential for broadcasting moving images. I wondered if daytime TV was quite what he had in mind. In Baird's era Helensburgh was a seaside spa town drawing thousands of day-trippers and city dwellers down the Clyde, thanks in part to the efforts of Henry Bell, the town's first provost and a pioneer of steam navigation. These days it was known primarily as a dormitory for Glasgow commuters.

'Aye, the town isnae what it was,' said Anne, nodding sadly as she cleared my plate away. 'Nowadays, 75 per cent of my trade is from the submarine base.'

In retrospect, trying to thumb a lift from a Trident submarine was a little optimistic. Britain's nuclear fleet was docked only a short bus ride along the shore from Helensburgh, at Faslane, but I suspected there might be a few security problems with picking up nautical hitchhikers while carrying enough warheads to obliterate a large city. Still, there was no harm in asking. I had fired off a speculative begging e-mail shortly before leaving Edinburgh, just in case the military spooks took it seriously enough to need security clearance/phone taps/CND membership checks. Then I forgot about it.

So I couldn't quite believe my luck, later that day, when a Royal Navy PR consultant met me just inside the infamous razor-wire fences and offered me a tour of a Trident submarine. Shaline Groves was the friendly face of nuclear fission, drafted in with her competent smile and immaculate blue trouser suit to wrest back some media limelight from the pacifist mums, clergy and even politicians who had a knack of being arrested in high-profile demonstrations at the gates. 'The only difference between the folk outside the fence and the folk inside,' she said, ushering me into her car for the short drive to the dockside, 'is that they believe in unilateral disarmament and we believe in multilateral.'

It was a tricky balancing act, spinning positive human interest stories while tiptoeing round the Official Secrets Act, but Shaline had done her best to persuade her paymasters to give me a ride. Unfortunately, she said, once a submarine had submerged there was really no easy way to 'drop me off' at my next destination – but she hoped that a full guided tour of the newest vessel would give me any information I needed. She said all this with a nervous frown, while glancing at my fleece-lined parka, jeans and walking boots. It occurred to me I probably looked like the archetypal protester. I tried to reassure her by enquiring cheerily after the health of one of the base's 'hunter-killer' submarines (nuclear powered but conventionally armed) which, according to a recent radio report, had been brought home for repairs after running into an iceberg.

'I think we actually said it was a "floating object",' said Ms Groves, with a tenseness that suggested this had not been her greatest public relations victory. 'But, yes, it was in the Arctic . . .'

We drove circuitously through a self-contained settlement of brick buildings and corrugated hangars, past gymnasia, accommodation blocks, various saluting sentries with rifles, and disturbing notices such as *Nuclear accident evacuation route* and *Gas chamber*.

'Gas chamber?'

'I'm never quite sure what that is, exactly,' said Shaline quickly. 'I don't ask.'

We parked by the docks, walked through a security gate and down a pier towards a vast matt black submarine, then immediately doubled back. 'That's *Vigilant* – we're looking for *Vengeance*.' It was an easy mistake to make, as the four Trident subs stationed at Faslane all had swaggering macho names beginning with V: *Vigilant*, *Vanguard*, *Vengeance* and, lastly, *Victorious*, which was away at sea.

'Officially that's a secret, of course,' said Shaline with a nervous chuckle. 'But if *Vengeance*, *Vanguard* and *Vigilant* are all here, it doesn't take a genius to work out which one is missing.' I reassured her that she had betrayed nobody, and we proceeded to the next wharf where I gave my mobile phone to a man in a shed, apparently in case I had any plans to broadcast official secrets.

Vengeance, the newest of the fleet at four years old, lay vast and menacing at the quayside, 150 metres long, her muscular flanks bulging like a whale on steroids. An officer in an immaculate white shirt with epaulettes led us up the gangplank past the conning tower and on to the surface of the submarine. It was entirely covered in black rubber sound-absorbing tiles, giving the look of something already charred by unimaginable heat. I stepped quickly across the lids of the missile tubes and clambered down a ladder into the belly of the beast.

Like many people of my generation and older, I had gleaned what I knew of submarines from watching film adaptations of Tom Clancy thrillers or *Twenty Thousand Leagues Under the Sea*. So I was intrigued and a little disappointed to find that there was no red lighting, no eerie sonar 'pling', not even a periscope with flip-out handles. Instead I was led down a well-lit corridor among glossy white pipes and tubes into an officers' mess furnished with floral armchairs and a silver tea service.

'I'm afraid what you see in most movies doesn't bear much

relation to reality,' said Lt.-Commander David Rich, as a crewman poured the tea. 'We haven't got any windows to watch the bubbles coming out of the back. And fortunately we also don't get sea monsters coming through the starboard hatch.'

This provoked dark laughter from four other senior officers filing into the room, who formed a horseshoe of chairs around me and proceeded to launch a sustained if gentlemanly assault on every other mass-media myth imaginable. They were irritated at being portrayed as faceless, soulless nuclear killers behind barbed wire fences; annoyed at the assumption that this was an outpost of English-dominated military Empire when most of them were Scots living locally; at pains to stress their family status and support for the local Rotary Club; and just as regretful as the next man at the necessary evil of the annual cost of Trident, widely estimated at £1 billion.

'We're taxpayers too,' said Commander Julian Ferguson, the first officer, whose native Glaswegian upbringing had somehow produced a remarkably aristocratic English accent. 'I'd dearly love the local comprehensive to be maintained properly, and my daughter to come home with state-of-the-art textbooks. But how do you put the nuclear genie back in the bottle? Getting rid of our weapons wouldn't stop us from being a target.'

It was all very civilised, sipping tea and munching Penguin biscuits with Her Majesty's finest, but none of it could quite blot out in my mind the close proximity of missiles designed to fly into space and rain down death on random millions. The 3-metre wide launch tubes rose vertically through the various decks of the vessel, two rows of eight with the triple bunks for the 140 crew members honeycombed among them, their exteriors as innocuous as boilers in a primary school basement. Following Lt.-Commander Rich down the uppermost deck, I noticed a poster taped to a bulkhead:

'Safety first'. It was a cartoon of a banana skin, which seemed to me a reassuringly old-fashioned sort of hazard when you were sleeping inches from a nuclear warhead.

My guide preferred to focus on the everyday running of the vessel. There was always one British Trident sub patrolling the world's oceans at any given time, its location a closely guarded secret. The nuclear reactor manufactured its own oxygen and drinking water, which made it possible to stay submerged for anything up to three months at a time. With nothing to distinguish day from night, the men fell into a routine governed by meal times, performing their assigned duties in the weekly weapons readiness test. They staved off boredom – and each other – with DVDs, gym training or by studying for exams.

'It's hard to get away from each other,' said Lt.-Commander Rich, pausing outside a spotless sickbay labelled *God's Waiting Room*. 'So there can be no backstabbing – it's all front stabbing. If someone's got a problem, everyone starts to take the mick out of them, tells them to grow up. There's only been one incident of fisticuffs in fifteen years.'

A large aerial towed behind the craft picked up Radio 4 and enabled each crewman to receive his allotted forty-word message a week. 'The families will tell you it's a very difficult thing to do – forty words without asking any questions,' he said. It seemed to me a little like being sent to prison voluntarily for a quarter of the year – except here you weren't allowed to transmit anything in return.

'The quieter we are the less chance of being detected,' explained Steve, a bespectacled sonar engineer, pulling his headphones off. 'As long as we don't make any noise, the sonar absorbent tiles make us almost invisible to other ships. But we can hear everything that's around us. Sound is our greatest defence.' He pointed out vague shapes among the fuzz of the sonar screen. 'The strong trace here could be a ship, or more likely flow noise coming round the supports of the pier. So you don't actually have to hear noise to see it's there. But my wife tells me I've got exceptional hearing. In the twenty-one years I've been doing this job I've learned to tune into stuff that's out of the ordinary.' At any given moment, four people were stationed here with headsets, just listening. 'We're hearing all sorts of things – everything from dolphins to shrimps to fishing vessels. Ships give a clattering, chattering sound. Dolphins are very high-pitched – in fact, dolphins are a nightmare. Once they surround you they're with you for hours, they won't leave you alone. They love riding on the pressure waves.'

He was a thoughtful man, as passionate about sound as any classical conductor. I thought of the strangeness of noises heard underwater – some muffled, some pin-sharp – and how peculiar it must be, sitting on a night shift, listening to echoes across a lonely ocean. 'The spookiest noise is a whale singing,' said Steve. 'When there's no ships around that's when you can hear them miles and miles away. It's the most haunting sound you'll ever hear.'

The ear was the only organ you could really trust at sea, for the vessel was effectively eyeless from the moment it left the Clyde. No portholes, not even an external camera to break the enveloping sonar sheath of silence, as it burrowed, blind as a mole, beyond the reach of daylight. 'At 60 metres you wouldn't see much beyond the boat anyway,' shrugged Steve. A curious myopia spread through the crew during the weeks at sea. The eye muscles grew lazy, never needing to focus further than the end of a corridor, to the extent that submariners were banned from driving when they first got back to land after patrol.

The job seemed to require a rather selective sensitivity: a willingness to sharpen your hearing while dulling your sight. It was, I reflected, something we all did to some degree — screening certain things in order to focus on others. Here it must surely work on a moral level too: sharpen your duty in order to dull your qualms. You focused on the specific job you had been given within the machine, rather than dwelling too much on the machine's overall purpose. The foreplanesman to operate the two lateral fins, an afterplanesman for the tail fins, both of whom used what looked like fighter pilot handles and spoke into a wonderfully antiquated brass cone. But neither could actually say he threatened to wipe out cities for a living. Mind you, somebody somewhere presumably had the mother of all responsibilities. I could restrain my morbid curiosity no longer.

'Can you show me the red button?'

The Weapons Engineering Officer — known as the WEO, rhyming with neo — lived in a high-security part of the vessel to which 60 per cent of his crewmates had no right of access. When I arrived he had covered up certain parts of his control panel with cardboard. 'It's just so we can allow you through the door,' he explained, ushering me in. 'The front and back of the boat are British, but this bit is US-made.'

Lt.- Commander Steve Young was Edinburgh-born, a personable, confident family man now living on the base. He seemed unsurprised and unembarrassed by my request. He turned a combination dial on a small safe above the console, and opened the door. Inside was a red Bakelite version of the handle of a Colt .45 handgun, connected to the launch system by a curly lead. It reminded me of the handset of a computer game, the kind of thing you used in arcades to shoot up cowboy assailants.

'And have you ever . . . pulled the trigger?'

'Actually, I pulled it this morning.'

Every week on patrol, and occasionally in dock, the Admiralty would put the entire crew through the launch procedure without telling them whether it was a test or for real. When the signal came through, an announcement was tannoyed around the vessel calling XO and WEO – Ferguson and Young – to the wireless room, where they would each pick up an encrypted message and take it to a central control room for decoding behind a black curtain, using codebooks stored in a safe within a safe. They would then check the results against information to which only the captain was privy, before hurrying to their separate stations to initiate the launch sequence.

'I have two keys, one for the computer console, another for the trigger. I have it round my neck on a black lanyard.' He slid back a plastic shutter on the control panel to show a keyhole. The other important key was carried by the commander, fitting a tiny keyhole in his launch console – a grey plastic box covered in lights indicating the various states of missile readiness. Once the WEO had keyed in the guidance codes for the missiles, and the captain had flipped the requisite switches on his console, the two would talk through the final stages of the launch over an intercom. Turning his key from 'hold' to 'fire', the captain would give permission to fire, and the WEO would pull the trigger, unleashing Armageddon.

Steve flipped open a laptop and showed me a computer-generated DVD film of what would happen next. Fired by compressed gas through a membrane on the launch deck of the vessel, each missile – a monstrous 13 metres long, 3 metres wide and carrying 60 tonnes of high explosives – engaged its own rocket as soon as it broke the sea's surface. Crewmen would feel it as brief tremor underfoot. On the screen before me, I watched a missile ditch its first stage rocket motor and climb beyond computer-generated clouds. There was a terrible balletic beauty to its drift through space, using star sightings to reach a predetermined point. Then the warheads, little cone shapes, began their freefall back through the atmosphere. I watched mesmerised as they fell towards the clouds, as harmless-looking as bits of gravel dropped into powdery snow. As they disappeared I braced myself, staring at the screen. After a few seconds Steve coughed. The presentation was over.

I was puzzled. 'Would you not see the flash of a nuclear explosion from that height?'

He looked embarrassed. 'I think that was very much the politically correct version.'

In fact, the specific consequences of the strike — even its intended target — were shielded from all those aboard. Only the politicians and those releasing the coded information at the MOD would know for sure where the missiles were going and whether they would be detonated on the ground or in the air.

I looked at the glossy exteriors of the sixteen missile tubes, ranged in two rows along the tail of the vessel, and realised that I could at that moment be standing within a metre of nuclear warheads. Steve didn't deny it or confirm it. There was physically space for 192 warheads on board, but patrolling vessels 'only' carried up to a maximum of forty-eight, each of which could deliver a 100-kilotonne blast. Which meant that within the womb of this single bloated war machine on that sunny afternoon lay potentially enough nuclear weapons for three hundred Hiroshimas — or around three times as much explosive as was dropped in bombs on Britain and Germany during the whole of the Second World War.

'To be honest, this is quite an awesome job for me,' admitted Steve, as we made our way back to the officers' mess. 'This is about £900 million of equipment, and I'm only thirty-six. It's quite a responsibility. Before coming here I spent a lot of time thinking about what is involved in this job and being part of the firing team. In the end it's a necessary evil. The ultimate defence of this country rests on an ability to present a credible threat to another country. I agree with the idea of deterrence because it's kept the peace for a long time.'

I felt almost dizzy with the idea of two men holding that much power and responsibility for the lives of others. 'Touch wood we won't lose any lives while I'm in the job,' shrugged Steve. 'Whereas my wife, working in intensive care, has lost several.'

'But doctors and nurses can't wipe out entire countries.'

'Neither can we,' said the commander, joining us in the mess. It was a shared burden, this power, even for those who pulled the trigger. A chain of command in which no single link was culpable. 'Ultimately the responsibility for whether these weapons are used or not is the PM's. You've got to have faith in the way the country is organised and led.' He smiled irritably. 'Nuclear war is not a nice thought, but if you're not prepared to do what's required then you shouldn't be here. If there's anyone who doesn't feel that way then I need to know about it so we can get rid of them. Doubt is the enemy of deterrent.'

Outside the base a knot of protesters appeared dumbfounded that I had so flagrantly exposed myself to enemy propaganda. Their own particular position was displayed on their placards: 'THEY BUTCHER BABIES TO CLAIM THEIR OIL PRIZE!' read one in blood-spattered crimson. 'BLOCKADE THE ARMY BASES! SMASH THEM UP!'

'We're known as the dangerous anarchist element,' said a twenty-five-year-old named Scott, posing in a Palestinian scarf for a press photographer. 'The lead-up to the Iraq war proved that just waving banners doesn't achieve a thing. If we'd even just had a thousand people cutting this fence at once we'd have achieved more. If you're lucky they have to evacuate everyone when the alarm goes off. It's about interfering with the everyday running of the bases as much as possible – encouraging other people to do the same so that the business becomes unworkable.'

I envied him his certainty, his righteous anger. Two of the older protestors were a little more sympathetic to my seesawing mind. Jim and Jane had helped establish the local peace camp two decades back, and protested the arrival of the first Trident subs by ramming them with a little rubber boat. But they'd got a mortgage in Helensburgh since then, and, though they were still passionately opposed to nuclear weapons, it was harder to be quite so dogmatic about the people on the other side of the wire. 'Some in the peace movement would say these people are all completely immoral, but it's not that simple,' said Jane, whose fleece and floral trousers seemed more school run than direct action. 'I now know lots of people living on the base, and a lot of the guys are good family men. I get on well with them, we run car boot sales together. A lot of them feel they're doing the right thing . . .'

Middle-aged protestors weren't the only ones feeling the chill winds of a complex new reality. The Cold War was over and the world that Tridents had been built to police had all but disappeared. The new enemies were stateless terrorists willing to strap explosives to their own bodies. What use were bombs big enough to annihilate countries? Nowadays weapons scientists were working on laser-targeted, bunker-busting weapons, and more shadowy innovations. It was only a matter of time for Trident. I wondered how many more years the two sides would stick it out, peering at each other through the fence.

Today's gathering dissolved harmlessly with little more than a few slogans and scowls from security guards, and I followed Scott back to the peace camp. A collection of ageing caravans clustered under trees, it was certainly more homely than the submarine, if a little lower tech. A bicycle-powered generator in a shed provided the only electricity, and the communal bath was a scorched tub propped on bricks in a clearing. 'You fill it with water, then light a fire underneath it,' explained Hoosie, a resident hippie. The compost latrine had been named George W. Bush to encourage regular bowel movements.

There were only five permanent residents, one of them in a wheelchair. 'It's not an easy place physically but it's great for support,' said Wheels, a Geordie with a pierced eyebrow, who lived in his 'wheelchair accessible bender' – an assemblage of tarpaulins and sticks. 'In cities nobody trusts anybody else. But here if someone has got a problem, we all sort it out together. Everybody looks out for each other.'

We huddled in the communal kitchen, sipping herbal tea. With its dark corners and rounded roof, it felt a little like what I had expected from the submarine: a small group of committed people with a clearly defined enemy, united by their certainty. 'At the end of the day we might never win,' said Wheels, philosophically. 'But at least we can say we tried.'

The conversation trailed off and was replaced by the sound of pattering on the tarpaulin roof.

'Bloody rain,' muttered Hoosie, deflated.

'It rains here 70 per cent of the time,' said Scott angrily. '*They* chose this location deliberately.'

7

No Urinating from the Poop Deck

Gourock to Crinan

Back in Helensburgh I boarded a ferry across the estuary to Gourock, another faded Victorian seaside resort. In its heyday, this hub would have given me the option of thirty-nine different steamships weaving across the Firth, back to Glasgow, or out to the islands. These days, with only three of them still running, I was going to have to be a little more resourceful. Sitting on a park bench on the deserted promenade, I unfolded my map and searched for open sea. The obvious route was to follow the Firth of Clyde down the inside of the Kintyre peninsula before rounding the Mull and heading north again. But there was also a short cut: smaller boats could weave through the Kyles of Bute to Ardrishaig and then across the peninsula using the Crinan Canal.

Crinan. The very name gave me goose bumps that afternoon. It felt like my portal to the past, to familiar touchstones of belonging. I warmed myself momentarily around a favourite memory in which family and friends gathered below a hurricane lamp in a little cabin on a Scottish island, playing cards late into the night, listening to the wind ... What was particularly compelling about this idyll was that I could potentially relive it within the next few days if only I could rendezvous with family friends in Crinan before they all went home. Out in the bay, triangular sails beckoned towards the silhouettes of distant Highland peaks. It was time to make something happen.

The MV *Menno* was not the most glamorous of vessels. Essentially a large, rectangular biscuit tin fitted with a crane and a necklace of tyres, she patrolled the Clyde keeping the 130 gas- and solar-powered navigation buoys in working order. Despite her looks, she commanded the sort of fierce loyalty you'd expect from the crew of an Elizabethan galleon.

'One day all boats will be shaped like this,' grinned Brian the skipper, throttling midstream on a retreating tide as the crane operator lowered a vast, weed-shagged buoy on to the deck. Outside the wheelhouse, a team in luminous orange boiler suits was demonstrating how many men it takes to change a light bulb. I counted eight. Apart from Brian and the crane operator, there was one man to attach a safety line to the buoy's fat anchor chain, three to scour the weed and barnacles from its side with instruments like wallpaper scrapers on long poles, others to daub the rusty upper section with new green paint. And of course the light bulb changer himself, climbing up the ladder past the solar panels, and tinkering inside the chamber.

Gregor the speedboat man had put me in touch with the *Menno* that morning at Greenock's container terminal. Brian and his crew had readily agreed to take me through the Kyles of Bute, if I didn't mind stopping to maintain the buoys. We were hovering in a bottleneck at the eastern end just now, flanked by rocks mottled with weird lichens, as the bladderwrack writhed in the current around us. The men bantered as they went about their well-choreographed tasks; one of them grinned up at me holding an orange starfish to his chest like a sheriff's badge. A 'happy ship', whose company might at any moment break into a chorus of 'Whistle While You Work'. Next to the lifeboat instructions, a brass plaque requested: *Will members of the crew please refrain from urinating from the poop deck.* There was something close to joy in it.

They dropped me at the quay in Portavadie, where I caught the thirty-minute ferry across to Tarbert. It was a glittering, breezy afternoon, and the whitecaps stretched away into invisibility behind a slight sea haze. Trapped in the armpit of the Kintyre peninsula, the water peaked and furrowed wildly, as if scenting what lay beyond the hills.

Tarbert, an eye-wateringly beautiful old fishing village which had found new life as a yachting destination, had sounded a likely place to pick up a ride through the Crinan Canal a few miles further north. But today most yachts were silent at their berths, and the only obvious candidates – an older English couple in expensive waterproofs – had already paid a man to help them through the lock gates. When I asked meekly if I might tag along anyway, they looked as terrified as if I had just invited them to a swingers' weekend. I backed off, apologising. Some people just didn't get this hitchhiking thing.

By five the wind was stiffening, and I realised that if I delayed any longer I might not make it to Crinan in time for my rendezvous with friends. With rather more haste than forethought, I accepted a lift from a couple of teenage brothers keen to show off their new speedboat. It was very like the one Gregor had driven along the Clyde, though with only one engine. If it was a car it would have had tinted windows, spoiler and fluffy dice. 'Make sure you've got all your stuff in dry bags,' said Darren, the younger of the two, leaping into the driving seat. 'You're going to get wet.' Cameron braced himself at the stern, looking nervously at his brother. As we roared out of the shelter of land, I understood why. The waves heaved loutishly against the boat, their tips breaking into spindrift under lowering black skies. I clung girlishly to Darren as he accelerated over the top of them, and thudded down into the troughs. 'Darren, either slow down or sit down,' shouted Cameron. Darren speeded up, the suddenly airborne propeller roaring hysterically before burying itself in another wall of water.

We finally pulled into Ardrishaig harbour to find a solitary figure watching us nervously from the quay. 'That's Dad,' explained Darren, typically blasé as he slid alongside. I waved guiltily, realising I had just accepted the maritime equivalent of a spin in his teenager's souped-up Ford Escort. But by the time I had climbed the ladder on the pier and hauled up my bags, the little boat was already speeding back into the distance, and Darren's dad had disappeared back up the coast road home.

Relieved, I wandered along to the canal basin and sized up the best place for a lift the following morning. Then it began to rain. Hard. Ardrishaig's main street was entirely deserted as I walked damply along it in search of lodgings. The only immediate opportunities for human contact were a hall full of Jehovah's Witnesses and a Spar shop which closed as I arrived. I was just beginning to feel really sorry for myself when somebody began to play a lament on the bagpipes. Soul-stirring as it may conceivably be when breasting a hilltop in the Highlands, this is not an instrument one yearns for when it's raining. I listened incredulously for a moment and started laughing. Ten minutes later the proprietor of the Grey

Gull Inn was surprised to have his nightcap interrupted by an inanely grinning Englishman who looked like he'd just walked out of the sea. I had made it to the canal — and that meant tomorrow I would be among friends.

8

Islands of the Mind

Crinan to Macaskin

Crinan Harbour had the topography of childhood. The almost-final destination on my first trip to Scotland, aged eight, it was etched on my mind like a sepia photograph: a boathouse, a landing stage, the beckoning sea.

But today it looked wrong, somehow. After hitching nine miles along the Crinan Canal with a couple of elderly yachties, I had arrived in a place I only half recognised. Standing at the edge of the basin, I vainly scanned the thickets of masts, trying to encourage the pooling of fragments. Where were the boathouse and the landing stage? Where were the friends I was supposed to be meeting? The only familiar landmark was the Crinan Hotel, stately and whitewashed on the road above the sea lock. 'It'll be the harbour you're wanting, not the canal basin,' said the barman, drying a glass. 'It's round the other side of the promontory – a wee walk through the woods.'

I followed his directions up a lane and turned right into the trees, intrigued at how the years had merged two separate places. I could hear only my own breathing and the rustle of foliage against my rucksack. Breaking out of the undergrowth, I stopped. Another single-track road ran straight along the forested edge of a bay dotted with moored yachts and dinghies. On it was the boathouse, built from breeze blocks. And at the far end of the road, on a floating pontoon, was a familiar cluster of excited children and adults carrying boxes and bags between the shore and a broad-beamed wooden motorboat. I walked towards them, feeling like an unseen ghost watching my own childhood holiday, until one of the figures turned and recognised me. 'Perfect timing,' said Lizzie, giving me a hug. 'We're just about to cast off.'

Lizzie had been a favourite friend in the innocent age before hormones kicked in. She still had the familiar giggle but was now well ensconced in motherhood with three kids and a towering husband. It was good to be known again. There was no need to introduce myself, or ask them for anything, or neuter my accent. I stowed my rucksack under a bench and made my way to the bow where Uncle Chris was fiddling around with the mooring line. He wasn't a real uncle, but the honorary title denoted the significance he had had in my growing up. 'Glad you made it,' he said with a grin. 'We were just trying to work it out — how long *is* it now since you came to The Island?'

The Island. We had always referred to it with those mythic capital letters, though somewhere out there in the haze it was real enough. It was called Macaskin, a rugged little scrap of land purchased by Chris's Scots forebears. Every summer for the past hundred years, various parts of their extended family had taken turns to invite friends to spend a fortnight in a cluster of wooden huts on its southern tip, living without running water or electricity and exploring the surrounding coves in small boats. To children reared in a London suburb it was pant-wettingly exciting, like finding yourself in the middle of *Treasure Island* or *Swallows and Amazons*.

We had set off in this same old clinker-built boat, *Wigeon*, that first summer in the late 1970s, our unsuitable luggage wrapped in binliners under the seats. Today, Lizzie's son Tom was learning to steer much as I had done then, a frown of concentration etched on his young forehead. Chris caught my eye and smiled. 'Good memories?' he shouted above the engine noise. I grinned back as the harbour fell away behind us.

Ahead, The Island materialised like a photograph in a developing tray. I watched the cliffs solidify above the rectangles and pitched roofs of the cabins, wondering how much I had modified the image in my mind. The rocky landing was still the same, a jagged sideways-leaning promontory, the purple kelp swirling in clear water, slapping against the grey stone. I walked up the path towards a familiar single-storey chalet with its huddle of shed-like outbuildings.

Inside, the room was smaller and lighter than I remembered it. I inhaled the aroma of old wood and took in the details, one by one. A stone fireplace my father had helped to build; wooden cupboards polished by use around their handles. Shelves of classic green and orange Penguin books. Binoculars and bird-watching guides. A glorious model sailing ship with intricate rigging. Tins full of bits and pieces, and up in the rafters — much closer to the top of my head now — bamboo fishing rods and tackle boxes.

And in the corner, the visitors' book. Dumping my rucksack, I flipped back to 1978. There it was, in the painstaking joined-up letters of an eight-year-old: 'My best holiday ever.' Scanning through the years, I discovered two further teenage visits, the loopy writing now leaning forward for speed. A proud mention of 'Fort Brackenhill' — our hideout built from old driftwood and heather.

In twenty-five years the place had hardly changed at all. The wood had darkened with handling, the windows had been enlarged, extensions had been built. But there remained no television, no electricity, no running water, and therefore the necessity of taking one's time over elemental tasks. An old mangle stood like a guardian of ancient values at the path that led to the toilet hut – known, for reasons lost in the mists of time, as 'Twenty Seven'. As in all the best children's fantasies, everything had a strange and quirky name. The zinc water flagons with their rope handles were 'Alice' and 'Alice's aunt', the shiny brass boiler which squatted over the fireplace was Bunty, and the sleeping huts were Grampus, Porpoise and Walrus. These traditions held solid from year to year, decade to decade. That was the beauty of the place, its fiercely defended *raison d'être*. It was an outpost which the modern world could not touch.

Sprawled happily in a deckchair outside the cabin that evening, I watched the three children making their own memories in the low orange sun. Dan, Tom and Caitlin were climbing the rocks on an old piece of fishing net, racing past the boulder where I had knocked the corner off a tooth at the same age. I shuffled through my own dog-eared collection of mental snapshots: my dad standing on the roof with a chimney cleaner's brush, pretending to be Charlie Chaplin; rapt faces crouched over rockpools; and the expeditions in search of 'crocodiles' (driftwood logs) around the rocky coves and bays.

After supper, when the children had gone to bed, we sat together retelling a few of the best stories, warming ourselves around our shared history. Later, washing by the light of a candle in a tin bowl, I felt a grateful ache. I loved The Island for the way it connected me, however tenuously, to the country I had chosen to live in. It was the nearest I would ever get to a Scottish childhood.

*

I stayed alone on the island the following morning, while Chris ferried everyone else back to the mainland. Not wanting to leave, I had offered to help him close up the cabin, which required that we both stay one more night. I shinned up a steep rock face behind the workshop and waved them all off towards the horizon. From this favourite solitary spot you could see a long way. At the height of my religious teens I had come up here to think and pray, all my senses sharpened and tingling with a sense of a Creator at large in the natural world around me. It was one of my strongest memories of what I would now call joy.

Two decades later I contented myself with listening to the gentle sounds around me: the sucking of the sea at the rocks below; a whispering of the wind in the sea pinks; and quiet tearing of grass from a sheep breakfasting a few feet away. *Wigeon* appeared in the distance shortly before midday, and I picked out her skipper through the binoculars, his head confidently thrust into the wind. I went down to catch his bows at the landing stage. We heated up some soup and leftovers for lunch, and set off to walk round the island together. It was a rugged piece of land, with cliffs, bracken-choked gulleys, rocky beaches, upland meadows and a small forest at the other end. Chris strode on ahead, exclaiming at the weather. The sky was an improbable blue, with downy clouds draped over the summit of Creag a Bhanan. We worked our way through waist-high bracken, stooping to drink cool, peaty water from the island spring. A breeze blew in over the sound, laden with the smell of greenery and budding earth, and set the meadows of yellow flag nodding.

On the forested north end we stopped at a little bungalow once owned by Sir Reginald Johnson, better known as the retired tutor to Pu Yi, the last Emperor of China. At one point, said Chris, the reclusive Buddhist had his rooms painted individually in blue, yellow, pink or mauve, so that he could meditate in a mood suited to the appropriate colour. On a garden bench were words inscribed in Latin which translated as: 'Never less idle than when idle; Never less alone than when alone.'

I found it a peaceful, encouraging sort of slogan, pleasingly mysterious. Chris would probably have preferred something more muscular, having spent his whole working life as a vicar in the clear-cut universe of evangelical Christianity. It was his passionate certainty that had sparked my early interest as a twelve-year-old on a Church youth camp. It was August 1982: a vivid, momentous holiday, dominated by my first crush (she didn't reciprocate), news of the birth of my sister, and an unexpected whiff of something interesting behind all the gospel choruses. I could still hear Chris's sonorous voice broadcasting the unconditional love of God across the marquee. Wracked with unrequited puppy love, I had willingly funnelled my emotions heavenwards, repenting of sins I've since forgotten (though scrawling *Adam and the Ants* on a school bench probably made it in there somewhere) and reciting Uncle Chris's conversion prayer with a fervour I might otherwise have wasted on the gorgeous Jo Edwards. As I knelt there mouthing the words, I felt a curious sensation – like the tingling of the scalp after the school nit lady had been to work, only better. Baffled but delighted, I tore around the campsite whispering *thank you* into the night air. It was as if someone had pulled a ripcord on my heart. One way or another I've been pursuing that feeling ever since.

We waded back up over the grassy, humped back of the island, through plateaus of bobbing cotton grass, talking tentatively about how our ways of thinking had changed. Chris had been knocked about by parish ministry but his faith was intact: a lean, weathered version of that crusading zeal, like a battened-down boat which had navigated through a storm. In his faith, as in his seamanship,

Chris was as single-minded as ever about pulling drowning souls aboard.

I listened silently, feeling vaguely inadequate. I missed the passion and the certainty, but over the years it had become claustrophobic, like a nuclear submarine requiring the exiling of doubt in order to focus on the urgency of Armageddon. I craved a roomier vessel, a glimpse of sky, the freedom to take back routes around the coves examining interesting existential flotsam. I was still sniffing the wind, following something just over the horizon, even if I couldn't quite see what it was.

But I had a feeling that in Chris's world I was simply adrift.

'We all have these doubts,' he said, nodding at my ponderings. 'But of course there's a danger that people get so caught up with the journey that they forget there was ever supposed to be a destination.'

Back in the cabin we cooked up a few last leftovers for dinner, listening to the shared liturgy of the shipping forecast, before turning in early.

I lay awake for some time that night, listening to the wind and the pattering of rain on the roof. The Island hadn't changed. But I had.

9

The Patron Saint of Wanderlust

Around Jura

The last steam puffer in Scotland hunkered down in the corner of Crinan basin like every little boy's bath-tub boat: a towering prow and a stubby red funnel spewing the sort of smoke best drawn with a black crayon.

'You can't possibly do a nautical odyssey around Scotland without going on a puffer,' declared her portly, bespectacled skipper. 'And as it happens we've had a couple of American passengers cancel this week – they think Europe's overrun with terrorists. So why not tag along with us for a few days?'

Nick Walker was precisely the eccentric entrepreneur you might expect to find at the wheel of this nautical *Chitty Chitty Bang Bang*. We spotted him at the helm minutes after coming ashore from Macaskin, his checked shirt clashing cheerfully with baggy mustard corduroys and a woolly hat in a manner which had once got him mistaken for a Romanian fairground attendant. Formerly part of a now-vanished wartime fleet which provisioned the island communities, the restored *Vic32* now sailed her old territory with a cargo of steam buffs on five-day working holidays.

I needed to be back in Crinan by the end of the week in the hope of joining a boatful of northbound Celtic monks, but in the meantime I had the perfect opportunity to eddy around some more southerly islands. I gratefully accepted Nick's invitation, waved Uncle Chris off on his long drive south and brought my bags aboard.

Once a simple receptacle for coal, cement or munitions, the hold of the *Vic32* had undergone a startling conversion. Above a lower floor of cosy passenger cabins was a kitchen and captain's quarters, and a wood-panelled passenger lounge with stuffed sofas arranged around a wood-burning stove. Interior décor was baroque veering towards bordello, with an upright piano, a plastic parrot perched on a set of wall-mounted stag's antlers and a little brass notice reading *Passengers will be flogged until morale improves*. A lovely old 78-speed gramophone played scratchy jazz with the aid of an assortment of pipes. 'We rigged it up to run off steam,' explained Nick. 'Almost everything is steam driven here – the engine, the winch, the tea urn . . .'

Steam wasn't something I had especially strong feelings about, which put me at a conversational disadvantage over supper that night. My eclectic fellow passengers included an anaesthesiologist, a town councillor and a white-haired former schools inspector – but they shared a perplexing passion for gaseous H_2O. 'Steam has a certain beautiful simplicity,' said one aficionado, looking into the middle distance as he bit off an asparagus tip. 'It's not like modern inventions where everything's hidden away and you've no idea why it works. It's more obvious, and much easier to understand where the energy is coming from when you've actually shovelled the coal yourself.'

He meant that literally, I discovered the following morning, as we assembled on the quayside before a glistening black mound of the stuff. 'Forty barrows should do it,' breezed Nick. 'Twenty on each side.' We slaved voluntarily in the sun for half an hour, emptying barrow after barrow down holes in the deck until we were ready to chug out through the sea lock.

A small crowd of tourists and steam anoraks had gathered on the wharf as one of the passengers emerged from below deck with a set of green velvet bagpipes. He flicked the reed a couple of times, then struck up 'The Skye Boat Song' as the water in the lock began to fall.

'Get away with you!' yelled a voice from above. 'Terrible stuff!' It was the manager of the Crinan Hotel complaining not, as it turned out, about the bagpipes but the fug of smoke that was engulfing him on his balcony. Nick waved back politely and grinned at the tourists, who clapped as an echo of the melody now tooted from a little row of steam whistles clustered round the funnel.

'People tend to forgive us for pouring black smoke all over their washing, because we're part of Scotland's history,' explained Nick, leaning over a chart in the wheelhouse as we coasted out on to Loch Crinan. 'Islanders tell us they used to stand and watch the puffers coming in – they were their lifeline. They knew to clear the rocks from the shore so they could beach themselves for unloading.' Meanwhile *The Tales of Para Handy*, the TV and print chronicles of a fictional skipper and his boat, the *Vital Spark*, had done for puffers what Captain Kirk had done for spaceships.

Outside, in the broad strait between the rocky mainland and the Paps of Jura, the wind was worrying the water into whitecaps. Behind the teak binnacle, where a tomato plant was quietly flourishing, someone had erected a primitive barometer. It was a small piece of rope nailed to a board titled 'Weather Station', accompanied by the following guide:

Rope vertical	Calm
Rope flapping	Windy
Rope horizontal	Stormy
Rope dry	Dry
Rope wet	Rainy
Rope white	Snow
Rope rigid	Frost
Rope invisible	Fog
Rope gone	Hurricane

'This is a force 6, gusting 7,' decided Nick, consulting a slightly more modern indicator. 'We'll head for shelter in Loch Sween tonight.' From below deck, barely audible above the wind on the wheelhouse roof, came the merest whisper of engine noise, like the sound of a sewing machine.

'Goes like a dream, doesn't she?' he grinned, opening the door and handing over to his first mate, Paul. 'An internal combustion engine uses explosions, but steam works on gas pressure. She's so quiet you can sometimes hear the porpoises out in the Sound of Jura.'

Down in the engine room, the heat hit me like a sandbag. Perched on a metal gantry, I surveyed a scene from Dante's *Inferno*. A figure in a blue boiler suit shovelled coal through an open door, his spectacles glinting crazily in the hellish orange light from the furnace. This bearded cave dweller didn't so much stoke the boiler as prostrate himself in veneration before it, hurling coal into its insatiable maw for at least two hours before every sailing. The slave looked up at me and grinned, mopping his forehead. His name was Keith.

'It can get up to II5 degrees down here,' he sighed happily, dropping his shovel. 'But it never loses its attraction. Once steam gets under your skin, you're hooked for life.' He had been working down here for six seasons, slaving through the Scottish summers, then flying home for a second blast of heat in his native New Zealand. 'Sweating's good for you — clears your pores out, gets rid of the good malt whisky you've been consuming the night before.'

A disembodied voice quacked through a brass pipe from above. 'Little bit more power?'

Keith pulled a lever. 'Coming up . . .'

The cramped room around me was full of brass tubes and valves and dancing pistons which spun the propeller shaft around with a *whuppa whuppa* sound. Catching my flushed, fattened reflection in the side of the 600-gallon idol, I was also beginning to see the attraction. The alchemy of fire and water.

'It's totally different down here when it's not working,' said Keith. 'A cold bloody lump of machinery. But as soon as steam starts coming through the main steam valve, she turns into this live monster! Burns about a tonne of coal every 50 miles, and if you have an emergency and run out of coal you can always start burning the furniture . . .'

The system had its drawbacks, of course, not least that it took those two hours of stoking to build up a sufficient head of steam to power the engine. The practical ramifications of this made themselves dramatically clear the following morning when I was woken by muffled yells and the clattering of the anchor chain on the outside of the cabin. 'The anchor dragged during the night — we almost hit the rocks,' said one of the galley staff as I came up to breakfast. Keith emerged some time later looking like a man who had dived into a coal bunker, much to the amusement of Paul.

'We had to wait more than an hour to get the boiler ready,' he tutted, doing his best to wind up his crewmate. 'I had to stave us off with a pole from the dinghy!'

Keith's eyes, panda-like with coal dust, narrowed. 'Bloody cheek coming from someone who can't even lay an anchor properly!'

We had moored close to a kelp-covered rock in the sheltered harbour of Tayvallich, where Nick was planning a historical morning stroll before we set off for Jura. By eleven o'clock we were all panting on a hilltop admiring the Paps of Jura across a cloud-shadowed sea, while, to our south, were forested valleys. 'It's quite Tolkeinesque, isn't it?' said Nick, putting down his bag next to a cairn.

From this height it was easy to see how the first Scots had turned out to be Irish. The two countries were just 12 miles apart at their closest point, and sometime in the fifth century a race of traders, known by the Romans as Scotti, had come across the Irish Sea in their skin boats and decided to settle. Nobody knows quite what prompted this sudden migration – whether land shortage, power struggles or simply wanderlust – but it was to spawn the powerful sea kingdom of Dalriada. In an age when land travel was arduous and the terrain rough, sea was evidently more a bridge than a barrier.

Traders weren't the only ones to cross the water. Steaming across the Sound of Jura that afternoon, we anchored briefly off tiny Eilean Mor, a grass-covered retreat apparently once favoured by a reclusive monk called Cormac. Seafaring saints had proved one of Ireland's most powerful exports over the centuries. The big names were St Ninian and St Columba, who famously converted the first tracts of pagan Scotland to Christianity and began the tradition of anointing kings at Dunadd, near Crinan. But this island's lesser known resident was more of an enigma. Where had he lived? There was a roofless stone chapel which had more recently been used as a whisky still, but St Cormac pre-dated both. It seemed he preferred a damp cleft of rock on the other side of the island. Two crosses were etched on the walls. There was barely enough room to lie down. We stood and stared at it.

'That's what religion does to you,' muttered Daphne, the ship's cook. 'He comes to an idyllic island like this and then lives in a hole in the ground. He must have been potty.'

Personally I rather liked the fact that a man with heavenly ideas had some dirt under his fingernails. Ireland's seafaring monks seemed to me to epitomise a robust, adventuresome kind of spirituality, their inner faith reflected in their outer journeys.

'You'll probably be interested in these nutters, too,' said Paul digging out a week-old issue of the *Argyllshire Advertiser* when we got back to the boat. He pushed it across the mess-room table.

ST COLUMBA BOAT DUE TO DOCK IN CRINAN

MID Argyll will have a special visit from a special boat next week. Irish-built curragh Colmcille will sail round the West Coast of Argyll on its epic voyage, replicating that of St Columba in 563 AD. The 37-foot curragh will be the transport of an international crew of 13 dedicated rowers from America, Ireland and Scotland, captained by the Irish Yachtsman, Robin Ruddock. The crew will depart from Ballycastle, Northern Ireland and sail to Iona via the Mull of Kintyre. They will eat the same food as sixth century monks, dress in robes and sing ancient hymns as they make their way to the island . . . The Colmcille will arrive in Crinan Harbour on Friday.

'Oddly enough, you're right,' I said, poring over the scant details. 'I'm due to join the crew on Friday.' If they were keeping to their timetable, the rowers would be across the Irish Sea by now, making their way steadily up the peninsula. If everything went to plan, the two boats — steam-powered and canvas-skinned — would dock in Crinan the same day, just in time for me to transfer my luggage and put on my cassock. Then it would be two days of rowing to Iona, more than 40 miles to the north-west.

Paul was looking at me with some bemusement. 'Rather you than me, mate.'

When we docked at Craighouse pier that afternoon, I rushed straight to the Jura Hotel and phoned the expedition organiser. I was diverted to his voicemail, which was disappointing if understandable: there was probably nothing more irritating to a monk under sail in a genuine curragh than to hear a mobile going off in the pocket of one's authentic robes.

After supper I ensconced myself in front of the bookcase in the ship's lounge for a little hagiography homework. St Columba was easy enough to track down — in the realms of Scottish sainthood he ranked as an A-list celebrity, with the added frisson of a reformed bad boy. Born in Donegal, the son of an Irish chieftain, he had gone to all the right monastic schools and quickly become a deacon. But things went wrong when he unleashed what amounted to a sixth-century copyright scandal: he had secretly duplicated a vulgate gospel manuscript from a bishop, only to be ordered to return it by the king himself. The impetuous prince persuaded his kinsmen into battle against the king, who lost three thousand men in the carnage. Penitent, Columba then sailed off into voluntary exile, pledging to save the same number of souls for whose death he had been responsible. The tradition was that he had stopped at Iona because it was the first place from which he could no longer be distracted by the distant sight of his beloved homeland. There he had established a sort of monastic HQ, from which he evangelised the Picts with a mixture of prophetic powers, earthy theology or spiritual conjuring tricks, depending on how much you trusted oral tradition and the airbrushing of Columba's seventh-century biographer, Adamnan.

In those days there was apparently nothing unusual about setting off in your boat with no particular destination in mind. In fact, *peregrinatio*, or religious voyaging, was an important part of Celtic tradition, a discipline which the holy men were expected to undertake as a kind of sea-borne pilgrimage. Some monks simply cast themselves off in coracles or curraghs – the favoured vessels, consisting of wooden skeletons covered in animal hides – trusting God to wash them up on their pre-ordained island retreat. Others actively navigated much further afield – St Brendan famously crossing the Atlantic. All were looking for a 'desert in the ocean', an island or isolated hideout in which to contemplate their Creator, a place where everything would make sense. The implication was that if you kept your eyes open you would know it when you found it. They called it *seeking the place of your resurrection*.

Cormac seemed to have struggled a little in this regard. Born into a Cork family of seafarers, he was, according to Adamnan, a good-looking but somewhat frustrated man, who 'not less than three times went in search of a desert in the ocean, *but did not find it*'. Evidently the damp crevice we had seen that afternoon hadn't hosted quite the spiritual resurrection its occupant had been hoping for. I found it strangely reassuring. It implied the man was at least human.

In fact, as I pieced together the few available facts about Cormac of the Sea, I found myself warming to him. Despite his looks and determination, he was one of the third division saints, never honoured with his own hagiography, but spliced into Columba's shining epic as the troubled friend who always looked as if he needed rescuing. In a typically strange episode, Cormac was four-

teen days into a determined northward sail when Columba, ever
attuned to the spiritual realms at his base on Iona, obtained
'prophetic knowledge' that his friend was in danger – under sting-
ing attack, as it happened, from 'a multitude of loathsome and
annoying insects, such as had never been seen before'. As Cormac
and his crew battled against the swarms of creatures – jellyfish,
perhaps? – which clogged their oars and battered the hull,
Columba called the faithful to prayer. And God obliged by reversing the wind to bring him back to Iona. Whether this was the
outcome Cormac was hoping for is not clear. Perhaps he would
have preferred simply to carry on without the jellyfish rather than
come back to base and start his search again? I felt aggrieved on his
behalf, instinctively sympathetic to his need to go on travelling, like
a naked hermit crab scuttling around in search of a roomier shell.

By contrast, there were moments when St Columba reminded
me of the sort of former traveller who, having enjoyed his rebellious phase on the hippy trail, is now in a position to be faintly
patronising about yours. Certainly, his biographer hinted at a
growing tension between the friends over the years. Cormac
launched repeat trips into the Atlantic and up towards the Orkney
Islands, searching for the place that would make sense of it all,
while Columba waited to tell him piously what he was doing
wrong. On one occasion it was because a crewman had departed
without asking his abbot's permission – a disappointingly bureau-
cratic quibble from the creator of the universe – while latterly he
seemed convinced his itinerant brother should simply go home.

'Though thou travel the world over,' he warned in a typically
finger-wagging prophecy, 'it is in Durrow thy resurrection shall be.'

I sat for a long time thinking about Cormac and Columba and
their different journeys. Why did one find spiritual fulfilment, the
other only traveller's angst? The books didn't say whether Cormac

eventually followed his elder's advice, but I rather hoped not. I liked his quiet defiance. It seemed to belong to a more modern age, this endless existential searching: I pictured a sixth-century James Dean scanning the horizon with restless blue eyes and the determination of a Grail Knight. Columba had probably meant well, an Uncle Chris dutifully nudging drifters homeward in case they forgot there was supposed to be a destination. But I took strength from Cormac, refusing to be rushed in his quest, despite the obvious questions: What exactly was your 'place of resurrection'? How did you know that you had found it? Or that you hadn't?

There seemed no clear-cut answers. But in the meantime, I had found a holy man I could relate to: the patron saint of Wanderlust.

10

Into the Whirlpool

Colonsay and Jura

'Holiday cottages!' said Charlie, jabbing a finger through the bus window at a pretty cluster of whitewashed buildings overlooking white sand. 'And *more* bloody holiday cottages! And look at that farm up there. Beautiful prime agricultural land, and what are they using it for?'

I took a wild stab. 'Holiday cottages?'

'Aye! It's criminal! Big fancy holiday houses sprouting up all over the place. It's going to become a holiday island very soon!'

Charlie's Bus Tour wasn't quite what I had expected. On Nick's advice I had ferry-hopped from Jura to Islay to Colonsay, one of the most beautiful of the Hebrides. I had joined a few other day trippers for the round-island journey, eaten my sandwiches looking over an empty beach and heard how Columba himself may have come here in his search for an island retreat. But now suddenly solitude seekers were the enemy.

'There's another one!' said Charlie, interrupting his commentary to point at a large white home on a hillside. 'Seven bedrooms, garages, what have you. Instead of buying the plot he bought the whole field so no one can build their home there.'

It was a problem in many of Britain's beauty spots. Everybody was looking for a place to resurrect themselves at weekends, but few wanted to think about the implications for settled communities. Here, nearly 40 per cent of the houses on the island were holiday homes, as incomers snapped up vacant properties at prices well out of reach of most locals. A little further down the road we passed a tiny cottage with flaking window frames and a dishevelled slate roof. 'That's the local teacher's home,' said Charlie. 'It's in a right state. Only eight in the school, and falling. In 1962 there were two hundred-plus people on the island. Now we're down to ninety-two . . .'

As the population shrank, and income relied increasingly on summer revenue from tourists, it became harder to sustain a year-round community. Farming, once the backbone of the island economy, was increasingly secondary to tourism. And Charlie wore more and more hats in an effort to keep his beloved island ticking over. Besides tour guide and bus driver, he was also a ferry docker, proxy vet, bin man, crofter, delivery man and undertaker. 'I'm a walking job centre!' he chuckled darkly. 'Used to do B&B as well, but these days we just don't have time, now that my wife and daughter run the bakery. Oh, and I look after old donkeys . . .'

Being an essentially urban creature, I had imagined life on a Hebridean island to be an idyll of bucolic pottering, interspersed with occasional sighs of spiritual contentment, rather like my holidays on Macaskin. It was something of a shock, therefore, to meet a rural gent whose multitasking made your average knife juggler look catatonic.

It wasn't outsiders *per se* who riled Charlie – he'd been one himself when he first arrived from Arran in 1962, and he now made his living off them. 'We don't mind people coming in if they're

going to contribute to the island,' he said, pulling up at Machrin's
Bay with a sigh. 'As long they don't try to *change* the place.'

Back on Jura, the islanders were still very proud of their most distinguished holiday rental guest. Eric Blair, a tall, gaunt writer with
a sickly disposition, had walked off the ferry in 1946 and taken up
residence in a remote farmhouse at the north end. These days it
was his pen name that pulled in the tourists: George Orwell. You
could buy a little yellow booklet about him at the Jura Hotel, while
the distillery by the pier was selling *1984 Whisky* – a 42 per cent
concoction for a heady £49.99 a bottle. Each year a trickle of lit-
erary pilgrims came to retrace the steps of Britain's most famous
novelist and essayist. Perhaps, like me, they wondered at the mysterious alchemy by which a wilderness as expansive as Jura could
spawn Orwell's nightmarish urban vision of a totalitarian state.
'Yes, it is strange, isn't it?' agreed Nick. 'We can go and take a look
if you want – the house is still there.'

We pulled out of Small Isles Bay the following morning on the
eleven o'clock tide, and steamed northwards at a safe distance from
the eastern shore. Jura was one of the emptier, wilder Hebridean
islands, dominated by the precipitous, scree-covered slopes of the
Paps, and occupied by thousands of red deer. Standing at the bow
rail, I tracked the shadows of clouds and a tiny red van beetling
across the naked expanse.

'I am anxious to get out of London for my own sake because I
am constantly smothered under journalism,' Orwell had told his
friend David Astor, owner of the *Observer*, who had an estate on the
island. 'I want to write another book which is impossible unless I
can get six months' quiet . . . somewhere where I cannot be tele-
phoned to . . .'

Barnhill, a house belonging to the Astors' neighbours, seemed to fit the description. I picked it out 23 miles north of Craighouse, a white block of habitation alone in a shallow glen. We anchored off the tiny hamlet of Kinuachdrach, rowed ashore and walked up the rutted farm track towards it. It was unoccupied though not abandoned — a two-storey whitewashed farmhouse overlooking the overgrown field where the author had once tried to grow vegetables. I pressed my nose to the window. The furniture looked as if it hadn't changed since Orwell's day: old stuffed horsehair couches, stiff wooden chairs and pictures lining the mantelpiece, including one of Orwell himself, presumably for the benefit of modern holiday rental clients. Back in 1947 it would have been more Spartan still. Sugar, butter, flour, bread, meat and sweets were still in short supply after the war, and Orwell's primary means of transport back into Craighouse was his famously unreliable motorcycle. There had been tensions with various houseguests who turned up during the summers, and his housekeeper left after a row with his sister. Not exactly an island paradise, then. I imagined a fire in the grate and the tapping of a typewriter from the bedroom above — and the hacking cough of his tuberculosis. Orwell, like the subversive hero of *1984*, must have had a keen sense that he was living on borrowed time, waiting for the knock at the door. What he couldn't have predicted was the unexpected way in which his island of resurrection would bring its own foretaste of death. As I was to see, that came quicker than he expected.

I got back to the *Vic32* to find a message from a monk. A man called Donald had phoned the ship's mobile. In a strange mid-Atlantic burr he confirmed that I was welcome to join the crew of the *Colmcille*, but there had been a slight change of itinerary. The curragh would now be leaving Crinan first thing *tomorrow*. This was a day earlier than planned, and several hours before the *Vic* was due to dock. I was in real danger of missing the boat.

After a short flurry of panic, one of the cooks came to the rescue – or at least her husband did. Michael Murray was a local tour guide who owned a twin-engined motor catamaran with a top speed of 16 knots. A bespectacled, curly haired man in a boiler suit, he came alongside at Kinuachdrach and we struck a deal. Before he took me back to Crinan, he would take me on a short but nerve-wracking excursion that the *Vic32* would never manage: we were going into the whirlpool.

The Gulf of Corryvreckan lay less than 2 miles around the corner between the north end of Jura and neighbouring Scarba. It was this notoriously turbulent tidal race – the only place on the Ordnance Survey map bearing the actual word 'whirlpool' – which had provided George Orwell's untimely brush with his own mortality. I had been through the place myself as a child with Uncle Chris at slack tide – the only navigable window of opportunity. Even then my memory was of a restless stretch of water marked with mysterious boilings and a little whirlpool which plucked at the dinghy we were towing and spun it round. Orwell was making a similar journey in an even smaller boat after a camping expedition with his nephew Henry, niece Lucy and three-year-old adopted son Richard, when he realised he'd miscalculated the tides. 'On return journey today ran into the whirlpool and were all nearly drowned,' he wrote sparsely in his diary of 19 August 1947. Aiming for slack tide, he seems instead to have arrived at the very worst time. When he rounded the corner and realised his mistake, the force of the current was already too great to turn back.

As young Henry later recalled, 'the boat went all over the place, pitching and tossing, [it was] very frightening being thrown from one small whirlpool to another, pitching and tossing so much that the outboard motor jerked right off from its fixing. Eric said, "the motor's gone, better get the oars out, Hen. Can't help much, I'm afraid". Rowing hard, Henry managed to reach a little island, and jumped ashore holding the rope – which was when a massive swell turned the boat over completely, tipping Orwell and the two young children into the water.

Speeding into the mouth of the rapids today, I was thankful the *Gemini* was everything Orwell's rowing boat wasn't: manoeuvrable, powerful, stabilised by twin pontoons. We were deliberately visiting the whirlpool at its most turbulent to see what Orwell would have encountered. The name came from *Coire Bhreacain* – the speckled cauldron – and it was easy to see why. The water around us seethed and boiled, mushrooming malevolently, carrying us towards the narrowest point of the gulf where the sea tore itself in two along a foaming white faultline.

'It's a complete tidal anomaly,' said Mike, keeping his eyes on the water. The flood tides from the Irish Sea ran up the Sound of Jura, building up a vast head of water which then forced itself westwards out through the gulf and hit the incoming Atlantic tide. 'There's a huge hole right in the middle, down to 219 metres. The pinnacle of rock which creates the whirlpool is probably a volcanic spout.' A sudden explosion of water pushed the whole boat sideways as surely as if we had been nudged by a tug. Mike turned the wheel and aimed us back into the eruptions in the middle of the gulf. A gull shot past, sitting serenely on the wind, an indicator of our own speed – about 6 knots. 'The sea birds love it because it throws up all these nutrients. Take the wheel a moment?' He grinned at my startled expression and darted out to take a photograph on deck while the wheel bucked and trembled in my hands. I watched the depth gauge: 42, 35, 34.8, then suddenly 100, where it froze. 'We're over an abyss,' said Michael, ducking back to the wheel. Dark water blorted suddenly with foam and we slid sideways as if on a conveyor belt. 'Look at that! We're basically sitting on a great knuckle of water from 100 feet down! The forces are mindblowing . . .'

The hairs on my neck were on end. It was the first time on my trip that I had felt genuinely afraid of water. Not far away the sea slavered around the blackened molars of rock where Orwell had foundered. The depths blossomed and convulsed like jellyfish. I tried to imagine the sheer terror of flailing about on the surface of such chaos.

'What would happen if you fell in?'

'Here in the middle of the vortex it would spit you to the surface, but if you went in at the edge, it would take you straight down to the bottom.'

Orwell was lucky. Grabbing his son as the boat turned over, he had managed to make it to the rocks with Lucy and struggle out of the water. Henry recalled that he maintained a calm 'Uncle Eric' face throughout the ordeal, muttering only, 'I thought we were goners,' before eventually attracting a lift from a passing lobster boat by waving a shirt on a fishing rod. 'He almost seemed to enjoy it,' remembered his puzzled nephew. Perhaps it was euphoria or delayed shock. Yet Orwell's own diary entry concludes cheerfully: 'Boat is all right. Only serious loss, the engine and 12 blankets.'

It seemed a remarkably routine near-death experience. Today, gripping the railing of the *Gemini*, I hoped I would prove as competent in an emergency. Another belch of bottle-green water burst from below, and I hung on as Michael spun us back around into the foaming overlay of two seas wrestling. Behind my exhilaration, I felt uneasy. However much you understood the physics of water, it was hard not to see a sort of malevolence in the churning depths, something primal that needed to be placated.

'Do you ever worry about playing with it like this?'

'I've gradually learned to treat it with more respect all the time. I was once on a smooth piece of water with a lot of elderly folk on board when a wall of water came out of nowhere and broke on the deck.'

'But you're not the superstitious type?'

'No. I used to have a forestry business and I was the one who cut down all the bloody rowan trees.' He grinned. 'And look, I'm still here.'

I gazed into the foam and the glassy caverns beneath. As *Gemini* nosed back towards Crinan, I realised I wanted it all to mean something more than physics, all this raw power that could so casually snuff out a life. Orwell himself gave mixed messages on metaphysics. A committed socialist, he disparaged organised religion for most of his life and seemed to pity those who, like Moses the raven in *Animal Farm*, distracted the masses from earthly justice with talk of an afterlife on 'Sugarcandy Mountain'. Yet he had dabbled briefly with churchgoing in the early 1930s, and retained a sort of nostalgia for the cultural form, if not the substance, of faith. Winston, the fictional hero of *1984*, emerged on Jura with a yearning for the old church bells. A few years after his narrow escape in the whirlpool, facing a more terminal prognosis, Orwell surprised those who knew him best by changing his will to accord himself a Church of England burial.

I felt I understood. It was not a deathbed conversion, perhaps, so much as a wistful hedging of bets.

II

Spiritual Warfare

To Easdale

There was no doubt in Donald McCallum's mind: a spiritual battle was in progress. 'We're under attack,' he confided, as we heaved at neighbouring oars. 'It's the obvious explanation for the problems we've had – we're being tested from another source.'

It was the third time I had watched Crinan harbour dropping slowly away to stern that week, and definitely the strangest. Having begun in a motorboat with Uncle Chris and progressed to a steam puffer with Nick, I was finally heading north in one of the simplest vessels ever invented: a flimsy wooden skeleton covered in a few layers of canvas and pitch. What I hadn't bargained on was theology to match.

In Donald's world, nothing happened by accident. Even my own last-minute arrival, I was disconcerted to learn, had been an 'answer to prayer': one of the crew wasn't feeling well and was now able to rest at the stern while I stood in at the oars. It was 'a miracle' that nobody else had suffered similar illness after the struggle to get across from Ballycastle in Ulster in the teeth of a relentless wind. 'We had to row until four in the morning,' said the sixty-five-year-old expedition leader, shaking his head at the memory. 'Just about finished us off.' Then, while the exhausted crew were ashore giving thanks for their safe crossing, a gale had dragged the *Colmcille* from her moorings and torn a hole on rocks. She had only just been salvaged. 'That was a nerve-wracking moment but – praise God! – we found a carpenter and were able to patch her up. Now she's good as new! So the Lord's really been looking after us!'

I tried not to think too hard about the divine DIY job currently keeping the sea on the outside of our thin canvas hull. Instead, I focused on the timing of our oars, which were unlike any I had ever seen. They pivoted on pegs protruding from the gunwales, their seaward ends tapering into sharpened wedges to minimise wind drag. It was like rowing with giant toothpicks. Sitting on a fixed wooden rowing bench, I almost fell over backwards with the lack of water resistance before learning to pull steadily in time with those around me, our feet braced against the latticework of the boat's internal frame. The boat climbed the waves easily, stabilised by a jumbled ballast of luggage stuffed beneath each man's bench: waterproofs, sleeping mats, watertight barrels for personal luggage. Also visible were the brown bundles of discarded monastic robes. They were almost impossible to row in – imagine a dressing gown hand-stitched from a car rug – but useful for cushioning the bare wooden benches.

Who were these people? They had seemed friendly enough folk when I met them at the pub the previous night – a mix of Irishmen, Scots and ancestor-hunting Americans recruited through church contacts, internet and newspaper ads. Donald's unorthodox retirement project seemed to have captured imaginations right across the age spectrum from college leavers to pensioners. They had graciously overlooked my non-Celtic blood, and enthused a lot about teamwork, but I sensed a little confusion about the precise aim of the voyage. The safe response was that it was a kind of adventure-cum-pilgrimage bringing together different sorts of Christians, but a vocal minority seemed keen on the word 'mission'. A bearded American called Ernest had even brandished a wad of printed tracts including a 'prayer of commitment' for potential converts. And now Donald was talking about 'spiritual warfare'.

In my rush to get involved I had agreed to wear robes and take part in services, which I took to mean a bit of hymn singing. Now, more than a mile from land, I was suddenly anxious to know exactly what else I had let myself in for.

'Well, on one level it's a re-creation of St Columba's journey,' clarified Donald, who had for some reason alighted on the 1440th anniversary of this sixth-century pilgrimage. 'But I guess the *real* purpose of the voyage is to rekindle the faith that he brought to Scotland so many years ago. I call it a spiritual odyssey, a kind of missionary voyage.' It was something of a homecoming for Donald, who left his native Kintyre peninsula at twenty to work as a naval architect in Maryland. He seemed unimpressed with what had happened in his absence. 'I read somewhere that by the year 2010 only 7 per cent of Scottish people will be attending church – that's one out of fourteen!' he said, shaking his head. 'So we're reaching out to the other thirteen in a small way, trying to share God's love.'

I stared at his weathered face, framed by distinguished silvery hair, and his brush-like moustache. For a moment he seemed less like a monk than a kind of nautical sheriff, with his posse of missionary desperados, riding back into town to clean the place up.

I had once tried being a missionary. A few days after my eighteenth birthday, fuelled with a potent mix of wanderlust and gap-year idealism, I had boarded another boat and set forth to heal the world. It was much bigger than the *Colmcille*, a 500-foot cruise liner converted into a hospital ship by a large religious organisation from the US. In Jamaica and later Central America, the ship's hospital offered eye and cleft-lip surgery, while the less medically minded of us were dispatched into the community to win souls.

As only a handful of us actually spoke the language of the people we were sent to convert, our Honduran evangelism took the form of a mime set to music, often performed in the middle of market places. It was as bizarre as it was colourful. I was cast as Jesus (white, blond) wearing, for theatrical reasons I forget, purple elasticated pantaloons, a glittery golden tank top and a crown. A pouting Satan had lured away a succession of rebellious souls (symbolised by their reversed baseball caps) and sealed off the world from its creator. My job was to break through the invisible wall of sin like a cat-burgling Marcel Marceau, and win the apostates back with lots of yearning hand movements. After a tug of war with Satan I was crucified and divinely resuscitated, at which point various repentant souls joyfully ripped reversible Velcro hearts off their chests and turned them over. Then we all hugged, gave high fives and lived happily ever after.

I don't recall any converts from these unintentionally camp theology lessons, though it's possible a few went on to develop a life-long fixation with gold lamé. Thankfully our audiences were usually too bewildered to be offended, but it was the beginning of the end for my wide-eyed faith.

Yet when I thought now of those five summer months in 1988, I felt both embarrassed and oddly wistful. Amid some very strange theology, I remembered generous and essentially well-meaning people – American students, an Indonesian doctor, a Mexican paramedic, a reformed Portuguese drug dealer who shared my cabin. I remembered the vividness of life: the scuttling march of large hermit crabs up the beach at sunset, the dolphins playing in our bow wave, laughter on the roof of a rural school as we nailed on new tiles. And I quite enjoyed being crucified, night after night.

That was the thing about fundamentalism. If you could keep the doubts away, the energy it gave you was all-pervading. It was all about certainty, about momentum, about having the secret formula. It was about knowing where you were going, and what you had to do to get there.

I recognised something of that spirit now in the adrenalin-fuelled banter of my crewmates. 'Right lads, keep rowing hard!' yelled the skipper Robin Ruddock at the helm. 'Don't let the white water worry you!' We bounced through the tidal race of Dorus Mor whooping like schoolboys, the wood frame of the boat twisting slightly, absorbing the pummelling.

Curraghs had been the transport of choice for seafaring monks for the same reason they remained in use among Irish fishermen: they were light and manoeuvrable and swift through the water. 'All the Celtic nations used them,' said Robin, an experienced sailor from the North Antrim coast. 'It didn't make sense to have wooden boats where there were no real harbours. You needed a boat you could carry ashore.' His only concession to the modern age in building *Colmcille* had been to use canvas instead of animal skins, which smelt terrible.

I found Robin a reassuring presence. His buzz-cut hair and barked orders could have got him mistaken for a paramilitary in the wrong kind of Belfast pub, but in fact his passion was peace-making through outdoor pursuits. Robin's day job was to put young groups of Protestants and Catholics in a curragh together and persuade them pull in the same direction.

Keeping well clear of Corryvreckan we turned north, hoisting

two ochre sails to catch a south-westerly up the inside of the island
of Luing. Nobody was exactly sure what Columba's original route
had been after landing on Kintyre, so our somewhat arbitrary
target for that day was the island of Easdale, which lay close to the
mainland, a stepping stone to Iona some 30 miles away. We were
all warm from rowing hard, and the sudden help from the wind
brought a gust of euphoria as we hooked our oars out of the water
and scudded along past low-lying islands and the occasional
derelict bothy. Someone dug out a small transistor radio and
turned on some Gaelic bagpipe music. Food appeared from various nooks and crannies.

'Pass me a couple of clams, Peter,' said a white-haired Scot in a
sailor's cap in front of me. John Martin had joined the expedition
at the island of Gigha, 30 miles south of Crinan. Back home he
was the church beadle and island carpenter, but he had evidently
done plenty of fishing too. He pulled out a pocket knife, slipped
its blade in under the shell, and worked it round the edge until the
thing opened. Scraping the black intestines overboard, he laid the
two halves on the bench.

'Ever had one of these before?' he asked me, peering at me over
a pair of battered Ray Bans. 'The white part is the flesh, the red
part is the nursery, the maternity ward.' He handed me a shellful of
mucus-like flesh and tipped his own down his throat. I gagged on
its saltiness, but managed to swallow it.

'De-licious!' said John, reaching for another. 'A dozen of them
and you can service a woman for hours.'

'There aren't any women here, John,' somebody reminded him.

Peter Macleod, a bespectacled twenty-something from Govan,
was perched behind us at the edge of the boat trying to urinate
downwind, with unsatisfactory results. By coincidence, he was the
younger brother of Colin in whose leaky rowing boat I had crossed

the Clyde. He was a quiet man who retained a simple faith. 'The preacher taught my granny, my gran taught my mum, and my mum taught me,' he explained, when I asked him why he believed. The religion of the hearth, passed down through generations.

Donald clambered around with a bucket of Mars Bars – a special treat for a crew otherwise limited to the more 'authentic' fare of bread, dates, smoked fish and clams. He came down unsteadily with a thud in the canvas bow, eliciting a wince from Robin.

'Back in Ireland we have a saying,' shouted the skipper, who knew just how easily you could step through the bottom. '*In small boats, move like a cat.*' Donald blushed and apologised. While he was technically the leader and originator of the voyage, he deferred to the expertise of his much younger skipper when afloat. It was an interesting dynamic.

In fact, the more I listened to my fellow crewmates, the more I noticed nuances of difference among them. James and John from Coleraine, another John from Argyll, and the aptly named Ernest all shared Donald's penchant for proclaiming things: prayers, itineraries, generalisations about the spiritual health of Scotland. But the rest of the crew seemed diplomatically noncommital in response. Tony, David and Emmanuel, three young Americans, joshed each other like college boys, while a trio of older Scots – Alistair the organist, Bob the landscape painter and John the clam-eating joiner – usually kept a sage silence. Did anybody else share my misgivings about our 'mission'? I would find out before long. But for now we were in the same boat, and that simple solidarity was enough.

12

The Celtic Renewal
Service

Easdale Island

Easdale was only just an island. It lay about 400 yards from neighbouring Seil, which was itself connected to mainland Argyll by a bridge. Coasting into a sheltered stretch of water between the two, we were greeted at the slate-lined quay by people with wheelbarrows: the local taxi service in a carless place. A short walk from the harbour, children of a wild, grubby, happy demeanour were playing football on a shared green between lines of old terraced quarriers' cottages. After the internal frictions of Colonsay, it had the feel of a community noticeably more at ease with itself. A few adults sat chatting on doorsteps in the sun, smiling as I passed. They didn't look to me as if they needed saving. At the corner of the green was a signpost like a totem pole, its splayed arms indicating an ambitious sense of global interconnectedness: Lima 6828 miles; Dunedin 12,613 miles; Oban 16 miles; Bar 48 feet.

I followed the last of these to the Puffer Bar and joined John Martin who was relaxing in the sunshine with his pint. A family passed along the quayside, the father pushing a laughing child along in the wheelbarrow with the shopping. If Columba or Cormac had made it here today, I found it hard to believe they'd have bothered going any further.

'A word of advice,' smiled John from behind his Ray Bans. 'If you're thinking about living on an island, don't visit on a summer's day. Go in the winter and get a bit of reality — that'll get rid of those romantic notions.'

Living on Gigha, he'd had a few illusions of his own until the day he came home from work and found that the doorframe of his cottage had been chalk-marked for eviction. The laird had decided to sell up. 'I couldn't believe this feudal law still existed in this day and age — it's medieval nonsense,' said John. In the event the laird relented with the eviction threats, but years of insecurity from a string of owners had brought local feeling to a head. When the island went on the market for the fourth time in 2002, new legislation and a windfall from the Scottish Parliament gave the inhabitants the real possibility of buying it themselves. With some nervousness, they grasped it with both hands.

'Feudalism still reigns, but in places like Gigha you can sense the difference,' said John. 'As soon as the news came, I saw folk painting doors and windows they hadn't touched for years. They suddenly changed gear and started taking responsibility for what was theirs.' In fact this was largely what had brought John on the voyage in the first place: apart from feeding his love of the sea, he was raising sponsor money towards the £1 million community buy-out. It had a nice symmetry to it: rowing to one island in order to help pay for another.

'Absentee landowners are a curse,' he said, looking over his shoulder at the harbour. 'Come the day this one decides to retire or sell up, these people could find themselves homeless. If they get any opportunity they should grasp it and buy him out.'

I suspected that for incomers like me, becoming an islander wasn't quite as simple as turning up with a trunk and claiming your new life. John took a swig of beer. 'If you're an asset to a community it doesn't matter where you come from. But I'm a great believer that if you're going to live in a place, you need to accept folk for who they are. If you go to a place which has accepted you, it's a bad idea to get your feet below the table and start saying this is how we do it somewhere else . . .'

It seemed an eminently sensible rule. It also summed up perfectly what was troubling me about Donald's mission: *If you go to a place which has accepted you, it's a bad idea to start saying this is how we do it somewhere else.*

The Celtic Renewal Service, as Donald was calling it, was scheduled for the following evening on a village green in neighbouring Seil. After a night on the floor of the community hall, we met that morning to organise it. It was an urgent, slightly furtive gathering. One of the men, an evangelical Scot, was convinced that a spiritual battle was under way. 'Last night in the bar there was a separation, as if local people were deliberately keeping away from us,' he said gravely. 'It's clear to me that these people are what you might call "nocturnal" in their attachments . . .'

John Martin, who had enjoyed a rather sociable night with the islanders, frowned and cleared his throat. 'I think we should wait and see,' he said bluntly. 'I hesitate to condemn.' There was an audible sigh of agreement from the less vocal majority.

Donald looked panicked. 'Amen! Nobody wants to condemn!' he said, ushering us on to some practised chants with Alistair the organist on his electric piano. Ernest, a slightly effete man in his fifties with a tonsured beard and long grey hair, wrapped things up with a closing homily from the life of St Columba. 'On one occasion, when St Columba came to an island he was told *Lay down your cloak and whatever it will cover is claimed for Christ,*' he said, smiling wisely as if imparting a deep truth. 'And the cloak grew and covered the whole island!'

Back in the Puffer Bar afterwards, I mused darkly on Columba's expanding cloak. Colourful folklore as it was, it simply underlined my doubts about such missionary activity, as if the human heart could be 'claimed' like a plot of land. It was feudalism on a cosmic scale, with God as absentee landlord.

I tried to explain some of my reservations to Donald over lunch, but he just frowned back at me. 'I'm not saying there's no God,' I said, biting down my irritation. 'But I don't see how you can be so sure He's personally sponsoring the expedition . . .'

Donald scraped back his chair impatiently. 'Of course He is.'

We donned our robes shortly before seven, observed by locals wearing sympathetic smiles. Most of us looked as if we were wearing picnic rugs tied up with string, though Ernest had pulled out the best of his already legendary wardrobe of period costumes. Today, in addition to his robe, he was wearing a crimson smock over his linen undergarments and a pair of little leather sandals.

'This is actually what Celtic monks would have worn,' he said proudly, fingering the quality of his garment. 'They loved colour.'

'Keep yer hoods up!' whispered Pete, more practically. 'It keeps the midgies aff!'

A cluster of perhaps forty people were watching as we clambered out of the boat on neighbouring Seil and processed across the car park chanting 'Kyrie Eleison' mournfully in time to a cowbell. Donald and Ern led the way, carrying an 8-foot wooden cross. I kept my hood well up.

In the middle of the village green, Alistair sat at a portable organ, helping us out with a kind of electronic chime when the long sleeves of his cassock would permit him to find the keys. The congregation looked friendly if nonplussed. After we had stopped singing, there was a brief silence punctuated only by a yelp from a woman as Ern's cross toppled sideways and caught her on the shoulder.

The Reverend Freda Marshall tapped the microphone. 'I don't know about you,' she began earnestly, 'but I really felt a tingle up my spine seeing the brothers here processing up the beach. I felt sure this was just how it might have happened all those years ago . . .'

The service was essentially a selection of hymns and choruses sandwiched with Bible readings. Donald raised an unintended laugh by feeling it necessary to explain that we weren't really monks, and we each had to take our hoods down and introduce ourselves, which most did with a simple greeting. I kept it honest and introduced myself as a writer who had hitched a lift with a hospitable crew. Donald looked at me as pityingly as if I were the disciple who had denied Christ.

'This voyage is kind of a dream come true, to repeat the voyage of Columba,' he said, when his own turn came. 'For me it's a symbol of how people can work together as the body of Christ. We hope you will be blessed as we repeat the voyage of Columba to Iona in a small boat like this, carrying the same message of God's love to all men.' His voice trembled with emotion, and he scuffed a stray tear from his cheek.

Other than this, things proceeded much as they were laid out on the notice sheet, until the first few spots of rain precipitated a crisis. A man leapt forward and covered the electric organ with a feed bag, and the various visiting clergy exchanged glances. 'I think with Donald's permission we'll skip forward to the final hymn . . .'

'Wait!' said Donald, his face reddening. Several members of the congregation froze in the act of putting on waterproofs. Our leader was standing in the middle of the green with his arms raised to heaven. At first I assumed he was feeling the rain, until I saw his lips moving and realised he was praying against it. There was an uncomfortable moment as the congregation realised this too. Lots of people studied their shoes. 'Look, it's passing!' shouted Donald suddenly, lowering his arms. 'Praise God, we can continue!'

It was true that the rain had stopped. In fact, as we finished the service somewhat stiffly as printed, and Donald issued his crucial invitation for 'ministry and prayer' and a 'new beginning', there was even a well-timed appearance of evening sun which came out and bathed the whole surreal scene in honey-coloured light. But if we had witnessed a miracle, nobody seemed to have noticed it. Instead, someone plucked up courage to ask for what they really wanted: a ride in an authentic curragh. Then dozens of people poured on to the quay, young, old, permed, bald, many of them requisitioning our robes for the full experience as Robin coached several boat loads back and forth across the harbour. The woman who had been clubbed by Ern's cross declined a healing prayer, insisting that her shoulder was 'absolutely fine'. Ern and Donald looked a little deflated as the truth sunk in: the entire gathering had been composed of local churchgoers. We had been preaching to the converted.

13

Rowing with God

Easdale to Iona

We woke at 5 a.m. and left the harbour before the village was awake, losing Easdale quickly in a fine sea mist. It was chilly to begin with, but the repetitive motion of rowing against the wind soon warmed us up, and we drifted into a collective trance of concentration. Soon we were rising and falling in an Atlantic swell.

It was eleven before we turned northwards around a stumpy lighthouse on the saw-toothed Garvellochs, finally hoisting the sails for a little assistance. Donald excavated the food barrel and passed round a few dates with a block of cheese and some four-day-old smoked fish by way of encouragement.

'Where's the bread?' asked Robin, frowning at what was being offered.

Donald flushed and rooted around in a couple of barrels. 'Ah, I guess we must have eaten all the bread before we set off this morning,' he said sheepishly. 'Sorry, guys, no bread. At least there's lots of smoked fish!' He laughed nervously into a silence broken only by the lapping of water at the bow and tinny haze of bagpipe music coming from John's radio. Robin stared angrily at the floorboards, then at his watch.

'Okay boys,' he said, finally. 'I'm afraid we're going to have to carry on rowing. The wind isn't strong enough, and if we're still crossing the channel when the tide changes, we'll end up right back where we started.'

There were sighs, some blowing out of cheeks as we all abandoned our long-anticipated rest and got back to the oars. The day wasn't going well. Apart from the adverse wind and the shortage of food, Emmanuel had been throwing up in the bow all morning, weakened by a nameless virus. Jim the bosun suddenly raised his arm from his oar, as if reaching up to grasp a favour from on high. 'Lord, it's a long journey and we've got a sick man on board and some of us are scunnered,' he intoned informally. 'If it's your will, it would sure be nice to have an east wind to help us know that you're behind us.'

It seemed a wager had been laid. Could prayer change wind direction as it had done for Columba, or would we continue to struggle onward like Cormac's hapless searchers? Were we dealing with Jim's attentive divine chum, or my essentially mysterious universe? At that moment, I was as eager as anyone to be proved wrong.

The wind grew more contrary, then dropped altogether. We rowed silently for the next few hours, the shore of Mull always tantalisingly distant each time we looked over our shoulders. Our movements became stiff and lopsided as we rolled away from painful sores or stopped for water. Emmanuel slept fitfully in the bow, wrapped in his monk's habit, waking only to vomit.

Donald looked back over his shoulder at me, embarrassed that God hadn't done the business yet. 'I think it's a test of our patience,' he said loudly, in case anyone was beginning to doubt.

'You're telling me,' muttered someone.

By four we could hear the faint hiss of breakers on the shore behind us. It was scattered with rocks the size of bowling balls, forming a level shelf which then curved upwards into towering cliffs. Robin coached us in to within 100 yards of the shore, careful to stay on the right side of the breakers. The tide, meanwhile, was already beginning to flow east – and even God seemed unlikely to interfere with that.

'We'll take a break here and wait out the worst of the tide,' he said, dropping the anchor.

'Why not hole up on the shore for the night and gather our energies for Iona tomorrow?' said Donald, tentatively. 'We could make a shelter and set out first thing in the morning, when we've rested . . .'

'We don't have enough food to keep going after tonight!' barked Robin angrily, overruling him. He was genuinely worried. 'You'd better let me provision the boat on the way back – these boys need Mars Bars and lots of fruit.'

Donald slumped under the public criticism. In the awkward pause that ensued, someone quipped: 'Oh well, if all else fails, there's always the outboard!' There was, indeed, a small outboard motor stowed on the floor of the stern, for emergencies. A few people laughed, including Donald – but he added nervously: 'That would kind of undermine the authenticity of the voyage.' There was a silence in which Emmanuel barfed.

Thankfully, Peter chose that moment to recall a bag of Sainsbury's pasta he had brought all the way from Govan. 'We could maybe share this?' he said, fishing it out of his drybag with a generosity that brought a lump to my throat. Jim gave a cheer and began boiling up a billycan of seawater over a Primus he pulled from below the benches. As miracles went, this one was up there with the multiplication of loaves and fishes as far as I was concerned. I shot Donald what I hoped was an encouraging grin. He

was more subdued than I'd seen him for a while, and I was beginning to feel sorry for him. His sunburned face was as red as a
baboon's arse, and his grey hair was matted in all sorts of directions. He grinned wearily back at me.

We were anchored in the retreating tide, dragged parallel to the
shore by the slow ebb. On the lower slopes a thatch of grey scree
and greenery gave the upper crags a silky opal sheen. High above
us on a bone-like branch sat two golden eagles, proud, regal, utterly
unconstrained by earth or sea. It was a magnificent scene, and it
made me feel both small and suddenly exuberant.

Peter doled out his pasta surprise (the surprise being that there
were a few pieces of grated cheese on top) and I took a plate each
to Robin and Jim at the stern. They were murmuring quietly
together, and attaching something to the outside of the boat. It
was the emergency outboard motor.

'We may be Irish but we're not stupid,' said Robin, winking at
me. 'If the monks can sleep in houses and eat Mars Bars, the
monks can use an outboard motor.'

'The Lord helps those who help themselves, eh?'

Robin pulled the starter cord, and the motor chuntered into life.
Donald looked up from his pasta in surprise. He opened his
mouth to speak, but Robin cut in first.

'There's no more food or water, Donald, and I've got to get
these boys to their beds tonight,' he said, tinkering with the petrol
input. He played a carefully prepared religious trump card. 'Look
at it this way: the only reason we *wouldn't* use the outboard at this
stage is out of *pride*. And you have to learn to swallow your pride
where the safety of others is concerned.'

We all waited for Donald to object to this moral *fait accompli*, but
he never did. Instead, Robin called the rowers to their seats and
slipped the anchor.

In fact, the outboard probably did more for morale than it did for our speed. It was a tinny contraption which spluttered and left the water entirely each time we breasted a wave. We had to row hard for the next four hours against the slowing tide. My muscles felt as twisted as rubber bands. The Torron Rocks drifted past in the mist, as insubstantial as ghosts on our port side, and the light was dying by the time we turned into Tinker's Hole, a passageway between the extremity of Mull and the little island of Erraid. Wordlessly, Robin cut the outboard and lifted it back into the boat.

'Right lads, this is the home strait,' he said. 'Let's get our habits on, and do ourselves proud.'

Pulling out into the Sound of Iona, we could see our destination rising gently against low skies littered with the last violet shreds of day. The outgoing tide was flowing as fast as a river in the centre of the channel, dragging us backwards so quickly that we had to row directly against it to make any headway.

'Pull hard, boys!' said Robin — and even Emmanuel managed to drag himself out of his sickbed to help. We inched past winking channel markers, towards the lights of houses on the shore of Iona. The lights were multiplying ahead of us. A crowd of people were standing waiting for us at the quayside pub with candles and torches, their cheers and applause pattering across the water.

A motorboat roared out to meet us. 'Welcome to Iona!' shouted a female voice.

'Praise God!' Donald shouted back. Many raised pint glasses as we pulled in alongside the ferry ramp, while others caught our lines. Some wanted to shake our hands, ask about the trip, so Donald recounted to anyone who would listen how the hand of the Almighty had been mightily evident. He seemed to glow in the darkness, a man on fire with the spirit and advanced sunburn.

As a final gesture he pronounced a homily while the men launched three captive doves into the sky as symbols of Celtic brotherhood. It was a nervous moment. One flew off while the other two flapped woozily across the beach and escaped to the roof of the pub. We took the hint, ditched our habits and got ourselves inside for last orders.

Nobody mentioned the outboard motor again.

14

Fingal's Cave

Staffa and Iona

It was a flawless day and the first ferry loads of tourists were tramping towards Iona Abbey in search of the graves of kings. I passed them, camcorders at the ready, as I walked briskly in the other direction, back towards the harbour.

It wasn't that I didn't love this little island. George Macleod, an inspirational minister who had brought unemployed workers out from Govan to rebuild its ruined abbey in the sixties, had called it 'a thin place', as if the veil between earth and spirit had almost worn through. I thought I knew what he meant. In fact I had visited Iona several times over the years, and always left feeling as if I'd been peeled.

Today, however, much as I admired the Iona community's earthy brand of activism — always more likely to be feeding the poor than trying to indoctrinate them — I desperately needed a rest before I left to begin my stint as galley slave on a square-rigged sailing ship in Oban the following morning. Waking on the floor of the village hall, I had lingered just long enough to hear Donald rallying his monks for another Celtic Renewal Service, before bolting for the pier.

The island of Staffa lay a few miles off Iona, but had been

drawing awestruck day-trippers since the Romantic Age. No Grand Tour was complete without a visit to Fingal's Cave: Walter Scott, John Keats, Felix Mendelssohn, William Wordsworth, Queen Victoria, Jules Verne, David Livingstone and Robert Louis Stevenson had all made trips here. Then as now, the main drawback was their fellow passengers. Wordsworth lamented that he had to share the experience with 'a motley crowd . . . hurried and hurrying, volatile and loud', while Tennyson remarked crabbily that Staffa was 'as interesting as it could be with people chattering and forty minutes to see it in'. Johnson and Boswell hadn't even got that far, as the sea was too choppy to land. Today the tourist launch was full of camera-toting pilgrims, pensioners, and American teenagers chewing their gum as rhythmically as cows. We motored along the Sound of Iona, past the old stone abbey and gentle hillsides dotted with sheep, and beyond the white sand of deserted beaches.

Staffa rose like a pie crust on the horizon, while the dark shadow of Fingal's Cave slowly grew beneath it. Its vast hexagonal basalt pillars were formed, according to the skipper, by the slow cooling of lava sixty million years ago. When we filed ashore and into its cathedral-like vaults, the sound of water was everywhere, the treble hiss of the foam undergirded by the booming bass of rollers barrelling into the yawning interior. Queuing along a handrail, I could hear someone humming faintly, but most were mute, even the Americans. Under the water, a few feet below our precarious walkway, the rocks wobbled pink and grey and luminous green. The columns enclosed the cave like ribs, as though we were hearing the ocean's fury from the belly of a whale. I shivered and went back to the boat.

'It affects people,' said the skipper, Davie. 'It's the power of the sound. People want to touch the sides, put their hands on it. We once had two blind folk on board; both made it to the cave unaided – they must have seen it completely differently to you or me.'

He was a thoughtful man, his face weathered but open beneath his peaked cap. Leaving most of the passengers atop the island, we chuntered out of the landing area and around the island for the benefit of three tourists unable to manage the stairs. He gave a wry grin when I told him I had arrived on the curragh the previous night. He had been on the quayside.

'It was nice to watch you boys coming in,' he said. 'All these strangers speaking to one another at the pub because they were waiting for this canvas boat with twelve or fourteen loonies on it.' He looked away. 'But to be honest with you, if anyone says to me they're a Christian, I look at them and think: *what are you hiding?* I think it's far better to stand up and say I'm a good human being.'

I nodded and waited for him to go on. Davie had good reason to doubt the efficacy of faith: his father had died rebuilding Iona Abbey. A sling had broken as he unloaded timber from a beached Puffer in 1955. 'My father pushed two of the other folk out of the way and got it himself. It was the wood for the cloisters which killed him.'

'No wonder you've got mixed feelings about religion.'

'Aye. But you can't turn the clock back. Anyway, there's worse things have happened to me . . .'

Only a few years ago five young men of the island were returning from a dance on Mull one Saturday night when a freak wave swamped their dinghy. One struggled to the shore to raise the alarm, the others never made it, Davie's son among them. I remembered the headlines at the time. Almost a whole generation of island men wiped out at a stroke. And for Davie, first father, then son, both lost to the sea. He winced when I alluded gently to the double tragedy, asked me not to mention it again. We stood in silence, watching puffins bobbing in the water.

'Most wars are started over religion,' he said presently. 'So I don't really look to anyone for their religious beliefs. If you speak to half a dozen folk on Iona that have been there as long as me you'd get half a dozen different answers ...' He looked at me suddenly. 'What do *you* think?'

'I struggle to believe,' I said, slowly. 'I think it's complicated.'

He nodded, swinging us back round towards the landing stage, ready to pick up the passengers for the return leg. 'It's this honesty thing – you have to be honest about what's there,' he said, a whimsical look in his eye. He throttled back, nodding towards the cave. 'Some folk look at Staffa and tell you those are vertical columns. But if you look more closely, a lot of them are subtly twisted or slanting. Truth is rarely a simple thing – it's all about perception.'

He had a point. The columns weren't straight, though the mind corrected them almost automatically. It was a shame really, because when you looked carefully, their kinks and slants and cracks were what made them interesting.

15

Square Rigged

Oban and Tobermory

She was a beautiful ship, even in the drizzle. I picked her out on the far side of Oban harbour the moment I stepped off the car ferry from Mull: a handsome two-masted, 100-foot brigantine with a navy blue hull and one of those old-fashioned bowsprits. I had first seen the *Jean de la Lune* ten years earlier in Leith, but only recently arranged a stint aboard. The deal was that I would earn my ten-day passage around the Outer Hebrides by working as a crew member – though I was a little vague as to what exactly this would involve. I wandered towards her with the music from *The Onedin Line* playing in my head – until I climbed aboard and met the bosun, at which point the Pogues kicked in.

'First tings first: do you *drink*?' said Shane, in a strong Cork accent, throwing down his vacuum cleaner to shake my hand. He was a seventeen-year-old with a round, open face, cheeky grin and tight black curly hair. He wore cargo shorts, bright orange wellies, and a T-shirt bearing the slogan *Monkey Business*.

'Drink? Um, yes . . . occasionally.'

'*Occasionally?*' He raised an incredulous eyebrow. 'What's the fecking point of that? Do you smoke?'

'No.'

He looked momentarily crestfallen, then the wicked grin returned. 'Ah well,' he said, rubbing his hands. 'We'll have to *educate* you a little.'

We were standing in an elegant wood-panelled dining saloon hung with aerial pictures of the Western Isles and a polished brass clock. Daniel, the other volunteer crew member for the voyage, appeared from the galley, a tidy looking seventeen-year-old who was using his gap year to train on tall ships. 'Roite den,' said Shane, suddenly businesslike. 'You two are *volunteer* crew, and I'm *permanent* crew – the bosun, in fact – which makes me da boss. So dump your stuff down below and get back up here so I can tell you what your jobs are.'

I don't normally take orders from seventeen-year-olds, but it was a tribute to Shane's winking charm and puppy-like harassment techniques that I did exactly what he asked. Four hours later I had vacuumed the lower deck, cleaned the showers and heads (head is the nautical name for toilets, perhaps because that's the part of your body most commonly aimed into them while at sea), polished a few brass rails, helped unload and store all the food from a super-market run, nodded briefly to the captain and his wife, and helped seven passengers bring their luggage aboard. I decided to grab a half-hour's nap before we set sail.

Crew quarters were at the front of the ship, and known ominously as the snake pit. Shane had already claimed two bunks, his unwashed laundry draped over every available surface like Dali's watches. I took the bottom bunk below Daniel, with about 6 inches headroom, a wee reading light and a high lip of wood to stop you falling out in a storm. I climbed in and pulled a long curtain along its open side. It was a bit like a coffin but at least it gave me a little privacy. It would be ten days before I

would be back in Oban, ready to head northwards to the
Caledonian Canal. Until then, I was effectively the property of
Captain John Reid, bound for the Outer Hebrides. That's all it
said on the itinerary – anything more detailed depended on day-
to-day wind and weather conditions. It was nautical mystery
tour, paid for in sweat.

I woke with a sudden panic, to the sound of the engine and a
strange motion in my stomach. How long had I been asleep?
Minutes? Hours? I scrambled up on to the deck to find we were at
sea, motoring across the Firth of Lorn, heading for the sound
between Mull and the Morvern peninsula. 'You missed the briefing,' said Daniel brightly. 'Captain wasn't very pleased.' Shane
shrugged, flipped his cigarette over the railing.

I found Captain John Reid in the wheelhouse. A solid, silent
man with close-cropped hair and a neatly trimmed beard, he
nodded when I apologised for missing the briefing, and continued
to peer at the flat screen in front of him, which showed our course
as a line crawling drip-like between two damp patches of land.
Technology sprouted from every surface: an autopilot, the technicolour layerings of an echo sounder, a Navtext spewing little
receipt-sized tickets. On the window was a bumper sticker: *Bad boys
drive bad ass toys.*

'How's the weather looking, John?'

I immediately regretted the 'John' – it sounded far too chummy,
even cocky. On the other hand 'Cap'n' could sound like you were
taking the piss. John ripped a weatherfax from the wall, studied the
hieroglyphics. 'Not so good for tomorrow,' he replied, levelly. 'A
cold front, and windy with it. I think we'll go to a sheltered wee
anchorage for tonight.'

I allowed myself a chuckle. 'Yes, I guess you don't want the passengers getting seasick – or the crew for that matter.' It was

supposed to be a bit of casual banter, but John's face hardened. 'If the crew are seasick they're off the ship at the next port,' he said, staring ahead. 'We can't have people lying around in their bunks.'

It was a pointed reference to me. I blushed and apologised again, but he again made no response. This was going to be trickier than I thought.

'Beautiful boat you have here,' I said, wheeling out the old fail-safe. 'Where did you find her?' Despite being the only working square-rigger based in Scotland, the *Jean de la Lune* was, as the name suggested, French. She was built in 1957 and used for years as a tuna boat before doing dive charters. John had bought her in 1988. 'I was pissed off with the rat race. I knew this boat from diving off her,' said John, warming up at last. 'I realised her potential. I put a whole new rig on in 1993–4, changed her from a schooner to a brig.' He laid his hand on the helm as one might pat the head of a faithful sheepdog. 'She's a very sound ship. She always gets top marks when it comes to survey time . . .'

A phone trilled and John picked it up. 'That's you needed in the galley,' he said, looking severely over the top of his specs. 'Better get down there sharpish.'

Jemma was cutting up vegetables in her stainless steel empire, listening to acid bagpipe music. She was a matronly, no-nonsense type with a twinkle in her eye. 'Feeling better after your nap?' she smirked. Once a land-based caterer, she had won a trip on the *JDL* and ended up marrying the captain. Now everything she knew about kitchens was subjected to the erratic buck and roll of the boat. Pudding bowls bulged from behind elastic restraints, pans of boiling water needed wedging on the hobs with remov-able metal rails. Knives in particular had to be carried as carefully as if they were sticks of dynamite, with an obligatory warning screech of 'knife!' until they were safely stuck to their long wall-mounted magnet. She set me to work washing up and peeling spuds. I braced myself against the deep steel sink, and groped around for cutlery in the greasy water, trying to banish the queasy feeling in my stomach by staring out at the horizon through the eye-level porthole. I needed to avoid seasickness at any cost.

'What did I just tell you about knives?' snapped Jemma. I stared mutely at the meat cleaver in my hand. I was suddenly five years old and had just broken my primary school teacher's scissor-carrying rule. 'Knife!' I offered belatedly.

Shane strode into the galley carrying four wine glasses at once. 'Oi, gobshoite! Don't use that dishcloth!' he barked, whipping me with my own sodden teatowel. 'Wineglasses need a special cloth.' I must have been looking either puce or crimson by this point, because Jemma took pity and sent me up to take wine orders. Maggie and Raymond (Sauvignon blanc) were chatty, witty Edinburgh lawyers; Nick (Shiraz), a friendly wildlife conservationist; Simon (Eighty shilling), a quiet highway engineer from Wolverhampton; Paul (Merlot), a recently retired computer programmer living in Geneva; Peta, a doctor, and her husband David (Sauvignon), a retired Scots engineer living in South Africa. They were standing at the rail watching our progress up a channel between heather-furred hillocks. Maggie asked me where we were going, and I had to confess I didn't know. In fact, I had hardly noticed anything outside the ship since boarding it. This was going to be a very different type of journey.

I had barely extricated the right bottles from the bar and stuck the whites in the freezer for a quick chill before it was time to drop anchor – in a sheltered basin known as Drumbuie. Shane worked the windlass, while Daniel showed me the anchor locker, where we monitored the flaked chain shooting out through the hole, keeping hands well clear. Then as soon as the engine died it was back to the dining room in matching blue sailing smocks to serve pork medallions and vegetarian stuffed peppers. We ate our own meal at a separate table within earshot of the guests, keeping wine glasses refilled, bolting the food in time to clear the table and scoot back into the galley to fetch desserts. Then there was the seemingly endless washing-up round, punctuated by nerve-jangling bellows of 'knife!' Finally, it was time to stagger up on deck to enjoy the evening sunshine and get the first proper sense of the passengers.

'What *are* you wearing?' hooted Maggie, laughing as Shane emerged in his orange wellies.

'Steel toecaps, industrial strength rubber, the dog's bollocks,' said Shane, kicking the air proudly. 'Ask any fisherman.'

'So what are *you* doing wearing them?' asked Ray with a wicked grin, sipping his pint. Ray and Maggie seem to have warmed to Shane already.

'Eight years I've been at the fishing,' he said proudly. 'Started when I was ten.' He smirked and dragged on his cigarette, enjoying the wide eyes of his captive middle-class audience. 'I can't read or write very well, but who wants to learn all that shite just to forget it again? Who needs books?'

Shane didn't look like the type to complain about lost childhood. He'd had too much fun on the trawlers, gutting and hauling, smoking and drinking, learning to put a good face on bad weather, getting his tattoos and bad habits in early. A bulldog tattooed on his shoulder dared anyone to contradict him.

'Fishing is feckin' *marvellous*. I've fished all over the place, all kind of boats, all kinds of fish. Pulled out some weird feckin' fish near Sellafield, I can tell you. Fish with two tails . . . A flatfish I was filleting had a second pair of eyes! There's some weird shit going on out there. Took it to a scientist and he gave me £75 and told me to shut up . . .'

The captain was chuckling to himself. Shane, on his third bottle of beer since supper, was only just getting started.

'Got rescued by the lifeboat people once,' he said, like a seasoned raconteur with that matter-of-fact voice which knows you'll be unable to resist. 'I gave them a tousand pounds, I was that fecking grateful! The fuse box caught fire and set off the rest of the boat. We were 67 miles offshore, and the diesel tanks went up too, so we had to get the life rafts in the water and wait till they rescued us. Wonderful people.' He waved a lifeboat-shaped moneybox under our noses. 'Contributions, anyone?'

'So how did you end up here?' said Raymond, fumbling for change.

'Easy. Got a text message from my brother Finbar – friend of John and Jemma's. *Feck fishin'* – *I've found a job for you here in Scotland!'*

I emerged from my bunk/coffin the next morning feeling fresh as a corpse. Truly, I had never felt so exhausted in my life, despite having skulked off to bed early. 'You missed a great session last night, gobshoite!' said Shane, still smelling of alcohol when I arrived to make porridge. I tried to explain that I was knackered after rowing for two days with some pretend monks, but Shane's uncomprehending squint convinced me to quit while I was ahead. But even monastic seafaring was probably more acceptable to him than the hideous social deformity that constitutes my real problem with late night sessions: I only ever have one drink.

It's not a moral thing, just a medical one. Since I developed migraine in adolescence, drinking a second pint of beer is like inserting an ice pick into my eye socket. It triggers an instant hangover, short-cutting to the rigours of the morning after, just when everybody else is starting to enjoy the night before. I've never looked for sympathy, just a little tolerance for a lightweight in the broad church that is your average pub. But I had a feeling that this wasn't really a shandy-drinking kind of place. One clue was pinned to the masthead in the dining room, just above the day's menu, presumably left by a satisfied passenger.

> Jimmy's prayer
> *Our beer*
> *Which art in barrels*
> *Hallowed be thy drink*
> *Thy will be drunk*
> *I will be drunk*
> *At home as it is in the local*
> *Forgive us this day our daily spillage*
> *As we forgive those who spillest against us.*
> *And lead us not into the practice*
> *Of poncey wine-tasting,*
> *But deliver us from alco-pops*
> *For mine is the bitter, the ale and the lager*
> *For ever and ever*
> *Barmen.*

Bad weather kept us in Drumbuie most of the morning, but at lunchtime John announced a quick dash across to Mull, which gave the opportunity to learn a few extra crewing jobs. As John manoeuvred towards Tobermory quay using a remote-control joystick, Shane showed us how to get wrist-thick mooring lines ashore by attaching them first to a thin rope and weighted ball. I fumbled the first one, but got the hang of it later as we cast off and redocked to make way for a car ferry. By the end of the afternoon, I was feeling moderately useful.

Tobermory was a cheerful looking port of brightly painted seafront houses on the northernmost coast of Mull, the opposite side of the island to the southern cliffs where we had anchored in the curragh a few days before. It had relied mainly on tourism since the decline of its herring industry, but Shane managed to track down a couple of trawlers and swapped a six-pack of beer for two bowls of tailed prawns. We feasted on them for supper, contentedly sucking garlic butter off our fingers.

After hours of serving and washing, there was a trip to the pub, most of which I missed by standing in a phone box on the edge of the pier while Ali wept at the other end of the line. Her grief for her father was still raw, and she was just about holding it together with the help of friends by taking time off work. It didn't help that I had left days after we had bought a new house, leaving Ali with all the paperwork. 'Do you want me to come home?' I said, feeling like the lowest form of male scum for not being there. 'No, don't do that – at least not yet,' she said. 'I just need you to listen to how it is for me.' I listened for an hour, until we were both exhausted but somehow connected again across the distance.

I couldn't quite crank out the necessary bonhomie when I finally got to the pub, shortly before closing time. Shane was on his sixth pint, hanging off Maggie and Ray's shoulders, cheerfully recounting how he had been driving cars since he was ten, and celebrating the second placing of the *JDL* pub quiz team ('Loonies Afloat').

'What took you so long to get to the boozer, gobshoite?' he asked, with an affectionate clout on the shoulder. I scrabbled for something suitably laddish to say in response, but in the end I just told him the truth: that I'd had a difficult conversation with my wife.

'Ali's her name, eh?' said Shane, his eyes rolling skywards, as if he was rummaging through a mental filing cabinet. 'Well, the last Ali I knew, I woke up next to her and found I had a pierced nipple. Hope it's not the same woman . . .'

16

Master and Commander

Tobermory to Portree

After various pub-induced declamations of nautical bravery, the passengers were rewarded the next day with their first taste of decent sailing. It proved to be more than they had bargained for. 'Make sure everything's stowed safely – it could get interesting out there,' shouted John, as we heaved out from the shelter of Mull and into the Sound of Sleat, I swallowed a couple of sea-sickness tablets and kitted myself up in waterproofs and safety harness. The ship's bell began to clang ominously on its own, until Shane tactfully removed the clapper.

'Roite, Nick, you take the main throat halyard,' he said, passing on orders from the skipper. He might as well have been speaking in Urdu, but luckily someone had glued little laminated labels beneath the splayed mass of ropes on a rack of brass pins.* I had

*NAUTICAL BIT: Later I would learn that there were nine sails. Three were jibs, called inner, outer and flying, at the front of the boat; three were square-shaped sails (which allowed the ship to be classified as a square rigger), the largest of them the course sail, above it the topsail, and above that the topsail gallant. And on the main mast were the main and upper staysails – both triangular – and the mainsail, which hinged around the mainmast on a yard and a boom. Halyards were for pulling sails up or down, while sheets were for controlling them once raised. So, with the assistance of Maggie and Ray, I was responsible for pulling up the mainsail.

just worked out which rope to pull and where to pull it from – me on the coachhouse roof, Maggie and Ray on the side deck – when John bellowed something which sounded like: 'Hauld the main throat halyard!' It was an urgent cry, but it was windy. Was it *hold* or *haul*? They meant opposite things. 'Sorry, John,' I asked, as cheerily as possible, at the top of my voice. 'Was that haul or . . .?'

'HAUL! NOW!' screamed John and Jemma in unison.

'One, two, HEAVE!' I shouted at Ray and Maggie, and we pulled in unison, bracing ourselves against any available upright as the boat pitched. It was important for them to think that I knew what I was doing, even if I didn't. The mainsail began to inch upwards.

'Come oan, gie't some welly, man!' shouted Jemma, her face furiously contorted. 'Two, six, HEAVE!'

Two, six, heave? I've never understood why mariners insist on having their own Masonic-style terminology, unless it's simply to show up ignorant landlubbers. When we'd yanked the thing as far as it would go, Shane shouted: 'Belay that!' Apparently that meant 'tie off the rope end'.

Ray and Maggie tied it off round the wooden pins, someone else pulled in a sheet and presently the mainsail grew elegantly round-bellied in the wind. You could feel the power transferring to the boat, which began to tilt beneath our feet. Within moments, we were heeled over so far that water was sluicing through the scuppers and the passengers were gripping the railings as if they were Zimmer frames. On our port side, Simon was silhouetted against the humped landmass of Eigg, hanging on doggedly to his allotted rope. A mild-mannered chap, he had the dazed expression of someone inexplicably teleported from a quiet afternoon of pottering in the garden. The bows pitched and lunged into a steep-sided wave, drenching Simon from head to foot. He shuddered and opened his mouth silently but held on to the jib sheet, shivering under his own personal storm cloud. 'Golly,' he gasped, finally.

'Simon!!! I've told you five times, get that jib in!' came Jemma's roar from the stern. Nodding mutely, he dragged the sheet as hard as he could, swaying uncertainly in the swell, tied it off, then tottered to the downwind handrail and discreetly vomited into the sea. 'Just getting rid of last night's beer!' he chuckled palely, before barfing again.

Other passengers weren't looking too good either. A few minutes later I found Nick hugging the toilet bowl in the forward equipment locker. I quietly congratulated myself on feeling fine.

'Right, who's still standing?' demanded Shane, unmoved. 'Get your harness on – you're coming up to unfurl the topsail and gallant.' Four of us climbed the mast – Shane, Daniel, Paul and me. We kept our backs to the wind, clipping our harnesses at each available rung, while the pitching of the boat amplified the higher we climbed. I followed Daniel out along the port side yard, balancing on steel cables strung below the beam, while bracing my thighs against the wood. Leaning over the furled sail to remove the ties ready for hoisting, I felt not fear but joy – that rare emotion which comes when you are concentrating hard on doing something else. Just beyond my fingers, fumbling at the knots, I could see the blurred fury of sea, 50 feet below, and a little row of white faces staring up at us from the deck.

Daniel grinned down at me as we climbed up to second and third yard and repeated the exercise. He had the bonus that he could throw all the right lingo around, having been on a square sail training course in Cornwall the previous year. 'Try holding the futtock shroud!' he'd say, perched on the outer jib as casually as if he were chatting in a pub. 'Mind your foot on the Flemish Horse!' I grinned blankly at him, enjoying the wind on my face until it was time to descend and hoist the sails.

Lunch was a tentative, white-faced affair over a table which slanted markedly to starboard and only retained its paraphernalia thanks to an ingenious rubber latticework. 'Tea, anybody?' asked Jemma sweetly, utterly transformed from the screaming harridan who had given orders earlier. Nick and Simon picked at their food bravely — eating 'little and often' was one of the better ways of staving off seasickness.

Back at the wheel, John had a faraway look in his eyes. Eight knots in a force 7 wind, powering through waves streaked with spume — no problem. 'The *Lord of the Isles* is having second thoughts,' he chuckled, nodding over the rail to where a luxury cruise ship had turned back in the other direction. We'd passed a few yachts too, their heavily reefed sails keeled over against the gale, hulls pitching like corks. But the *Jean de la Lune* was in her element, a miniature throwback to the windjammers which once pounded through the roaring forties.

I washed up the lunch things with my legs braced apart and water sluicing up the side of the sink, Thin Lizzie blaring from the stereo. By the time I finished, the coast of Skye was closing in as we approached the Kylerhea narrows, where the island came closest to the mainland. Squalls moved across the water like a magnet over iron filings, etching strange spirals and patterns among the wavelets. 'Better get the sails down before we get through the narrows,' shouted John. And so we did the whole procedure in reverse, a little less traumatised by the bellowing of the captain, a little more confident up in the yards. Some time later, after gliding under the Skye Road Bridge, we dropped anchor in Plockton, a tree-lined bay dotted with yachts.

After supper John ferried us ashore for folk night at the Plockton

Inn. There was a flautist, a mandolin player, two fiddlers, and a uillean piper, all hunched earnestly round a table lined with pints.

The atmosphere was warm and smoky, and I might well have nodded off had Shane not chosen to insert his tongue in my ear for one of the passengers' snapshots. 'Can you play "The Wild Rover"?' he yelled, as another folk lament twiddled to an end in a round of polite clapping. 'Maggie, you'll take a dance?' he said, and dragged her, laughing, into the middle of the pub. The two of them developed a sort of waltz in which Maggie stood on the steel toe caps of Shane's orange wellies as he stepped around the room. Half the pub joined in the roaring rendition. The folk band played through gritted teeth, as if they had been asked to pipe up with 'The Birdie Song.'

I watched through drooping eyelids, until I was shaken awake in the corner at closing time. 'Bit of a party animal, are we?' said Shane. I flushed and apologised. Even by my own spectacularly unriotous standards, this was a bit lame. It didn't bode well.

'What happened to sharing anchor watch, Nick?' said Jemma, looking daggers at me when I surfaced to make breakfast the following morning. Shane appeared to have spent the night lying on the dinner bench.

He opened his bloodshot eyes painfully as Daniel arrived. 'I tried to wake those two up but they were feckin' *dead*.'

Anchor watch? I blinked and looked from Jemma to Shane. I felt like the victim of some weird conspiracy. Shane filled me in, irritably. Apparently the anchor had slipped a little in strong winds the night before, necessitating a round-the-clock watch to alert the captain if it slipped any more. I was supposed to take over from Shane some time in the early hours of the morning, though I had no recollection of being asked.

Jemma looked disgustedly at me for a moment. 'That is *out of order*,' she muttered, shaking her head as she walked into the galley.

'Look,' I said, following her. 'I'm sorry Shane's ended up doing the whole watch, but I really can't help unless I'm actually *conscious*.' I thought back to the missed briefing, when I had again been blamed for being asleep. 'I do sleep deeply, but it's not that difficult to wake me.'

'Aye, well,' said Jemma icily. 'There's no fucking way you'd have slept through *my* shift change. When you're crewing a ship, you learn to sleep with an eye open, right? A *real* sailor's always got part of his mind on the ship.' She softened a little, seeing my sagging expression. 'But dinnae worry the noo. Just get that bloody porridge served up.'

Outside it was raining steadily, and several of the guests retreated to their cabins to nurse hangovers as we motored across the Kyle of Lochalsh to Skye. I tried to redeem myself with Brasso. I rubbing the stair rails, doorknobs, ship's bell and nautical instruments with the stuff until I could see my own furrowed brow in the gleaming surfaces.

'Okay, tell me what's wrong with this,' said Jemma, the moment she saw the ship's bell.

'Surprise me.'

'It's supposed tae point its name forward, ye great numpty!'

She grinned at me as I unscrewed the thing and turned it round. I didn't grin back. 'Everythin' okay?' she asked. 'Seems like you're pretty knackered . . .'

I reached for this scrap of human feeling. 'Maybe I'm not cut out for this galley slave way of life,' I said. 'I'm not used to being yelled at one minute as if I'm an idiot, and then treated as if nothing has happened.' In truth, I hadn't felt so thin-skinned since

Test-driving *Thistledown* with Craig at Linlithgow *(Katy Lee)*

The futuristic Falkirk Wheel scoops up a passenger boat from
the Forth and Clyde Canal *(Nick Thorpe)*

Zeepaard skipper
Don Penfield
directs a canal diver
to the mattress
springs around his
propeller *(Nick Thorpe)*

George Parsonage, aka The Riverman (rear), patrols the Clyde with assistant Mark Gash
(Nick Thorpe)

Crossing the Clyde in a hand-crafted yoal with Govan boatbuilder Colin Macleod *(Stuart Wallace)*

Gregor Connelly ups the pace downriver towards Helensburgh
(Stuart Wallace)

Trident submarine
HMS Vengeance
looms in the
Clyde estuary
(MOD)

The biscuit-tin-
shaped *MV Menno*
on maintenance
duty in the Kyles
of Bute Credit
(Nick Thorpe)

The *Menno* crew
prepares to de-
slime a navigation
buoy *(Nick Thorpe)*

The steam puffer *VIC32* on approach to Crinan Harbour
(Brian Fair)

Bad habits: the author (left) kits up for the 'Celtic Renewal Service' on Seil with seafaring organist Alastair Chisholm (centre) and expedition leader Donald McCallum
(Nick Thorpe)

Retracing St Columba's journey in *Colmcille*, a wood-and-canvas curragh
(Nick Thorpe)

Lubber as scrubber:
The author begins his
assigned duties aboard
the *Jean de la Lune*
(Wattie Cheung)

Anchored in the
Shiant Isles, where
the birds are in
charge *(Nick Thorpe)*

The fabulously
square-rigged *Jean de
la Lune* shows off
her full plumage
(JDL Marine)

The 60-million-year old basalt columns of Staffa form Fingal's world-famous cave
(Nick Thorpe)

Kayak instruction en route to Fort William with Ken, Pete and three million midges . . .
(Gary Doak)

The author, dressed as a woolly bear, contemplates Loch Linnhe with a sinking feeling
(Stuart Wallace)

Weeding the Findhorn Foundation vegetable garden in search of its once-famous 40lb cabbages *(Nick Thorpe)*

The Last Lighthouse Keeper: Angus Hutchison at home in Stromness, Orkney *(Nick Thorpe)*

The fishermen of *MV Resolute* lower her trawl doors in search of herring shoals east of Shetland *(Nick Thorpe)*

Peter Morrison (right), owner of dungarees once coveted by Mick Jagger, with crewman on the *Vivid* near Montrose *(Nick Thorpe)*

Robert the Bruce contemplates another declaration in Arbroath *(Nick Thorpe)*

Tom Gardner enjoys a stint at the helm of the *White Wing* near Anstruther *(Nick Thorpe)*

working as a spotty seventeen-year-old sales assistant on the M&S underwear counter.

'Tweat me nicely, boys!' lisped Shane, who had come up the stairs behind me.

Jemma shot him a glance, but didn't join in the fun. 'That's what you southerners don't understand about us Celtic types,' she said. 'It's all banter. Here you tell your best friend to piss off, and it's a term of endearment.'

'Absolutely,' grinned Shane, slapping me on the back. 'You're a worthless gobshoite – but it's all good!'

17

Midsummer's Day

Portree to Scalpay

The Shiant Isles bit through the horizon, a row of jagged molars in a miasma of wheeling sea birds. Stranded in The Minch between Lewis and Skye, they harboured no permanent human residents, though the corrugations of old lazybeds on the livid green hillsides showed where the long-departed crofters had once farmed. These days it was the birds which really owned the place. Their racket grew as we approached, from a faint echo on the wind to an aural assault ricocheting off 100-metre cliffs.

They came from all directions, razorbills, oystercatchers, puffins and cormorants, circling in the air above us, spattering the decks, plunging like scimitars into the water around us, the wind acrid with guano, salt and seaweed. From below they seemed little more than a chaotic swarm, thousands of individuals, each following its own plan. But once ashore and looking out from the tops of the cliffs that afternoon, I saw the bigger pattern: a vortex of thousands of birds, following the same anticlockwise ellipse along the edges of the cliffs, out over the bay and back along the edge of a rocky peninsula. It was both awesome and practical, presumably evolved to minimise collisions, like some vast airborne skating rink. Only the odd thrill-seeking chancer refused to keep to the rules, slicing through the midst of the oncoming traffic like the speed freaks in ice-hockey boots who dart around spraying chipped ice. I watched a puffin emerge from a burrow on the cliff edge like a novice skater, plunge uncertainly into the circling masses and look around immediately for an exit. Twice, three times it approached its precarious ledge-side burrow, each time aborting its landing to make another circuit, its stubby wings flapping frantically like a cartoon character poised above a ravine.

Last to the dressing-up box of evolution, puffins seem to me comic but slightly melancholic creatures. I watched a group of them standing round uneasily on the cliff edges in their formal dinner jackets and striped carnival masks, as if coerced into attending an old school reunion they were now regretting. I peered closer through Simon's binoculars at those sad, mascara-streaked eyes, and decided I had a met a few puffins in my time: playing their cheery role with brave desperation, somehow stranded in the wrong life. The beak itself was a talking point, but why the gloriously redundant colours? Was it an evolutionary cry for help? There was probably a revealing fable in there somewhere: *How the Puffin Got His Beak*.

'I'd love to see them underwater,' said Simon, in his wistful, Eeyorish tone. 'They're crap at take-off and landing — just sort of fall off things and hope for the best — but once they get underwater they can move like lightning. They're like different creatures.' Simon seemed a little puffin-like himself, when I thought about it. I realised how little I knew of our passengers — how the quieter ones had simply faded into the background.

As I followed the other passengers across the summit of the hill, picking my way through sphagnum bogs dotted with white cotton-tops, I heard a honk of disdain from behind me. 'Early warning,' said Nick, as a large brown and white bird scythed overhead. 'You don't want to get on the wrong side of a great skua.' If puffins were the clowns of the bird world, then skuas were the assassins. They dive-bombed unprotected human scalps if their young were threatened, and occasionally skewered an incompetent puffin for breakfast. We skirted their territory warily and made our way down to the rocky beach, the sun filtering weakly through the ribbed clouds, and our lifejackets now polka-dotted with birdshit.

The Shiants gave no safe overnight anchorage, so we motored on westwards across the Minch to Scalpay, a tiny boat-shaped island just off the south-eastern corner of Harris. 'These folk are seriously religious – no drinking, no working on a Sunday,' warned John, as we dropped anchor in the quiet natural harbour. Not a soul was in sight, just a string of well-kept pebbledash houses strung along a single-track road. I was intrigued to see a powder blue soft-top Mercedes parked outside one of them. The four hundred islanders had a reputation for innovation and enterprise, having both modernised their fishing fleet and nurtured a thriving textiles cottage industry. They were also known, like Presbyterians across the Western Isles, for their rather severe take on life. Sex, joked their detractors, was dangerous because it might lead to dancing – and other satanic hobbies. The very suggestion of more open-minded interpretations had historically caused whole sections of congregations to calve off like icebergs to become new churches with confusingly similar names. On the plus side, I had also heard that Gaelic metrical psalms had an austere beauty about them. And the next day was Sunday.

But John showed no intention of letting anyone ashore. 'I don't

even see a pub here!' he said pityingly, shaking his head like a colo-
nialist reporting lack of sanitation in an African village. 'Better to
wait till we get to Barra tomorrow – at least that's Catholic, so they
won't mind a drink.'

So that was that. We had supper and brought our hallowed
drinks out on deck and peered across at this unknown village from
our anchorage in the bay: two cultures entirely failing to meet.
Nothing and nobody moved in the midsummer night, except the
occasional bird flapping lazily across the crimson skies, reflected
almost perfectly in the gently stippled water as the light dissolved
in pink mist.

'Roite, it's da longest day of the year, which means *nobody's*
allowed to go to bed,' announced Shane. 'And dat means you too,
gobshoite. It's time ta party!' There was something both enter-
taining and compelling about Shane after three beers, like a
leprechaun with a pump-action shotgun. I decided tonight was
probably the night to let my hair down, and poured myself a
second pint of shandy.

In a sense, I consoled myself, we were following an equally
strong tradition of the Western Isles. The Scots sailor Martin
Martin reported in 1695 that among 'persons of distinction' it
was considered an affront to your host if you failed to drink yourself unconscious:

> 'The manner of drinking used by the chief men of the isles is
> called . . . a 'round'; for the company sat in a circle, the cup-bearer
> filled the drink round to them, and all was drunk out whatever the
> liquor was, whether strong or weak; they continued drinking
> sometimes twenty-four, sometimes forty-eight hours. It was reck-
> oned a piece of manhood to drink until they became drunk, and
> there were two men with a barrow attending punctually on such

occasions. They stood at the door until some became drunk, and
they carried them upon the barrow to bed.'

Shane deviated a little from this traditional format by appearing
at one point dressed in nothing but a binbag and orange wellies,
with fishnet stockings drawn on his hairy legs. But there were some
suitably salty sea shanties, a dirty joke contest and even a drunken
duel with water pistol, before we all collapsed into our bunks in
the culturally sensitive manner prescribed by the island chiefs.

18

Blame the Dolphins

Mingulay to Oban

The deserted island of Mingulay looked the perfect cure for cabin fever. After a rather subdued day motoring south through mist and hangovers, we dropped anchor in a wide bay where white sandy beaches were slowly burying the shells of a ruined village. The stalling of the engine left a haunting silence.

The little community of 150 people had dwindled from the beginning of the nineteenth century due to a combination of epidemics, overcrowding and the fact that even the hardiest folk disliked being cut off for half the year because of the lack of a pier. At one point an unfortunate rent collector had been left there for a year with only the corpses of plague victims for company. It's a mark of how much I needed solitude that the story only made me more eager to get ashore and wander through some nettle-choked ruins. No matter how immersed I was in communal life, a part of me would always need to escape. It was like holding one's breath underwater.

Roaming through the grounds of the roofless school, now strewn with old fishboxes, I looked through the window of a padlocked bothy, probably used by a visiting sheep farmer. I could make out candles in plastic shrink-wrap, armchairs bleached ash-white, worn through to a froth of stuffing, a threadbare carpet, and a table with a Calor Gas oven on top. And just inside the window, a slightly shrivelled balloon animal, which completely ruined my melancholy mood. The desolate sound of the wind whipping through the grass, and the lonely cry of the oystercatcher were somewhat compromised, I felt, by the squeak and grunt of auld Wullie the crofter struggling to make another balloon giraffe by candlelight. It cheered me up no end.

I wandered back along the beach with a grin on my face. Back at the ship, the passengers were exultant from their walk to the top of the hill, which revealed, apparently, a sheer drop into the sea, as abrupt as this eastern side was gentle.

John promised to take us round that side when we weighed anchor, and Daniel and I climbed to the top of the mast for the view. There was nothing but sea between here and America, and the waves had built over hundreds of miles into majestic swells, kneaded by wind. Before us sheer cliffs plunged 200 metres into the foaming sea. Birds wheeled below us, before us and above us, a breeding colony of guillemots and kittiwake, while on the green summits occasional white specks indicated thrill-seeking sheep. Wedged in behind a stay, and harnessed for safety, we clung on and howled at the wind as the mast swung from side to side, grinning insanely down at the furrowed white faces of our fellow passengers, braced against the railings.

And it got better. I was just setting the table for supper when the boat swung suddenly to port, accompanied by a shout from John. 'Whales!' Maggie gasped with delight and went off to call Raymond, who appeared blearily on deck dressed only in his fluffy white towelling bathrobe, and we all followed the sudden sliver of black, arching crescentlike above the waves, and then another, a little way behind. 'Looks like minkes,' said John, as we followed them. Shane noticed another two on the other side of the boat, all keeping their distance, though John had turned down the engine to a steady low chunter. The evening light had a luminous, magical quality to it. We had been circling, transfixed, for what seemed like about half an hour when Jemma rushed to the back of the boat, and we made another turn. Out beyond the whales were two dark fins, much steeper than the curves of the minkes. The first cruised more or less straight through the water while the other slalomed floppily from side to side. It was with a shock that I realised both belonged to the same, very large fish. 'That,' said Jemma, 'is a basking shark.' The biggest fish in UK waters was a solitary roamer slowly sieving the seas for plankton. Climbing to the first crosstrees of the mast as we edged nearer, I glimpsed for an instant its huge, mottled body between the dorsal and tail fin, and the gaping mouth that seemed to glow an eerie luminescent green. It turned a final time and was gone.

Something changed in me that day. The remainder of the voyage seemed gentler, less resistant somehow, as if I was no longer pushing against the flow but travelling with it. The time passed in a slow scrolling of islands, punctuated by washing up and polishing, as we made our way back towards Oban. We stopped at Barra, then Canna, a lush little haven where I slept for hours in the long grass and watched otters playing in the kelp. Then it was on back towards Mull past Rhum, Eigg, Coll and Tiree – we counted them off, one by one, always at a distance. I had only grazed the edge of island culture, meeting the odd barman or coffee shop owner. But I was beginning to make peace with this – my real journey had been among the foreign cultures aboard the ship. Now, with a day and a night to go, I felt almost at home in this little floating outpost, despite my inability to share its primary rite of communion. It was, after all, the longest I would spend in one community for the whole of my trip. John remained a distant mystery, but Jemma and Shane were less barbed these days — or perhaps my skin had thickened. I had even come to like my cosy coffin bed, its containment and safety.

When we were within sight of Mull, Shane attracted a pod of dolphins as he lay in the net of the bowsprit. They wove in and out of the sparkling bow wave, flashing their white bellies at us as we snapped pictures for a magical quarter of an hour. Something about dolphins always moves me: that uninhibited spirit of playfulness, perhaps, with that long, beaky, flirtatious smile. Or maybe it's the sadness of realising how rarely as adults we attain that childlike spirit.

It was a warm, windless day, and by the time we entered the Sound of Mull the water pistol had been produced. Shane and Jemma rushed around like hit men before abandoning the pump action gun for buckets hurled from the top of the cabin. Daniel and Maggie both got one in the face, and by the time we turned into the wooded haven of Lochaline for our final night, several of us were laughing helplessly and sopping wet. It was a good ending. I think we had the dolphins to thank for that.

Back in Oban harbour the next day, the little shipboard community quickly dispersed, leaving Shane in charge of a top-to-bottom clean of the ship ready for the next trip. As I wielded my toilet brush for the last time, my successor arrived: a blonde German backpacker called Melanie.

'Hands off this one, she's mine,' whispered Shane, with a broadening grin, as Jemma showed her round the galley.

'Aye, right, in your dreams,' said Daniel.

'Welcome aboard,' said Shane, involuntarily rubbing his hands as Melanie sat down with us at the mess table. 'Important question: do you drink?'

'Not really,' said Melanie, looking puzzled. 'A glass of wine occasionally wit my meal, but . . . not much.'

'Smoke?'

'No,' said Melanie, firmly.

Daniel and I smirked at each other as Shane nodded carefully. 'It's all good,' he shrugged.

And it was.

Oban was enjoying a rare heatwave. Along the quay, teenage boys in cut-off jeans took turns to leap into the sea, tensing their wet torsos for the watching girls as they scaled the iron ladders. High on the hillside above, the town's famous fake Colosseum, raised by a vain nineteenth-century banker, peered down on a harbour basin that seemed to simmer in the sun. Fishing boats and ferries lined the quay. Surely *someone* would take me to the entrance of the Caledonian Canal?

'Fort William?' frowned a man offering seal-spotting trips. 'Don't know anyone goes up that way.' He said it as if I'd asked to get to Kazakhstan, rather than a major town barely 30 miles to the north.

'How about fishermen?' I asked.

'Naw, they all just go out to sea and come back in.'

The harbourmaster, a friendly matron with an enormous bunch of keys jingling on her belt, was similarly unhelpful. 'Naw, darlin',' she said. 'I think ye could be waitin' a lang time. I cannae think of anybody who goes that way.'

I phoned the local yacht club and got an answer machine. I asked in the ferry office, at the dockside, in the newsagent's, in the tourist office. 'What's wrong with taking the bus or train?' said the information officer, eyeing me testily. 'You can do it in less than an hour.'

Scanning the streets disconsolately, I fanned the tiny hope that something would come up, something I hadn't yet considered. I had to get on to the Caledonian Canal to meet Ali in less than five days' time. It was 4.55 p.m. when I noticed the answer standing on the pavement in front of an outdoor suppliers' shop like a big pink exclamation mark.

It was a sea kayak.

19

The Mighty Midge

To Fort William by Sea Kayak

Anyone glancing beyond the blur of their windscreen wipers in Oban's modest rush hour the following morning would have noticed three long and luminous shapes nosing out from the harbour towards a greasy expanse of rain-pocked sea.

I had met Ken and Pete, two local canoeing instructors, over a hastily arranged pint the previous night, and, like most outdoor pursuits fanatics, they needed only the smallest of excuses for an outing. They not only agreed to loan me a kayak, but to accompany me on the trip, which would take two or three days. It had seemed the perfect weekend adventure in the previous evening's golden sunshine. The weather forecast for the day was less encouraging.

'One hundred per cent precipitation,' confirmed Ken, shaking the drips from an internet gizmo he had hanging in a waterproof wallet round his neck. 'Still, it could be a lot worse. At least we've got wind and tide on our side.' I wobbled out of the shallows past the *Jean de la Lune*, where I had spent my last night, and waved to Daniel and Shane, who were watching my departure. Shane, bare chested and baggy trousered, twitched a half-smoked Regal by way of farewell, shaking his head with a hung-over half-smile. Daniel squinted through his digital camera from below the peak of an expensive waterproof. There was no sign of Melanie. As the ship fell astern, I felt a spreading sense of freedom. I was beginning an entirely different kind of voyage. On the *JDL* I had been a team cog. Here I was captain of my own boat, if not quite my destiny.

My turquoise kayak had sealed compartments for my luggage and elastic netting for a bottle of water and rain mac within easy reach. I had never canoed in open sea before. The boat wobbled disconcertingly, but it did at least have a foot-controlled rudder to help with steering. I wore borrowed wet-suit bottoms, a splash top and a life preserver.

'If you happen to capsize, just knock on the hull three times to say you're okay,' said Ken, affably, as the harbour walls fell away behind us. 'Otherwise we'll assume you're drowning.' The waters of Loch Linnhe were relatively benign for a man who was happiest canoeing vertically down waterfalls. 'Up on the River Falloch I once went so deep into a plunge pool my eyeballs got squeezed by the water pressure,' he reminisced as we drifted along. 'I remember seeing the end of my canoe above me, and above that the daylight. All I could do was hope it spat me out again.'

Pete was the quieter of the two men, a downshifting Yorkshireman with a pierced eyebrow. He was being coached towards his final exams by Ken, who needed him as a senior instructor in his new company. 'I'd always prefer a kayak to a bigger boat,' he said, as we wove past a couple of yachts. 'You get closer to the wildlife because there's no engine noise.'

The quietness was indeed wonderful. Just the occasional splash of a missed stroke, or a gull flapping across the wide stretched flatness. More sublime and startling still was the scenery below us, where hundreds, perhaps thousands, of blue neon jellyfish hung like planets in the dark water. I paddled on quietly through the migration as if through deep space, awed but uneasy.

My biceps were beginning to ache pleasantly by the time we pulled into a deserted bay for lunch, wedging the boats between rocks cushioned with bladderwrack. Never had bread and cheese tasted so phenomenally good. I could almost feel the internal alchemy as blood sugar became muscular energy, powering me into the afternoon. Ken showed me how to improve efficiency by avoiding a splash of wasted energy at the beginning of the stroke. It had an elemental simplicity.

The tide was on our side, carrying us inland, but the wind was getting up. Waves began to slap the underside of the canoe. A grey cloud ceiling impaled itself slowly on the spike of a radio mast as we steered round the end of an island and made for shore. 'If it gets any lower it'll be fog,' said Ken. 'We'd better look for a camping spot.'

Camping had seemed a great idea after a couple of beers the previous night, but in the incessant rain I began to dream of log fires in hostelries. My fingers were squeaking a little on the blades, the skin white and prunelike, and my sodden sleeves flopped about, scooping up water. Unfortunately, we were miles from any settlement, and the light was fading. We eventually settled on a wide and deserted storm bay with signs of a stream for cooking water. The only thing it lacked, apparently, was exposure to a steady wind to keep the midges away. It was to prove a pivotal omission.

I began to feel pinpricks on my face and ears even as we pulled the kayaks up the beach. 'Midge net?' asked Ken, tossing me a sort of mesh bag to put over my hat. Thank God for that net. Even through the dark netting I could see the little buggers swarming like thickening columns of smoke. 'I've never seen them this bad,' admitted Ken. We unloaded the tent from the canoe and hurriedly thrust pegs into the ground. Once we had all the gear inside, Pete and I sealed ourselves in the tent while Ken cooked dinner in the insect-infested drizzle on one of those improbably small meths burners favoured by mountaineers. 'It's very simple and works in any conditions – a bit like me,' breezed Ken stoically, from inside his midge net. Peering gratefully through the tent mesh, I could see hundreds of insects swarming on his exposed hands, which swelled slowly like pink rubber gloves.

I had been shrugging off the warnings ever since I left home. If you were caught in a swarm with no cover, said the wide-eyed doom-mongers, the only thing to do was run. Cattle had been known to throw themselves off cliffs rather than endure the feeding frenzy. I had laughed this off as a melodramatic exaggeration. Surely even the female Highland midge couldn't possibly be that bad. Now, imprisoned in the tent, I should probably have eaten my hat, had I not needed it to keep the little vampires off. It was going to be a long night.

By 10 p.m. we were definitely losing the battle. After Ken's delicious but midge-peppered meal of tomato pasta, onions and olives, brewing a cuppa had been a definite mistake – we were only invulnerable as long as our bladders could hold out. Even with a coordinated tent entry and exit procedure, the besieging army swarmed inside each time one of us plunged out through the opening. Worst of all, I later needed to answer a rather more substantial call of nature, which meant squatting hurriedly in the long grass while flailing and slapping like a dervish. Imagine a toilet seat made of map pins and you're close. On my return I had to track down the ones I had let through the tent opening. By the time I felt it was safe to go to sleep, the canvas walls were speckled black and red.

Only Pete seemed oblivious to the carnage, having drifted off to sleep almost immediately after eating. The midges seemed as repelled as anyone else by his cataclysmic snoring. I lay awake analysing the various stages of this affliction with something verging on awe. It went in cycles, gradually decreasing from phlegmy thunder to a quiet rumble, until the breathing itself slowed into a pregnant silence. Then, after five seconds or so would come an extraordinary explosion of noise, like a Rottweiler savaging a jelly-fish – and we were back to rattling full volume again. The rain drummed an accompaniment on the canvas most of the night, along with the whining of midges in my ear. I dug out some foam plugs, wrapped my head in a sleeping bag liner and eventually dropped off.

In the morning Ken was putting a brave if rather blotchy face on it all, having slept in a balaclava. 'Time for thum coffee, I think,' he lisped. His lips were so swollen from midge bites that he looked as if he'd had collagen injections. He rustled up some bacon butties uncomplainingly outside the tent, where a cold wind had dispensed with the last insect stragglers. 'I slept like a log,' said Pete cheerily.

We decamped and restuffed the kayaks by 8 a.m., and threw ourselves back into damp clothes and a second day's paddling. It proved an unexpected tonic. A mere 80 per cent precipitation forecast turned out to be wrong, meaning no rain, and the predicted force 3–4 wind from the north blew from the south instead, so that the wavelets chased us. I began to get the hang of using my paddle as a rudder, and timing strokes for the moments when the nose dipped down the far side of a swell. You could coast for ages on a good one, as long as you didn't let the surge turn you sideways. 'We're going to make it to Fort William today after all,' said Ken, around mid-morning.

We stopped for lunch at the Corran narrows, slopping as unobtrusively as possible into the local hotel bar. The landlady glared at us for dripping on her carpet, but gave us fish and chips anyway, along with three plastic bags to sit on.

Later, as we coasted through the forested valley, breathing in the greenery and smell of seaweed, a family of seals surrounded us, snorting and curious. The hills swelled higher and closer until, at about mid-afternoon, the houses began to multiply on the loch side, and the sigh of traffic signalled our approach to Fort William. A town of ugly square concrete houses rose ahead of us, its waterfront hogged by a dual carriageway. Behind it, Ben Nevis was masked in a midge-net of cloud. We paddled straight past the town, past a long concrete pier used for training deep-sea divers. 'Don't fall in, now!' yelled a diver cheekily from the back of a rib inflatable. The sudden slap of his wake caught me by surprise and I twanged a muscle wobbling frantically for several seconds, furious that I was about to capsize within sight of my destination.

But I didn't. Instead, we coasted to a weary, victorious halt by the black-slimed lock gates of the Caledonian Canal, gently applauded by Pete's wife. I helped load the boats on to the roofrack of the family Volvo. It had been a companionable way to spend the past two days, I thought, as I waved them off back to Oban. And so far at least, I had even stayed the right way up.

The receptionist of Fort William McBackpackers was a New Zealander with a pierced tongue. She turned down the grunge music long enough to smile briefly and take my £10. 'You're in the Mr Men room,' she said, resuming her bored expression. 'Mr Nonsense.'

I found my bunk bed, labelled in primary colours with the appropriate children's character. I was above Mr Small, whose trainers reeked, but I was too tired to care. I made myself some supper from leftovers in the communal kitchen, and turned in for the night, noting absently in my progress from shower to bed that my underpants were peppered with dead midges.

20

The Yellow Submarine

Below Loch Linnhe

'GO DIVE!' read the advert. 'Experience Intense Adventure! Learn to Scuba Dive Today! (Warning: May lead to high levels of excitement and adventure. Not intended for those who still rely on their floaties, or channel-surfing couch commanders).'

The phone number at the bottom was a local one. Having completed my kayak trip in two days rather than three, I could afford to wait an extra day before tackling the Caledonian Canal. After travelling so far upon the surface of the water, it was about time I ventured under it. I made a phone call and wandered down towards the sea, marvelling once again at the way in which the city fathers had imaginatively cut off the most attractive feature with four lanes of traffic.

Don McGregor, the managing director of the Underwater Centre, agreed that Fort William wasn't the most obvious place for a world-class diving facility. 'Trouble is, if you take someone and train them in Portugal or Barbados, does that really prepare them to dive in a north of Scotland environment?' asked the affable Geordie, whom I recognised as the same man who had goaded me from his inflatable. Today he sported a smart suit and a heavy cold. 'Whereas if you can learn to dive in Scotland, you can dive anywhere.'

This wasn't a holiday dive course. Don trained rig divers, MOD divers, divers from all over the world. 'We'll fail people if necessary,' he said, leading me down the pier. 'We'll take their ten grand and fail them if they're not up to it. We can't afford to let shite out there.'

The men on the pier pushed past in body-hugging wet suits, peeling off sodden rubber helmets to reveal raw faces and shaven heads. There was an animal vitality about them. 'These guys are insane,' said Don proudly, looking a little out of place in his suit. 'If you go to 100 metres on Heliox, you've got to take three or four days to decompress, otherwise you'll get the bends.' Next to the decompression chamber was a small medical centre with an operating table for the times when things went wrong. 'What sort of operation?' I wondered, nervously. 'Intubation,' said Don. 'Drilling a hole through the chest bone to get air directly into the lung.'

I decided to put off the diving and try out the centre's submarine. Outside, a crane was lowering the *Morzh* into the water. She was a bright yellow contraption with red and white hatch covers, giving her the cartoonish look of the original Yellow Submarine – though with three-person capacity, this one would have struggled to accommodate all the Beatles. Don passed me a strange outfit to change into. 'You wear it over your clothes to stay warm and protect you from the silicon grease.' The furry all-in-one reminded me of the kind of gorilla costume you might find in a downmarket fancy dress shop. Someone came into the Portakabin as I was struggling with the zip. I half expected it to be a nun or a rooster.

'Alexander,' said a blond-haired man in heavily accented English, thrusting out his hand. 'You go in my submarine, no? I am her pilot.' His bosses at a Russian nautical institute had given him the *Morzh* in lieu of several years' pay. 'We bought it off him,' cut in Don. 'Then brought Alexander over to operate it.'

Climbing down through the conning tower in my gorilla outfit, I was unnerved to find that the first crew member was here on a work placement. 'I saw this advert – submarine pilot – and thought I'd give it a try,' said Michael, an Aberdonian, as I folded myself into the cramped passenger seat. Another socked foot felt its way past me on to the driving seat. It belonged to a Ukrainian assistant pilot called Yevgeny. Alexander had decided to direct operations from the surface, which didn't sound to me like a vote of confidence.

'Pliss?' said Yevgeny, gesturing that I should put my head down while he bolted the lid on the dustbin-sized conning tower. I put my furry feet against the curved metal before me, and looked through the small round windows at shin level, feeling the first stir-rings of claustrophobia. Nothing but silt and a vague outline of the pier leg ahead of us.

Yevgeny flipped a few switches. A small wall-mounted fan began to whirr. There was a hiss of increasing air pressure and my ears popped. A radio crackled into life in Russian as Alexander gave directions from the pier above. The flat screen booting up on the bulkhead above was at least familiar: a Windows 98 desktop. It promptly flickered into a psychedelic sonar screen of morphing inkblots. 'That's the pier,' said Michael from behind, pointing to a solid brown blob. 'Yevgeny flies on his compass and sonar. Visibility is about 10 metres, sometimes worse. Depends on tides, and what the river brings down with it.'

I looked up through the tiny window in the lid of the conning tower, watched the luminous figures on the pier shudder and fade as we dropped beneath the water. There was a crunch as Yevgeny ran into the leg of the pier, and a couple of crushed mussels dropped out of view past the window. A bark of Russian radio abuse suggested Alexander was not very impressed. 'We just moved the sonar today,' explained Michael, noticing my white knuckles. 'It looks like it's not picking things up properly.'

Before I had time to panic, a dazzling light shone through the window at us. 'Smile for the camera!' said Michael. A yellow ROV, or Remotely Operated Vehicle, about the size of a large Flymo, hovered outside for a moment like an alien probe, presumably part of someone's training. Then we were tilting, turning, falling away from the pier. The windows showed only a faintly luminous green. Starfish came briefly into view on the sea floor as we whirred down a gentle slope. Then, at 10 metres depth, something loomed large in the silted twilight. Yevgeny jerked the joystick backwards, allowing us to hang before the long, barnacle-encrusted object, on which violet peacock worms waved campily like a crop of cocktail umbrellas. What was it? A sunken log? A shipwreck? 'It's a Centurion tank,' he said, as if such things were found routinely on the floors of Scottish lochs. 'Now we go deeper to see a little *Titanic*.'

While the tank had been dropped into the loch expressly for the enjoyment of scuba divers, the 'little *Titanic*' turned out to be a real sunken fishing boat, the *Nanque*, now colonised by sea life. We glided over dark holes in her rusting fabric, catching the convulsions of jellyfish against the glass, and momentary glimpses of faster fish fleeing our headlights. It was more like science fiction than seafaring — a trip to another planet, complete with alien lifeforms and constellations of starfish. The crackling Russian voice, the bamboozling numbers on gauges, slow-motion landings on grey wasteland . . . I could have been hovering above the surface of the moon.

We touched down again, struck something more solid than mud, and Yevgeny jerked us back and forth in irritation, throwing up silt like snow in the window like a boy racer spinning his wheels. 'We go back now,' he said sullenly. The water began to lighten from bottle green to lilac, and there was another thud as we came up under the pier again. Yevgeny hung his head as a stream

of invective broke from the radio. It had not been his best driving
lesson. Eventually, the sky rippled into view through the conning
tower lid, and with a sucking hiss, we were free.

I must have had a slightly haunted expression as I climbed the
ladder, because the pier manager asked with a smirk if I still
wanted to do the introductory dive. I didn't have the balls to back
out now. He beckoned me into a Portakabin with TV monitors
showing eerie underwater arc lights and ghostlike figures moving
about below us.

It wasn't the kind of scuba diving I'd had in mind. Instead of
drifting over stippled reefs of technicolour sea life, these men were
used to perching on the submerged legs of oil rigs. Outside, a row
of brightly coloured umbilical cables snaked over the railings and
down into the murky water. 'Air, pneumohose, audiovisual, hot
water,' counted off the instructor. I wedged myself into a wet suit so
constricting that my arms stuck out like a scarecrow's. Over that I
wore a second rubber suit with what looked like a kitchen tap fitted
on the hip, along with a heavy oxygen cylinder and a pair of wellies.

After a quick pep talk and basic instruction came the astonishing weight of the helmet. It felt as if it was made from solid brass,
like an old-fashioned outfit from a Jules Verne novel. Someone
showed me how to twiddle a nostril-blocking implement from outside the glass to prevent my eardrums bursting. Only idiot male
bravado prevented me shouting that I'd changed my mind as the
neck brace clipped the helmet in place and all sound was muffled
except for my own panicked breathing.

Descending the iron steps required huge concentration, and the
attendant kindly put down her *Daily Mirror* and came out of her
shelter to pay out the fat liquorice coil of my life support cables.
My helmet was full of the eerie sound of Darth Vader breathing.
A radio crackled into life in my ear. 'Can you confirm you're okay?

Over?' said a voice. I put up a thumb in the way I had been taught. Then, rather wonderfully, I turned on the tap at my hip and felt a guilty thrill of hot water gushing between my inner and outer layers, down into my boots. It was like wetting yourself, but without the neurosis. Equally wonderful was the way in which the enormous weight of my helmet simply disappeared underwater. 'Okay, Nick, descend the ladder and wait at the bottom for instructions.' I climbed ponderously downwards, able to see only the rungs in front of my mask, trying to keep my balance. I could see hot water spilling from my sleeves and gloves, in little blurred eddies. Only my hands registered just how chilly the loch actually was. The last few metres of ladder to the loch floor felt like a descent from a moon lander.

I was standing among dozens of starfish. 'Just make your way over to the other divers at the welding bench,' said the voice in my ear. 'You should be able to see the arc lights.'

I looked into the murk around me. I could see no further than a few metres, and there were only the vaguest suggestions of tonal shadows. I walked a couple of slow-motion steps.

'Hot,' said a voice.

Were they guiding me? I took a few more steps.

'Cold,' said the voice. I stopped.

'Sorry to bother you again, control, but I can't find any divers and I'm not sure I'm understanding ...'

There was a slow expelling of breath in my ear. Hot and cold, it turned out, was simply the welders' way of instructing operators on the surface to turn electricity on or off.

'Ah. Thank you. I'm afraid I may now have wandered in the wrong direction.'

'What can you see?' said a voice.

'Um, not a lot just now.'

It was true. More significantly, I couldn't see the ladder either. I suddenly felt extremely tired, and only marginally interested in the fact that I was lost on the bottom of a loch. Everything was heavy and slow. My mask was beginning to steam up. It was a bit like being depressed.

'Just go a little further and you'll start to see the glow of the welding irons,' said the voice, patiently. I stumbled sideways slightly and found myself kneeling. Someone above pulled me back to my feet with a tug on my umbilical cord.

I never did find the welding bench. I was fiddling with the tap, trying to reduce the now uncomfortable heat around my groin, when one of the divers tapped me on the shoulder like a friendly police constable and escorted me back to the foot of the steps. It was all I could do to get one foot above the other under the returning gravity of my helmet, before hands reached down and grabbed me and I was escorted to the pier surface for de-kitting.

Looking over the edge to where the welders' cables were still dangling into the water, I realised I had got lost in an area of approximately five square metres. Yet I was so exhausted I had to ask a man to help me pull my wet suit off, which is easy to misconstrue in the shower. I hurried away, defeated. I had hoped to feel at home in the water, to sense its essential kinship – I was, after all, 80 per cent H_2O myself. But never had it seemed such alien territory, so hostile to human endeavour.

From now on, floating on top would suit me fine.

21

The Great Glen

Fort William to Laggan

I vacated my Mr Nonsense bunk well before eight the next morning, and wandered along the canal bank to the first lock. With my newcomer's grasp of nautical hitchhiking, I had discovered locks were the optimum lift-blagging spot. Any boat took at least ten minutes to negotiate both sets of gates, and that was a long time for anyone to ignore a plaintive looking backpacker standing on the quay. Today it was more urgent than usual, as I needed to rendezvous with Ali the following day. But I was also particularly optimistic, as I was standing at the bottom of Neptune's Staircase – a 500-yard flight of eight successive locks lifting boats 64 feet over the course of an hour and a half. Surely that was long enough to woo even the stoniest-hearted skipper?

In the event it took about thirty seconds. First in the queue for the swing bridge was *Eala Bhan*, a lovely old converted herring drifter taking tourists up the canal to Inverness. The curly-haired skipper peered out of the cabin window at me from behind his oblong sunglasses as I offered my line-handling serv-

ices in return for a day's passage. 'Aye, why not,' he grinned.
'Hop aboard.' We gunned towards the lock in a fug of diesel,
joining two yachts and a fishing boat of bare-chested fishermen
in wraparound shades. I tossed my first line up to a lock keeper,
who looped it over a hook and dropped the end back to me.
The skipper grinned and nodded. It felt good to be crewing
again.

It was a staggeringly beautiful day. From the top lock we could
see down Loch Linnhe, with Fort William tactfully obscured
behind trees and hillsides, while the peak of Ben Nevis was for the
first time unveiled. The canal was just as impressive. It was
Thomas Telford who had first connected the string of natural
lochs, creating a short cut between the Atlantic and the North Sea.
Unfortunately, short cuts are never as short as you think. By the
time it opened in 1822 it had taken nearly twenty years of con-
struction, which meant vessels were increasingly too big for it, and
the advent of steam made it possible to navigate the treacherous
northwest coast more safely. These days it was better known as a
leisure route, unique among canals in the UK in that it ran down
a valley and was therefore flanked by plunging slopes, guaranteeing
breathtaking scenery.

We reached the end of the canal section and emerged into
Loch Lochy (a name seemingly invented by committee at the end
of an uninspiring Friday afternoon) where the water was magnificently turbulent, raked by a wind that swept down the valley
towards us. Two yachts bobbed around, their masts flicking back
and forth like volume indicators. Wooded hillsides rose steeply
from the loch.

The whole valley was a diagonal tear across the geological map
of Scotland, formed when the north-western and south-eastern
sides slid more than 60 miles towards each other along a faultline

later smoothed by glaciers. The ice retreated around 8000 BC, eventually leaving the string of lochs – Lochy, Oich, Ness and Dochfour – which Telford was to link with canals.

'That's the Gaelic side – what I like to call the civilised side,' grinned Iain pointing to the north-west. He was originally from Lewis, the son of a shipwright, now working as a management consultant. He had found the *Eala Bahn* (Gaelic for white swan) mouldering in Stornoway harbour, and promptly bought her. 'My friends thought I was nuts. She was in a bit of a state, but the hull was pretty good. You learn to look at the lines of a boat rather than the superstructure, and underwater she was nearly wine-glass shaped. I fell in love with her there and then.'

Built in the early sixties, the herring drifter had previously plied the Western Isles for more than thirty years before Iain restored her and fitted her out as a tourist boat. It had taken ten years of Zen-like discipline to craft each fitting from scratch. The main mast was a single sitka spruce, obtained from a friendly forester, seasoned every day for a year with a mixture of paraffin and linseed oil.

Iain reminded me of others I had met on my trip, driven, meticulous, and single-minded in their grand love of a boat: Don on *Zeepaard*, Nick on *Vic32*, John on *Jean de la Lune*, and now Iain on *Eala Bahn*. It seemed to be a guy thing. What better way to satisfy those contradictory urges for the comforts of home and the freedom of a stretched horizon? And to keep the restless mind busy with the next challenge on a list. *You have to keep moving to recharge your batteries.*

'It's been a labour of love,' Iain was saying, as I shouldered my bag ready to jump ship. 'Ten years is a long time. But now I've got my eye on an old paddle steamer.'

Hopping ashore at Laggan Lock, I waved him off towards Loch

Oich brimming with renewed nautical ambition. Until now I'd been reliant on others' expertise. Tomorrow, however, Ali and I would navigate towards Scotland's darkest waters on a boat of our own.

22

Monsters and Gods

On Loch Ness

Father Gregory Brusey was strolling companionably through the loch-side gardens of Fort Augustus Abbey, deep in conversation with a friend, when they were rudely interrupted by the world's most famous monster.

'We saw quite distinctly the neck of the beast standing out of the water to . . . a height of about 10 feet,' said the startled monk in 1971. 'It swam towards us and after about twenty seconds slowly disappeared, the neck immersing at a slight angle. We were at a distance of about 300 yards . . .'

Steering our little fibreglass cabin cruiser out of the bottom lock, past the empty abbey and towards that same spot more than thirty years later, it struck me that belief was a strange and unpredictable thing. Father Gregory was dead now, his Benedictine brothers and pupils were gone, but the monster he thought he saw was still attracting huge congregations of tourists.

After the idyllic lochs and stretches of canal, the wide, bruised wastes of Loch Ness held a sort of primal dread. The steep, enclosing hillsides were hunched against a dour horizon, the forests gashed with rockslides or scabrous with scree. Ali and I had spent a rich if emotionally turbulent few days getting reacquainted aboard our hire boat on the northward dawdle through Loch Oich, stopping to chat to ancestor-hunting Americans and men with bison-like physiques tossing cabers at Invergarry Highland Games. The *Dunstaffnage Castle* had become as cosy as a campervan, with its folding furniture and beige leatherette décor and familiar looking steering wheel. Now it felt as substantial as a foil pie dish. A wind whipped at us from behind, heaping waves against the stern, and sucked us off course whenever I took my hand off the wheel. I looked into the water and shivered. It was black with peat, utterly opaque and deep enough to submerge the Eiffel Tower. Nowhere in Britain was there so much fresh water enclosed in the same place – and so much room to hide a monster.

Apart from Father Gregory's sighting, the epicentre for activity seemed to be at the northern end of the 23-mile loch. In fact the very first sighting had allegedly been in the River Ness, in around AD 565, when none other than St Columba had reportedly confronted a great beast and sent it packing. Since then more than a thousand sightings had been logged, most of them in or around Urquhart Bay, whose ruined castle provided appropriately gothic scenery.

We reached the shelter of its little harbour in three hours, and found it full of plastic boats identical to ours – all due back in Inverness the following day. Our fellow holiday-makers were busy making themselves at home on the crowded quay; a couple were fishing, while four passengers were dragging a picnic table to the back of their boat, observing a nautical version of the British tradition that one should never bother traipsing to the countryside when there's a perfectly good lay-by available. There was even a pay and display meter on the dockside. I backed into one of the remaining spaces while Ali looped the mooring lines around the cleats and fed the meter. The boat next to us was a red motor launch with *Nessie Hunter* emblazoned on the side; the white one next to that bore a logo of a microscope and the words 'Loch Ness Project'. We plumped for the more scientific sounding option and phoned the number.

Adrian Shine had a long white beard and unruly hair which contrasted oddly with his smart suit. He had first arrived here as an amateur naturalist at about the same time as Father Gregory's sighting, and was still trying to get to the bottom of the mystery thirty years later, as director of a research institute known as the Loch Ness Project. He reminded me of the druid Getafix in the *Asterix* books.

'You'd better see our exhibition first,' he said, when he pulled up in his purple van to collect us. 'Save you asking a lot of pointless questions when we go out on the loch.'

Drumnadrochit, less than a mile up the road, was a kind of tartan Jurassic Park. We overtook a large fibreglass plesiosaur standing on the roadside, drove past a string of giftshops and something called the Nessie Experience, and pulled up in front of an old hotel that Shine had transformed into an exhibition called Loch Ness 2000.

He ushered us into the ticket hall and through a curtain. 'I'll see you at the end.'

We followed the crowd through a succession of rooms and video or slide presentations, all bearing Shine's resonant commentary. 'Should we always believe what we see? Have the scientists overlooked something? Today we must be naturalist and detective, judge and jury . . .' I was hooked. There was archive footage of the manageress of the very hotel in which we stood, recounting her sighting in 1933 on the way to Inverness. ('I yelled to my husband, "Stop! The Beast!" It rose out of the water with water rolling off it.') There were more than a thousand other eyewitness sightings over the years, and tantalising shots taken by visiting scientists: a grainy gargoyle-like face; something that could have been a flipper. In 1981 Shine's own team was surprised to discover a hitherto undetected fish population of Arctic charr living at a depth of more than 700 feet, which only increased the curiosity about what else was down there. In 1987, he borrowed a whole fleet of cabin cruisers like ours, fitted them with sonar equipment and set them to work for a week, combing the loch for unexplained contacts in a media-saturated experiment known as Operation Deepscan. Among a handful of interesting results, one echo seemed to show a 'large and moving' object 200 feet down, which had yet to be explained.

But at the same time other investigations had exposed many sightings as tricks of the eye or mind. Film footage demonstrated, for instance, how on the mile-wide loch, boat wakes from long-passed craft could look like the moving humps of a sea serpent, while swimming deer or water birds could easily be mistaken for the neck and head of a monster. Another thesis was that the classic sea beast first encountered by St Columba in the River Ness was a wandering sturgeon, an ugly fish which grew up to 3 metres long. Even the quintessential Nessie photograph, taken in 1934 by a Harley Street consultant, had been discovered to be an elaborate hoax involving a remote-controlled submarine.

We emerged into a giftshop feeling a little confused. Shine appeared from among racks of stuffed Nessie soft toys, hats, confectionery, whisky, T-shirts and key rings. 'As you can see, we've got an extensive range of everything you might want to give to someone else,' he said with an ambiguous smile. 'What we're trading off is the undoubted reputation of Loch Ness – but if at the same time we can make our investigations, so much the better.'

Recently Shine and his team had been getting interesting data on other fronts. Due to the heavy and undisturbed silting, core samples taken from the loch bed were proving an invaluable historical record – even the radiation from the Chernobyl disaster in 1986 was recorded there. The previous year he had located the wreck of John Cobb's *Crusader*, which had disintegrated during his fatal attempt on the world water-speed record in 1952. But I got the impression he was basically diversifying to keep himself in a job, like a vicar who loses his faith but can't quite imagine leaving his parish.

'There are still anomalies we can't explain,' he reminded me, as we got back into the van, along with other day-trippers. 'But that doesn't mean we won't explain them. Some of the deepscan sonar results have turned out to be fixed objects, pieces of debris – a submerged buoy, for example. And the sightings continue. But the human eye, associated with the human brain, will often produce an image which is much more satisfactory than that produced by a camera.'

We drove down to the harbour and boarded the observation boat. A skipper in plaid trousers manoeuvred us on to the loch. I was beginning to feel a little cheated, which surprised me. It seemed that I wanted there to be a Loch Ness Monster, or at least didn't want there *not* to be one. The skipper switched on the sonar to show the bottom of the loch, and we watched without hope as the fuzzy coloured lines scrolled past blankly.

'So in thirty years, you've never actually seen a monster yourself?' I asked, sitting back down beside Shine. He must have caught the disappointment in my voice, because he didn't give a direct answer. 'My first expedition was to Loch Morar, where there was a tradition of a creature the locals called Morag. On my first visit there I was rowing along the shore in a flat calm when this black hump came out from behind the promontory, moving steadily out towards the centre of the loch. It stopped, and I stopped and began to back on the oars to move back towards this object and take a photograph. As I got nearer to it, it didn't look like a hump any more, it looked like a huge head.' Several of the other day-trippers were listening intently.

'I closed ever more gingerly on it . . . and it was a rock. It was an optical illusion – the reason it was moving was because I was moving.' He paused, and I got a sense of how angry this man of science must have been with himself for allowing his excitement to get in the way of his cool reasoning.

'It taught me two things. That what you see and remember may not be what is there. And that if you see something unusual, you should pursue and follow it to the end. Which is what I'm doing here.'

It had become something of an obsession. 'At the beginning I thought it was something that could be sorted out in a couple of years. But it grew on me really. First it was twenty years, then thirty years.' I wondered at what stage in that period his emphasis had changed from being a study of an elusive monster to a study of the human mind. In recent years his team had taken to testing per-ception using sticks and boat wakes. They found that people saw mainly what they wanted to see.

'There are still some controversial sonar results in Loch Ness,' admitted Shine as we disembarked from the pier. 'There are three where we still don't know what they are. But the longer you're here the more things you understand, so the fewer monsters you see. Because of course, in the end, "monster" is just a name for some-thing you don't understand.'

A little like 'God', I reflected, as we motored away from the har-bour later that afternoon. Perhaps men of the cloth understood

Nessie better than scientists. After all, if there was one thing more elusive than conclusive proof that He existed, it was conclusive proof that He didn't.

Father Gregory knew this well. 'We ought to leave the monster alone,' he told the *New York Times*, after his sighting had made him famous. 'In this technological age, we've placed a label on everything. I am a champion of the unknown. Mystery intrigues people, and so it should remain.'

23

Death and Destruction

Inverness and Culloden

Culloden Moor seemed not so much a place as a penance. It had awaited me like an appointment for root canal surgery ever since I arrived in Scotland. Like many Englishmen (not to mention quite a few Scots), my supposedly rounded education had left me entirely ignorant of the sins for which my country was responsible: a quick and bloody massacre, followed by a sustained campaign of ethnic cleansing which sped the collapse of the entire clan system. It was time to make amends.

Squatting on the outskirts of Inverness, the place was largely unchanged since the battle, save for a tourist walkway, a few flag-poles and a road which had been built across the outer limits. It had also acquired a Visitor Centre, and a sign asking visitors not to pick the heather. The life-sized mannequins in the entrance hall set the tone for the orgy of feel-bad which was to follow. In the red corner for the bestial Brits, Butcher Cumberland, a slob of a man squeezed into his redcoat uniform and with a face like a roasted pig. In the blue corner for the romantic Jacobites, the well-proportioned figure of Bonnie Prince Charlie.

We shuffled bleakly into a room where lots of little painted soldiers and clansmen were squaring up to each other in a large glass cabinet. From a video presentation next door came the sound of forlorn bagpipes and blood-curdling screams. 'Are you sure you want to do this today?' said Ali. We had dropped off the hire boat in the rain that morning feeling a little blue already. She bailed out to read a book in the coffee shop while I wandered out on to the battlefield.

It could easily have been different. The exiled Charles Edward Stewart had fared rather better than expected, having landed in Moidart after a disastrous crossing from France in 1745 with a paltry seven men. Within weeks the Young Pretender had raised a Highland army fierce enough to put even Londoners in a panic, making no secret of his determination to seize both the English and Scottish thrones for the Stewart dynasty. They had marched as far south as Derby before retreating tactically northwards again, winning a decisive victory en route at Falkirk. By the time Charles reached Culloden, however, things were going distinctly pear-shaped. Through a series of colossal misjudgements, his hungry, sleep-deprived men faced the redcoat enemy on sodden terrain in foul weather with defective artillery.

Even a greenhorn like me could see it was a terrible site for a battle. I followed the path through its maze of boggy tussocks, and joined a huddle of tourists on the far side of the moor. A guide in Highland dress was pointing out the positioning of the Campbell clan – one of a significant number who had fought *against* their fellow countrymen on the side of the British throne. The Campbells in particular had never been forgiven for this treachery, having also wiped out the Jacobite MacDonalds of Glencoe in another infamous massacre a few decades earlier. 'We hate the Campbells,' said Michael the Highlander as I arrived.

'Worse than the English?' I asked, a little too hopefully.

'About the same,' he said, gripping his sword theatrically, to a ripple of nervous laughter. 'There's not much to distinguish a Campbell from an Englishman.' His straight face made it difficult to tell if he was speaking in character or from personal grudge.

It didn't really make much difference. For an Englishman Culloden was like original sin. A terrible decision made by your forefathers, like Adam and Eve eating the forbidden apple, for which you must repeatedly beg forgiveness, even though in your heart you knew it had nothing to do with you. All paths led back there in the end.

Michael the Highlander was grimly explaining how the British army had deliberately used lead bullets which spread on impact and caused maximum internal damage. The loss of the battle itself, he admitted, was mainly due to a succession of bad decisions by the French prince and his deputies. In particular his incompetent quartermaster, William O' Sullivan, made Homer Simpson look like Einstein. He was the one who chose the battle site, meaning that any advance had to be made uphill against Cumberland's mortars, in the teeth of a biting northeasterly wind. And as if to skew the odds even further, he failed to provide rations for the troops, and brought the wrong sized cannon balls. On 16 April 1746, with only six thousand hungry and exhausted men against Cumberland's well-fed nine thousand, and disastrous communication breakdowns in the field, the Jacobites were set up for defeat. 'More men died in the line waiting for the order to attack than died in actual hand to hand combat,' said Michael, gloomily. Within an hour, 1200 Jacobites lay dead, while their leader fled.

Cumberland, however, did not know when to stop. He earned his nickname as the butcher by ordering his men to give 'no quarter' to their opponents even when the battle was over, leading to the subsequent massacre of not only wounded soldiers but hundreds of innocent men, women and children in the surrounding area. The aim was to crush the clan system altogether: chiefs could no longer legally call on their tacksmen as soldiers, Highland dress was banned, and even bagpipes were classed as 'engines of war'.

The trouble with Culloden was that, while its stark theatrical colours stood out well from a distance, you only had to get a little closer to see the various tensions that cross-threaded it: Catholic vs Protestant monarchy, Lowlanders against Highlanders, individualists vs communitarians. So why did history always seem to boil down to the same stark 'England vs Scotland' fixture?

I cornered Michael at the end of the tour. 'The clan system would have disappeared eventually,' he admitted, once the crowd had dispersed. 'But it wouldn't have been so sudden without Culloden. When the clan chiefs lost their power they found it easier to kick people off their land. And if all the clans knew what was going to happen after Culloden they would all have been here on the day. The prince would have had a huge army.'

He kept his conversation polite but clipped. I got the impression that people like me still represented the problem to Michael. But surely, 250 years after this bloody mess, we could put it behind us? Now that Scotland had a Parliament, wasn't there a possibility that auld enemies could get on a little better again?

'I'm a Scottish patriot,' said Michael, unmoved. 'I think the whole reason the Parliament was built was to calm down the divisions.' Whereas he hoped to emphasise them. 'If we got a Conservative government again in London it would completely split the country,' he said, his voice conspiratorial and low. 'Think about it. A Labour administration in Scotland and a Tory government. It would be unworkable! People would vote for full independence.'

There was no disguising the yearning. Michael wasn't happy

with this semi-detached living arrangement. He wanted the full divorce.

Back in Inverness, I waved Ali off on the train home and sought a bed for the night. It was an attractive city of tree-lined roads and elegant Victorian buildings, and my hostel overlooked the River Ness, where surf canoeists played in the fast-flowing shallows of the city centre. The streets were packed with tourists in search of their heritage, and the locals were serving up the usual refried tartan. There were kilt shops, bagpipe makers, clan ancestry centres, even a place called Highland World which boasted a Gaelic-speaking 'animatronic head'.

I wanted to keep heading north towards Orkney and Shetland, but as ever there was more than one way to do it. Whether I hitched straight there or tagged east along the Moray coast in search of northbound fishing boats would depend on what I found at the harbour. More immediately I wanted somewhere peaceful to stop and think for a few days, gather my thoughts.

I went to get my hair cut. It is one of the unsung miracles of the world that wherever you are there's always someone willing to massage your head and talk about your holidays for less than a tenner. I closed my eyes and let a sixteen-year-old with a pierced belly-button spray me with warm water.

'New in Inverness?' said Mel, the somewhat older proprietress, wrapping a black bib round me.

'Just passing through. Nice place to live, though, I'll bet.'

She blew out through her teeth, and snipped away a stray hair. 'Och, Inverness is jest weird. It's like this modern city trying to take off, but the whole place is run by a lot of churchy old biddies. We had a concert in the park last night – a great wee celebration, you'd imagine – except that the biddies are already complaining about the noise, even though it finished at nine! Then it's two extremes: biddies at one end, and New Age nutters at the other. You can spot Findhorn folk a mile off. They're usually tie-dyed in some way.'

The Findhorn Foundation was a regular in the newspapers, variously described as a commune full of free-range hippies or a forward thinking pioneer of ecological house building, depending on whether you worked the tabloids or broadsheets. It had first hit the headlines back in the sixties after successfully growing enormous 40 lb cabbages in the unpromising sandy soil – allegedly by asking advice from the 'plant spirits'. These days its residents were more famous for building recycled homes out of hay bales and whisky barrels.

'Nice enough people, but not quite of this planet,' said Mel. 'You should drop in there on your travels. It's right on the Moray coast.'

24

The Stricken Vessel

Adrift in the Moray Firth

I caught my first glimpse of Findhorn's forested shores from the deck of a yacht called *Water Vole*. It was a homely wee craft with a shopping bike wedged in the cockpit, and a couple of pinecones hung from fishing line knotted on the shrouds. 'Our weather station,' explained Julie, a feisty nurse who had left Hull to sail round Britain with her husband Dave.

The weather wasn't at its most predictable, even with the help of a pinecone. We had motored out of Inverness, under the towering Kessock Bridge and into the Moray Firth, waiting for a southeasterly that never came.

'The shipping forecast was wrong,' observed Dave, a genial fifty-something with a bushy mariner's beard. It was an almost cloudless day, and we sat in the hot white light of the cockpit, watching the coast recede as the estuary broadened. A cormorant stood like a gothic cross on a large red buoy, its black wings held outstretched in the sun, and a school of dolphins surfaced not far away, their grey backs squeaky wet in the sun. The seaside town of Nairn was a hazy line of distant houses, giving way to a dark green line of pine forests underscored by golden sand. And somewhere among the trees was an alternative society.

Unfortunately, we seemed to be sailing past it.

'Findhorn's got a tidal harbour and we've got a five foot draught,' explained Dave apologetically. 'I don't fancy it, I'm afraid.' He was a careful sailor, not effortlessly confident, and had been studying the pilot book for an overnight berth. The next non-tidal harbour was Buckie — a 24-hour access port several hours further on.

My heart sank. This was where boat-hitching differed markedly from road-hitching: you couldn't just pull over whenever you wanted. Jumping off relied on the next landfall, unless you fancied a swim. 'Well, at least we might get a bit of a sail once we're round this point,' said Dave shrugging. 'Let's get the jib up.'

I hadn't realised just how much I had set my heart on the hippy commune in the forest until I watched its golden sands slide astern. It sounded just the kind of open-minded place I needed to gather my thoughts, and it had never occurred to me that I wouldn't get there. I was still yearning fulsomely for it when, by odd coincidence, the engine coughed and died.

'That wasn't supposed to happen,' said Dave, frowning. 'Here, take the helm.' I took the tiller as he fiddled with the throttle, tried to start the engine again, once, twice, three times. But there was barely a cough. Dave's brow furrowed above his specs.

'Just bloody typical,' he muttered. 'Right by the bloody rocks!'

'Oh don't be so melodramatic,' said Julie.

But I could see his point. A few hundred metres astern, the sea was breaking into froth over a patch of submerged skerries. We were facing away from the shore, positioned to catch any wind in a broad reach. But the sea was as flat as oil and the jib hung limp as a rag.

'We'd better start praying for some wind,' he said quietly. I fixed my eye on a wisp of seaweed in the sea beside us. We were actually moving backwards in the water. The rocks were getting closer. Stripping down to his vest, he clambered down into the cabin to take the engine cover off.

'What's wrong with it?' said Julie, her voice tinged with panic.

For the next hour we lived in agonising slow motion. As Dave fiddled with the engine, occasional gusts of wind would push us out a little way, only to die again. Then we could only watch as we lost the ground we'd made up. The sun bounced inappropriately off the peaceful seascape and gulls windsurfed across the powder blue evening skies, completely oblivious to our peril.

At about 6 p.m., Dave's face appeared white and haggard in the doorway. 'I think it's time to call the coastguard.'

'Oh God,' said Julie. 'Tell me this isn't happening.'

Dave sat with his head in his hands for a moment, then picked up the radio handset. 'This is *Water Vole* calling coastguard, do you copy, over?' His voice was controlled, affable, the sort of voice one might use to call fellow CB radio hacks to tell them a passably funny anecdote. We waited. The radio crackled into life. '*Water Vole*, this is Aberdeen coastguard, over.'

'Sorry to disturb you on such a lovely afternoon, but we've got engine problems – it won't go. We're about half a mile from the skerries. Any advice? Over.'

The coastguard asked for our size (30 feet) and vessel type (Bermuda sloop), then went silent for a moment, before coming back on air.

'We'll put a call out to any vessels in the area who can assist. Failing that, we'll request the launch of a lifeboat.'

'Er, that sounds a bit heavy,' said Dave. 'We just need help to a local landing.'

But the call was already going out to all shipping in the area.

Within minutes two yachts responded: *Boracic* and *Stravaig* — faint
white triangles on the horizon. 'Proceeding to the scene,' crackled
a response. 'Will be with the stricken vessel within the hour.'

'*Stricken vessel*?' hissed Julie. 'Apparently we're a stricken vessel —
this is so embarrassing!'

I looked at her in bemusement. The wind was keeping us off
the rocks for the moment, but she seemed almost more worried
about being rescued than shipwrecked. 'You don't understand the
yachting world,' she said when I hinted at this. 'Being rescued is
absolutely the most shameful thing that can happen to you!'

'Guess we'd better tidy up a bit,' muttered Dave.

Stravaig got to us first — a gleaming white, broad-beamed yacht
with a motor that purred like a Jag. The driver brought her non-
chalantly alongside, a tanned, handsome man in aviator sunglasses
who waved and passed a line to Julie on the bow like a calm uncle
assisting a small child.

'Thanks very much,' I offered, weakly, in the absence of anyone
else saying it. He nodded, and continued watching Julie, who was
struggling to tie the line after getting entangled in the radar reflec-
tor. *Boracic* arrived soon after, and circled impatiently.

'They're *loving* it,' muttered Dave, ducking as Julie severed the
tangled string. 'Every minute of it. They'll be relating it over their
pints to their friends tonight.'

Eventually the tow-rope tautened and *Boracic* sped off, while
Stravaig dragged us back towards Lossiemouth — which, I was quietly delighted to notice, was a neighbouring port to Findhorn. As
we rolled home in the beautiful evening light, Dave sucked ruefully on a bottle of beer, and I mused on what I had learned about
the yachting world. I had always romanticised nautical types as a
kind of classless fraternity, but today I had stumbled on a water-
borne *Good Life*, as full of intricate social codes and one-upmanship

as any suburban cul-de-sac. Dave and Julie had left their old lives to get away from all that. Yet here they were, the Tom and Barbara Good of yachting, mortified at being rescued by Margot and Jerry.

25

Teapots and Fairies

The Findhorn Foundation

I stood in the sunshine and read the sign again. It was the sort of glass-fronted notice board that cornershop customers use to advertise second-hand pushchairs or office cleaning – except that this one was screwed to the outside of a health food emporium and offered 'Shamanic drum journeying' and bottles of Chinese herbal tonic. Most useful and intriguing was a postcard in the accommodation section:

Mo's House – £15 – B&B
(Look for the yellow teapot)

I memorised the scrawled map and set off down the path. The Findhorn Foundation Educational Trust was a little like a seventies holiday camp, a leafy network of quiet walkways running between prefabricated homes and caravans with names like *Aslan*, *Divine Will* and *Shirley's Temple*. There were a lot of wind chimes.

I stopped outside a well-tended place, with a little pond in the front garden where water dribbled over pebbles and foxgloves hummed with visiting bumblebees. Once evidently a simple box-like prefab, it had sprouted various extensions and outhouses. Most gratifying of all, it welcomed the visitor with a foot-high yellow teapot perched on a stone. I went up to the door and knocked. It was opened by a stern-looking woman with oblong spectacles and a Germanic accent.

'You must be Mo . . .?'

'No!' said the woman, outraged. 'I am Helga-Marina!'

'Oh. Sorry. I was wondering about the B&B . . . will Mo be back soon?'

'Mo is in Australia!' We stared at each other over this non-sequitur for a moment. Then Helga-Marina said: 'How long do you vant ze room?'

It was a very small bedroom with a bunk bed in the middle, but it had a little writing desk by a window, overlooking the tinkling pond. I took it. By the time I had washed and stowed my gear, there were three women sitting out on the picnic bench under the apple tree, sharing a vegan salad.

'You must meet your housemates,' instructed Helga-Marina, who was actually Belgian. 'Rita and Agnes.'

Rita, middle-aged and blonde-haired, flashed me a motherly smile. 'Agnes lives in the shed,' she said, in a northern English accent. 'Just in case you thought you were sharing a room.'

All three women hooted with laughter. Agnes, a lithe German twenty-something with a shaved head and saffron trousers, offered her hand. 'It's true! Come and look!' She ushered me over to the small garden shed and opened the door to reveal a sleeping bag.

'I have everything I need!' she said, happily. 'And you?'

'Pardon?'

'Why are you here?'

Rita and Helga-Marina looked at me enquiringly. 'A place to recharge the batteries,' I said, hesitantly. 'I'm writing a travel book, but I want to stop travelling for a few days.'

Helga-M frowned. 'You are going to write about us?'

'Maybe. Is that okay?'

Agnes looked delighted. 'Then I *must* tell you about my ascendant master called St Germain – he speaks to me and tells me the future!' I stared at her blankly. 'An ascendant master is someone who has attained perfection in past lives and no longer needs to be reincarnated,' she explained. 'Are you going to write that down?'

'Um, okay.' My head was beginning to swim. 'So that's – what? – Buddhist?'

'I don't know,' she shrugged. 'I don't really need to give it a name. This is the Aquarian age, where structures no longer matter. But I must go and practise my violin . . .'

She wafted off to her shed, from which the exquisite sound of concert-standard violin practice soon emanated. I made my excuses and got up, keen to look around the site. But Helga-Marina was not finished yet.

'Tell me, vat is your birth date?'

I gave her the information warily.

'Aries,' she nodded, as if confirming something to herself. 'And thirty-three is a *very* important age for a man: the age when Jesus was crucified!'

I laughed nervously and put on my day pack.

She smiled and wagged her finger. 'Yes, this is the age when you decide if you will be *resurrected* or not!'

I blinked at her for a moment, then made my escape.

The Findhorn Foundation had begun somewhat unpromisingly as three unemployed hotel managers living in a caravan. Peter and Eileen Caddy had settled among the sand dunes in 1962 with three children and a Canadian friend, Dorothy Maclean, and started growing vegetables to supplement their dole money.

Initially ridiculed by locals for expecting anything of value from such sandy soil, they were attracting attention within a few years for their remarkable crops of vegetables, herbs and flowers – most famously their enormous 40 lb cabbages – and their extraordinary explanations. Dorothy had discovered that she could commune with the plant spirits – or 'devas' – and was receiving direct instructions on how to get the best yield. The spinach deva, for example, suggested helpfully: *If you want strong natural growth of the leaf, the plants will have to be wider apart than they are at the moment.* Eileen, meanwhile, spent most nights meditating in the public toilets (the only private place), and her 'inner guidance' convinced the group that their caravan would one day expand into a world-renowned spiritual centre.

Sure enough, word spread and a mixed bag of New-Age experimenters, religious devotees, ecological pioneers and drifters joined the settlement. By the end of the 1970s it had been transformed into a 'university of light' offering courses in things like meditation, herbalism, healing and 'sacred dance'. There were unsubstantiated tabloid rumours of free love and underage sex, and the occasional naturist wandering out of the sand dunes. But these days the locals in nearby Findhorn village seemed to accept their neighbours as benign if eccentric.

It was a broad and surprisingly leafy campus, more California than Caledonia, set among sand dunes and pine trees. Hundreds of people were living in a mix of old caravans, prefabs, and eco-homes – made from bales of straw, or in a few cases from old whisky vats. A wind generator called Moya whispered overhead. People wandered around purposefully, very ordinary looking folk, with only the occasional tie-dyed shirt. In fact, the place was

increasingly attracting the attention of businesspeople with its radical ideas on sustainable living and workplace practices. I was keen
to find out why.

The Phoenix Shop sold organic food, herbal medicines, fairly
traded textiles and books. I browsed through titles like *Raising
Psychic Children*, *Crystal Healing For Animals* and sections on
numerology, fairies, ley lines, dream sharing, dousing, chakras,
wicca . . . It was like entering an existential supermarket without
a shopping list. After twenty minutes I settled on *The Kingdom
Within*, a sort of beginner's primer on Findhorn itself, and wandered back to Mo's House, where I sat out in the now-deserted
garden to read it.

> The new age will have two hallmarks: An open view of spiritual
> seeking which tolerates the use of ideas and practices from more
> than one tradition, rather than a closed system in which individu-
> als are tied to a single all-purpose philosophy. And an emphasis on
> experience as well as faith. Our view is that we are entering a time
> when spiritual insight is not just given to a few theologians, adepts,
> priests or shamans, but is available to all.

Conservative believers always shrank from the words 'New Age'
like vampires from garlic. They called it a slippery slope with no
handrails or signposting – a 'pick and mix' spirituality, danger-
ously unstructured. But what did fundamentalists offer by
comparison? The certainty from which to fly planes into sky-
scrapers? At least this open system seemed candid about its
shortcomings:

> Not everything that arises from such a grand mixing together of
> elements is going to be beautiful, functional, useful or healthy.

Some of it will be silly, frivolous or even toxic. But at the same time, there will emerge from this exploration new insights and combinations that will be holy, powerful and transformative.

There seemed a refreshing absence of *fear* in what I was reading. No demons, no original sin waiting to lure you into the bushes. Just lots of different paths, some wiser than others – and the assumption that you would learn from them all.

Was it humanly possible, I wondered, to keep an entirely open mind? Instead of steering vigilantly towards what I already knew, could I allow myself to push off in my coracle and simply see where I ended up? I decided that, for the duration of my time here, I would at least try.

I was sitting under the apple tree pondering all this when a nun looked tentatively round the hedge. 'Hello there,' she said, peering over a pair of stylish sunglasses. She had a shaved head and was dressed in long burgundy and saffron robes. 'Is Agnes around?' Her accent was unmistakeably Glaswegian.

'Fraid not – but I think she's due back soon.'

'Do you mind if I wait?'

I grinned and shook my head. 'No problem.' A perfect opportunity for open-mindedness. 'I hope you don't mind me asking, but are you a Buddhist nun?'

She laughed and wandered over to the picnic bench. 'I'm glad you recognised me. A guy I met last week thought I was a Partick Thistle supporter.' She put her hands together and nodded the Buddhist greeting. 'I'm Kelsang Machig.' Then she sat down gingerly opposite me.

It was Machig's first holiday at Findhorn since her ordination earlier that summer. Until then she had been known as Gabrielle McGuire, a learning support teacher at Glasgow Academy. 'I keep meeting people who knew me as Gabrielle, when I had big hair and make up and long dangly earrings. I've been coming here for years, so it's a bit of shock for them. And you should see people's faces when I walk around the supermarket in suburban Giffnock. It's a riot!'

Despite her lack of make-up, the buzz-cut silvery hair, and presumably her total abstinence from sex or alcohol, she seemed luminously peaceful. Her face radiated friendship.

'So how did you decide to become a nun – if you don't mind me asking?'

'How long have you got?'

Gabrielle had always had what she called a 'spiritual impulse'. While other children were obsessing over dolls, she was begging to go to mass – which she attended faithfully for thirty years, before getting a little more experimental. 'I've pretty much tried everything there is in the whole New Age thing: crystals, therapy – firewalking was my hobby for a while. But none of it's a patch on Buddhism. That's what got me though the break-up of my marriage.' She paused. 'It was basically a choice I made to have a compassionate view of things, and I realised that it was teaching me a lot about attachment. That in itself took away some of the pain.'

Instead, she had salvaged a friendship with her ex-husband, and won the lasting respect of her teenage sons. 'They think it's cool to have a Buddhist mum. My parents weren't quite as enthusiastic. My dad said: "You're going to cut all your hair off? I know exactly what you're up to – you're attention-seeking!" I told him I could think of easier ways.'

Her decision to get ordained had grown, somewhat improbably, from a romantic holiday in Venice. A week of candlelit dinners and gondolas had climaxed magnificently in a marriage proposal from a wealthy and handsome suitor – with the offer of a luxury Venetian apartment as her wedding present. Oddly, though, she found herself pining for a break she had taken earlier the same summer: alone this time, in complete silence for three days, in a hut in rural Dumfriesshire.

'What I had found on Buddhist retreat was total peace of mind. And when I compared the two types of happiness – a simple happiness that came from within, and a glitzy happiness that was dependent on circumstances – I realised I would choose the hut over the hotel. So I turned that dear man down and became a nun!'

She grinned mischievously, like one who has played an outrageous trick on the world and got away with it. 'I used to have a wardrobe crammed full of clothes – now I've got one outfit. I tell my friends that burgundy is the new black! Cutting off my hair gave me an amazing sense of freedom and liberation. I'm now realising how much I relied on my appearance . . .'

It occurred to me that I was being evangelised. Machig shook her head at the suggestion. 'You know, Nick, one of the most important teachings of the Buddha was: *Don't believe anything just because I'm saying it*,' she said. '*Go out there and find out for yourself if it works*.'

Outside a low-roofed wooden building in the trees, a row of shoes indicated that the afternoon group meditation was about to begin. I slipped off my own boots and went inside. In the centre of the room was a table with candles and a bowl of flowers, with chairs circling it. A couple of other people stayed cross-legged and serenely silent, their eyes closed. I sat down and waited.

Presently there came the sound of quick footsteps on the path outside, the ripping of Velcro sandal ties, and a woman appeared wearing a sun top and a beatific smile. She walked into the centre of the room, folded herself into the lotus position and introduced herself as Adriana.

'As we connect with the earth through our own breath, may we allow the light to shine through us,' she said. Then silence.

Keep an open mind.

I tried hard to think what Machig had told me about meditation – then remembered that thinking and trying hard were both exactly what I was trying to avoid. The idea was to *be*. I tried focusing on the breath coming out of my nostrils. In, out, in, out . . . a marvellously simple thing. No shopping list of angst-ridden requests to a God you only half believed was listening . . . But dammit, I was *thinking* again. No wonder the Buddhists called it *monkey mind*. I quietly ignored its gibbering, and focused on my nostrils again, feeling the coolness, the heat on the inhalation and exhalation . . .

After fifteen minutes of this, I felt oddly calm, almost submerged – like in the diving suit but with less sense of failure. The only real instructions we'd had were to imagine our inner light beaming across the world and granting us compassion to our fellow humans. No single deity had been invoked – which meant none was excluded. Adriana gently bonged a gong to signify the end of the meditation. I stretched and opened my eyes.

Down in the wooden community hall, supper was about to begin. Around a hundred people were holding hands in two concentric circles. I joined the outer one as a cook introduced the meal: an elaborate vegetarian extravaganza involving beans and cracked rice. We all stayed silent for a moment. Then a few people said 'thank you'.

Who were we thanking? The cooks? The earth? God? Buddha? I scooped up a plate of food and asked a bespectacled Irishman in an apron. 'All of them, I guess,' he said in a gentle brogue. 'Though I'm an atheist myself.'

Aidan was from Tipperary. He had arrived at Findhorn looking for information about homeopathic medicine before deciding, much to his own surprise, to make his home here. 'In the end I look at the results of the place,' he shrugged. 'Whether you call it God or energy or wood fairies, there's something inside that we tap into here. I don't know very many places in the world where there's so much love. The relationships are honest and direct – you know there's very little backstabbing.' He chewed pensively. 'Put it this way: it's the only place I've ever felt homesick for when I'm away.'

He got up to do his kitchen duty and I finished the meal in rich silence. I wandered out into the evening sunshine, where people were sitting round chatting, and a group of kids were jumping through a garden sprinkler. It was a scene of eye-watering tranquillity. Almost to my surprise, I felt myself opening up inside like parched soil.

I was woken next morning by a rising screech and a thundering that shook the very foundations of the house. 'Awful, isn't it,' said Rita, as I emerged bewildered from the shower. 'We're right next to an RAF air base – that was a Nimrod taking off.'

Savouring the irony of a utopian pacifist community sharing a fence with a military base, I wolfed down some cereal and toast and hurried off to find the famous community vegetable garden. I was intrigued to find out how a morning's work at Findhorn would differ from a morning's work anywhere else – and the gardening was where it had all begun. It was now a vast vegetable plot which somehow managed to avoid looking like an allotment by retaining magical looking thickets of wild trees and bushes.

We met outside a potting shed – a mixture of long-term residents and nervous looking visitors – and formed a circle. Circles were evidently a big Findhorn tradition.

'Let us all stand for a moment and be thankful for the sun on our faces,' said Mark, who was the garden 'focaliser', which was a way of avoiding the word *boss*. We all stood silently for a while, feeling the sun's warmth, and the wordless comfort of another human hand. Then someone said 'thank you' and we all joined in. Again, there was no reference to who exactly we were thanking. It didn't really seem to matter.

Still in a circle, we did some 'attunement' – another standard part of a Findhorn working day. 'Listen with your eyes closed and see which your heart calls you to,' said Mark, as various members of the gardening staff stepped forward to tell us about the jobs that needed doing that day. I sat on my scepticism and allowed my heart to pass over weeding the cucumbers, putting manure on the vegetable patch or watering the courgettes. I quite fancied weeding the lettuces so I went for that – though I was surprised to see all the other jobs willingly taken too. Someone apparently felt 'called' even to the manure.

Keep an open mind.

There was something rather special about kneeling in the companionship of strangers, not obliged to make false conversation. I saw no sign of 40 lb cabbages, but the organic lettuces were certainly squeaky and firm, and the weeds were easy to pull from the sandy soil. We had a break in the middle, when everybody smothered huge heels of bread with organic peanut butter and jam, and drank tea in the sunshine with dirty fingers. People talked a little, but mostly we were all just enjoying the feeling of benign human fellowship – a woman from Glasgow smoking Silkies with her eyes closed; a shy, shambolling hippy called Dave who had left his job to come here; and a family of Austrians who came back every summer. 'If you work in the garden you are allowed to take things for yourself,' whispered a Colombian woman, pulling up a carrot and handing it to me. It was the sweetest carrot I have ever tasted.

Four days passed in a blissful round of manual labour, healthy vegetarian cuisine and curious 'alternative therapies'. Aidan the atheistic Irishman invited me to his little caravan (*Dolphin*) for some 'energy work' which involved lying on his doctor's couch with a piece of dry pasta between my lips while he placed magnets on my chest for reasons I failed to grasp. He concluded that I should give up wheat and coffee, drink more water and chew my food. Helga-Marina, meanwhile, took it upon herself to try and cure my migraine.

'Most ailments can be cured by natural remedies, or by emotions,' she claimed, thumbing through a rainbow-coloured book. 'Here! Migraine! *Causes: A resistance or emotional blockage, an inability to sit in the flow of life; a sexual dysfunction.*'

'I see,' I said hesitantly. 'And what does it suggest I do?'

'Practise letting go in the flow of life,' she read, then flushed. 'And, it says, er . . . masturbation may help . . .' Rita laughed so hard she snorted tea through her nostrils. I scurried out, to the sound of uncontrolled cackling.

For all its battiness, there was something about the place I liked. It reminded me of the feeling I had at the campsite as a twelve-year-old. That unsolicited immanence of something like joy, felt on the skin, in the air. A sense of mystery and mischief – a little like being in love.

'When I first heard the talk about fairies, I too was condescendingly amused and very sceptical,' said Brian the potter. 'But as you'll see, they responded so conclusively I could no longer deny it.'

He ushered me into an armchair in the middle of his pottery, a barrel-like man, clad in pink shirt, voluminous dungarees and a snowy beard, like Father Christmas in mufti. He spoke in an educated BBC-announcer voice, observing me soberly through large square spectacles. Brian had come to Findhorn with a group of bohemian teachers in 1970, excited about living in an experimental community but a little unsure about the wackier fringes. He had caught his first glimpse of the little people when Dorothy Maclean had asked him to illustrate her book about 'plant devas'.

'As an artist I sat down not knowing where to put the dots,' he said, pulling a sheath of papers from a shelf. 'But I ended up with these.' He handed them to me carefully. They were black and white pointillist sketches: a marigold deva with wide eyes and petals for hair accompanied by a pointy-eared elf with pixie boots; a daffodil deva, rose deva, gorse deva, oak deva each dreamily intertwined with their own plant or with a retinue of fiddle-playing pixies.

'They're beautiful,' I said, carefully. They seemed to me to be well-executed but fairly conventional representations of fairies and sprites, the sort Brian might have seen in children's storybooks as he was growing up.

But they were only the beginning. In the weeks after sketching them he became abnormally aware of the perfume and colour of flowers, even of being greeted and caressed by invisible hands as he walked in the garden. It got stranger. Walking through Edinburgh's Botanic Gardens one day, he glimpsed Pan himself, replete with hooves, hair and horns — and the same afternoon he was greeted in a suburban dell by a group of elves. 'They seemed androgynous and very beautiful, wearing clothes very like those depicted in fairy stories, in colours of russet, gold and green,' he had carefully recorded in a written testimony of the event. 'They wore hats with high peaks and pointy shoes with curly toes.'

It was the phrase *like those depicted in fairy stories* which bothered me. Even with my credulity wedged open, I couldn't help thinking that the textbook conventionality of Brian's little people somewhat undermined his story. 'A sceptic might say that your imagination just borrowed them from what you already knew,' I ventured.

But Brian turned my thinking on its head. 'My theory is that these beings use our categories to present themselves to us. They're not *really* like tiny humans — they're beings in their own right outside human comprehension. So they inhabit vehicles we understand, which is why they take on the somewhat medieval appearance, wear medieval clothes — because that's the last time they were taken seriously.'

I nodded dumbly and took another sip of tea. 'It's basically a matter of becoming conscious of signals you're getting all the time. Our consciousnesses are attuned to a very narrow range of information. If you took in everything your eye is seeing you'd be overwhelmed. We tend to close off from things which have no survival meaning, or social meaning.' I thought back to the sonar submariner who sharpened his hearing even as his eye muscles atrophied. In the same way, perhaps most of us had lost our elf-sensing muscles.

This was presumably why nobody else noticed that when Brian boarded his bus back to Inverness after that Edinburgh weekend in 1971, he was accompanied by a small elf called Merlando. 'The feeling of incipient madness, consternation and sheer amusement that this gave me can be imagined,' he admitted. 'I was concerned that someone might want to sit on the seat he was in and I really could not figure out whether I would have the courage to say, "Excuse me but that seat is occupied." In the end no one chose to sit there. Perhaps he had some way to influence them unconsciously?'

Only a select few could see the nature spirits, even at Findhorn. Brian himself tended to get fewer 'communications' these days, though his invisible friends had grabbed his attention recently while he was walking through the herb garden. They were annoyed at a thoughtless plan for a kitchen extension. 'As I got to the halfway point it was like being punched in the solar plexus, a sort of psychic blow,' said Brian. 'When I looked inwards there was a clamour of voices saying, *Why are they neglecting us, what is going on?*' They had asked him to alert the gardeners, and at least hold some kind of ceremony if their domain was to be covered in concrete. 'The garden team received it with some warmth and put things to rights,' said Brian. 'And in the end the extension went in the other direction.'

I sat in silence. If there was a muscle for belief, I was fairly sure I had sprained it.

Brian smiled sadly when I explained this. It was a feeling he understood well. Three years after meeting his first nature spirit, he had fled Findhorn for nearby Pluscarden Abbey to become a trainee Benedictine monk.

'Why?'

He sighed. 'Mainly because I felt threatened by these psychic experiences I was having, and was looking for a way that was safe.'

'You thought this place was dangerous?'

'It *can* be dangerous — but so can too much religion — you only have to think of current fundamentalism. Everything can be dangerous; it's a question of balance. If one doesn't go helter-skelter seeking all kinds of psychic experiences but uses discrimination . . .'

'So what brought you back?'

'I think it was probably artistic temperament,' he said, rising to his feet with a wry smile. 'I went into a deep depression about six months before I was due to make my final vows. I guess ultimately my inner self couldn't take the reduced horizons — the sense that I knew exactly what I'd be doing at any time of day for the next fifty years. And also, I don't know of any church community where love is so consistently demonstrated as it is here. So I left.'

It was mid-afternoon and Brian needed to get back to his kiln. I shook his hand on the doorstep. 'Do you ever worry that people can misinterpret these experiences, won't take them seriously?'

Brian shook his head tolerantly: 'I feel I'm old enough not to give a damn.'

I walked through the woods, down a dappled path I hadn't taken before, feeling strangely light-headed. I listened for a moment — to the cooing of a dove, to the quiet scutterings of unseen things among the branches — and then wondered to myself. Then I chuckled and waded on into a labyrinth of dunes, through wiry clumps of grass, following the sound of the sea.

Findhorn village was a cluster of stone cottages and a harbour perched on a wide inland bay. Today it was thronged with people, in the midst of a summer fête, its grassy sea frontage dotted with stalls: bat the rat, tombolas, Punch and Judy, and some definitively non-vegan hot dog and burger stands. I drank it all in, glad of the change of scene. It was the first time I had left the Foundation since I had arrived. Here there were few signs that it even existed save for a rainbow-coloured book titled *Spiritual Growth*, jostling with dog-eared copies of *Jaws* on the second-hand bookstall.

Down on the old stone quay a group of sailors were rigging a long wooden boat for rides around the bay. I wandered down with an ice cream, hoping for a sail. The *Bien Trouvé* was a replica of a French eighteenth-century captain's gig used for community team-building. She was immaculately painted in navy blue and white, her oars and rowing benches varnished the colour of honey. 'She's a great sail training boat because she needs a crew of thirteen,' said one of the men, welcoming me aboard. 'Everyone has a job.' I took responsibility for hauling up the terracotta mainsail, under the tutelage of a friendly, Harry Potteresque teenager.

'Halyard!' shouted Harry, as we drifted out on to the sparkling water. I yanked the lugsail to the top of the mast, while he hitched the halyard in a polished cleft of wood. As the wind filled it, the boat accelerated quietly to 12 knots across the shallow bay. I sat watching the seaweed writhe from the sandy bottom like motorway foliage at our passing. There was almost no noise, just a quiet bubbling of our wake. With each four-sided sail pulled taut, the boat leaned slightly, slicing the water. No froth, no waste, no speculative metaphysics. A different kind of energy, shorn of resistance.

The next morning I went in search of the shipwright, hoping for a lift. Martin Cruden worked among the sand dunes in a workshop raucous with resin fumes and radio hits. He had fashioned the *Bien Trouvé* from a single larch trunk, and now he was hunched over what looked like a glider wing, propped on trestles.

'Actually it's an aerodynamic mast – basically a vertical wing,' he said, scraping epoxy resin off his fingers. 'An ordinary mast creates disturbance in the air behind it and slows you down, but this generates more power to push the boat along.'

With his sun-bleached dreadlocks, beard, sandals, even a tie-dyed T-shirt, he looked exactly the sort of person you might expect to find in the meditation room – which was ironic, because Martin didn't really have much time for his New Age neighbours. 'I worked at Findhorn on two of the Barrel houses, and found the working practices a little strange. They were a bit too relaxed for me. I'm a go-ahead kind of guy, used to working eight till six, getting my head down. But at Findhorn you spent twenty minutes attuning at nine, then another twenty minutes detuning at five and nobody feels any particular rush. I got depressed, felt like I was being held back, taking eight hours over something that should have taken one hour. So I went into boat building instead.'

Speed, a low priority at the Foundation, was Martin's Holy Grail. He looked at the elements as energy to be harnessed with maximum efficiency. His best attempt yet was sitting outside the workshop. It was a bizarre looking contraption even before you took in its glam tigerskin paintjob – an apparent collision between a canoe and a frame tent, its winged upper body teetering on a slender 10 foot hull. 'I named her *What Is It?* because that's the first thing anybody asks when they see her.' You could understand why. Among the stately craft of the Findhorn Yacht Club, she stood out like a leather catsuit at a Women's Institute meeting.

'At first I made an arse of myself capsizing her several times a day, but when I got the hang of it people stopped laughing and told me I was going too fast. In a good wind she can hit 30 knots.'

Unfortunately, *What Is It?* was only big enough for one person, which made it rather pointless to ask for a lift up the coast. But walking back along the beach, I found something changed for me. For the first time in days, I found myself gazing out to sea.

26

Gone Fishing

Along the Moray Coast

Back in neighbouring Lossiemouth, I begged a lift on a tub-like prawn trawler called *Clarness*. The skipper was a big man with a pudding-bowl haircut and an aversion to eye contact, but he was friendly enough. 'You're in luck,' he said, as his men wound new nets on to the drums. 'We'll be heading out for a few days, but first we've got to go to Buckie for ice.'

Buckie was 12 miles east, about quarter of the distance to the large fishing port of Fraserburgh, where I had my best chance of catching a boat north. I clambered gratefully aboard, and dumped my rucksack in the dim interior, where a crewman with sideburns offered me a beer. 'Squid are a seasonal thing, but they seem to be early this year,' he said, pointing out the new nets. He lowered his voice, jerked a thumb upstairs towards the wheelhouse. '*He's* getting steamed up because other guys are catching squid and he's not. It can go for £200 a box.'

'Is it the restaurants driving the price up? For calamari?'

He squinted at me and took a long draw on his cigarette. 'I've really nae idea what they do with them.' Bitterness and smoke hung about him.

We clambered up to the wheelhouse. 'Jaws here has spent longer than anybody on this boat,' said the skipper. 'Seven years – that's pretty good in this day and age. Mostly you're lucky if you get the same crew for two or three weeks.'

Opinion varied on the cause of the current state of the fishing industry. Fishermen usually blamed the quota cuts on weak government negotiators selling out to foreign boats in the name of European unity – and ocean scientists being unduly pessimistic about fish stocks. Others said the fishermen had plundered the seas and were paying the price for eighties lifestyles and expensive cars. But most agreed on one thing.

'I wouldn't want to be going into it now,' said Jaws. 'Fishing's stuffed.'

Colin ran chunky fingers through his mop of hair as we manoeuvred out through the harbour entrance. 'It's been a good job to me. I've never been anything else but a fisherman. But when you count up the value of it, it can be a kick in the teeth. Fifteen years ago you were getting twice as much for the product as we're getting now. Everything else has gone up by two or three times. The product is coming down in price, but the overheads are doubled. I can bring in £3500 of product a week. That's before fuel, crew wages, overheads. There's not a lot of give and take in it . . .'

The job seemed closer to currency speculation than fishing – all about *product* and *margins* and *overheads*, about watching markets and available stock. Knowing when to switch nets for the get-rich-quick currency of squid, before the rest of the fleet joined in and sent the prices tumbling.

We fell silent, listening to the sporadic fizzing of the VHF as the coast became a hazy strip of sand and greenery, rolling hills and chipped cliff faces. Gulls wheeled overhead and Colin stared out through the salt-stained window, occasionally quizzing me on what I was doing, places I had been. It was mid-afternoon when a harbour wall loomed and a deckhand slouched into view and positioned himself by the mooring line. 'That's my boy,' muttered Colin darkly. 'Does it without even taking his hands out of his pockets.'

Once brimful with boats, Buckie was losing its soul. A group of retired fishermen huddled in its harbour office like refugees at an embassy, one of the few places on the foreign soil of modern life where they still found their language spoken. They emerged from a fug of cigarette smoke to point out the £2 million fish market now empty; the five local boats awaiting dismemberment in the latest round of decommissioning; and up above the harbour, the cut-price shops helping locals make the best of it.

'There are just less fish,' said one man, who had reaped the benefits of the boom in the seventies and eighties. 'It's like anything else — it had to run out some time. Norway, Faeroe, Iceland, they all put restrictions on long ago and they've still got the fish. We never had the restrictions till now, and we're paying the price. We're all fished out. The boats got bigger, the nets got bigger, the engines got bigger — everything got bigger.'

Adam Main was thinking smaller. His squid boat *Shaligar* was less than 10 metres long, and he cut crew costs and overheads by taking her out single-handed. Unlike his cousin Colin, he fished on short overnight trips, so I tracked him down on the dockside just before 10 p.m. and asked to tag along. He was surprised at the request, but glad of company, so I clambered aboard. He rushed about casting off mooring lines, then darted back to gun the engine. The wheelhouse had the friendly, cluttered ambience of a floating bachelor pad, its dashboard piled with binoculars, disposable gloves, wasp spray, tissues and a Tupperware box full of loose change. Once cast off, Adam left his wellies outside the door, pre-inserted in the rolled-down legs of his yellow waterproof dungarees ready for action. Inside, he stepped into a homely pair of carpet slippers.

The light was dying fast as we left the harbour, with only a pink glow on the horizon to silhouette our competitors. 'Eleven!' he said, his brow furrowed, counting their boxy profiles. 'Festooned with boats! This time last week there were three. News travels fast.' There was energy in his voice. He'd started fishing at sixteen, and at forty-three was not about to let a bit of competition throw him.

'On Friday I got seven boxes of squid – that's a good bit more than £1000. Last night I got two boxes – but even that earned me £350, which isn't bad for a night's work for a one-man band. Unfortunately, when the big boats move in, we may as well go home.' He said it cheerfully, like a man putting coins in a slot machine while insisting that gambling was for mugs.

'Strange creatures,' he said, as *Shaligar* gurned out into choppy water. 'We dinnae really know very much about them. They come into shallow water, they spawn and then they die. Predator by night, prey by day. They reckon a squid eats its own weight every day. Imagine that! If I was a squid I'd be eating 14 stone of crap every twenty-four hours.'

He grinned, kicked off his carpet slippers and jumped into his boots, pulling up the dungarees as he strode towards the stern. 'Time we shot our nets.' High above the stern, the net drum began to turn, paying out the net quickly into our foaming wake. Presently, with a clanking and a shudder, two shackled iron 'doors' dropped over the back of the boat. They disappeared under the surface with a screeching of the pulley, the wire veering outwards suddenly as if carrying a fleeing fish. Their function was to open the neck of the net. Adam kept his hand on the winch switch until only the ends of the towing ropes remained on the drum. Then he strode back to the wheelhouse.

'That's us for a while – just trawling and hope we pick up something interesting,' he said. 'Cup of tea?'

He switched to autopilot and went below, leaving me to watch the darkness outside the windscreen, with the green-over-white lights of other trawlers moving slowly in relation to us, all labouring up and down the coast, like tractors ploughing the same large field. Adam re-emerged with two mugs. His was proudly inscribed *Captain*. 'You'll have to have this one,' he said, handing me one marked *Cabin Boy*. We sipped companionably in silence, eating on pancakes smeared with marge and jam, watching the psychedelic scrolling of the depth gauge as Adam puffed his way through a box of Regals. I thought of the big-eyed squid, rising like ghosts in the darkness beneath us, attracted by the moon. Suddenly the engine noise changed and the boat wheeled round to starboard.

'Shite,' muttered Adam, pushing the throttle forward until we straightened. 'Probably caught on an old lobster pot.'

There were obvious disadvantages in working alone. The previous night he had run aground for two hours, finally rescued by two men in a creel boat who came to his aid. 'You rely on the other small boats – stay in contact all the time.'

A mile or so past Cullen, he steered the boat in a wide arc, and began following the orange sodium lights back towards port. The wind had come up, blowing offshore in angry whitecaps, splashing up through the scuppers. It was past midnight when Adam stepped back into his wellies and began to haul in the catch, watching impatiently as the net slowly emerged from the darkness. Finally, the bulbous teat of the net end – the *bag* – came into view, its contents indistinguishable but pulsating as Adam winched it up above a steel funnel. The slime of a red jellyfish hung like dog drool.

Several wide, angry eyes stared disconcertingly through the mesh. 'That's a poor catch,' muttered Adam, frowning as he hinged down his stainless steel sorting counter. He worked quickly, unhitching ropes and levers to allow the catch to cascade across it in front of him. His rubber-gloved hand darted back and forward, sliding jellyfish and crabs back out into the sea through a letterbox-sized hole at the end of the sorting counter, throwing the squid into buckets, their eyes bulging grotesquely from phallic bodies, their tentacles limp. 'Not even sure that'll fill a bucket, let alone a box,' he said, shaking his head. Other skippers checked in on the short-wave radio. 'Two buckets at most,' said *Alexander*. 'Four bloody squid!' said another.

We motored back into the harbour, where the gulls gathered like hoodlums below the sodium lights, waiting for scraps. 'Sounds pretty rotten for everybody,' said Adam. 'But I'll see what the dawn haul brings.' I bowed out and hurried back to my B&B through the quiet, rainslicked streets, wondering at his gambler's optimism. But it paid off. Next morning the harbour master told me he'd pulled in three boxes. At £200 a box. Not a bad night's work for a man working alone.

Not everybody was so lucky. Early next morning I hitched a lift upon a rusty 12-metre trawler whose solitary crewman had paid the ultimate price. 'I usually rent her out to a feller on the west coast, but this year he died on her,' said the skipper, Jim, as we set off for Fraserburgh. 'He was working out of Troon on his own and must have got his hand caught in the winch. It dragged him in and crushed him under his own nets.'

Looking aft at the empty net drum, I felt the hairs prickle on the back of my neck. The *Patsy B* had motored on pilotless for 15 miles until she ran aground on a beach in Arran. 'Someone saw her and called the coastguard to investigate. And that was how they found him. By the time he had twelve turns of rope round him he'd have been a goner. You shouldn't really work these boats single-handed – there's nobody to help when it all goes wrong.'

Jim had brought her home through the canal the week before, but he'd lost heart in her. You could feel the drag of sorrow, encrusted like barnacles on her hull. 'After what happened, I just want rid of her. I'm thinking I'll beach her somewhere, touch her up underneath, then sell her on,' he said, staring ahead. 'Maybe get a smaller boat instead, more of a diving set-up.'

He looked ruefully at his deckhand, who was asleep in a reclining seat. 'Johnny's father and uncle both died at sea too, eh Johnny?' Johnny woke up and yawned. Ignoring Jim's question, he reached up and turned on the small television. With his shaven head he could have been twenty-five or forty. He opened a bag of crisps and ate slowly, staring at a daytime chat show. He wore a shell suit, and his carpet slippers – seemingly as reassuring to a fisherman as a working echo-sounder – bore little embroidered portraits of Bart Simpson.

I ducked out of the wheelhouse and sat on the hatch cover, watching the coast unfurling. Every now and then I turned to stare at the empty winch at the back of the boat, trying not to see the man hanging there. The surface of the deck was mottled red and green from all the repaints – in sixteen years she'd been a clam boat, pilot boat, diver charter boat and fishing vessel. A few metal panels were growing waferlike with rust and decay at the corners. Everything changed, everything decayed, our lives evaporated like surface water – I knew all that. Yet I was unsettled by the suddenness of this nameless crewman's death. No time for mended relationships, goodbyes, thankfulness, regret. What routine thoughts had he been chewing on as he wandered to the stern to start hauling? How would he have lived that last day differently if he had known it was his last?

I reeled my day in experimentally, morsel by morsel, in the balmy afternoon: the benign seas, the clouds wispy and tufted as if grasped at from below. Gulls sailed along the tips of the waves, wing tips centimetres above the water. I savoured each sensation, feeling a pleasure tinged with unease. I wasn't ready to give any of it up. Not yet.

Half an hour later, as we navigated our way into the mazelike interior of Fraserburgh harbour, Johnny jerked from his recliner like Frankenstein suddenly plugged into the mains. Putting on his trainers and rucksack, he climbed impatiently to the bow. We had barely touched the quay before he was off up the ladder, stopping only to throw a grudging loop of mooring line round a bollard.

'Can I help with anything?' I said, as Jim scrambled between stern and wheelhouse trying to moor his boat single-handed.

'Thanks,' he sighed. 'That's supposed to be what crewmen are for, but I just can't get him to do any work. Everybody knows fishing's finished.'

We watched Johnny running down the quay, as if from death itself. He didn't look back. I couldn't help noticing he had taken his slippers with him.

27

The Cod Crusaders

Fraserburgh

The *Fraserburgh Herald* was doing its best to cheer up its residents. Sitting in the beachfront café, I scanned stories laden with the forced gaiety of an ebullient auntie. *Villages Gear Up for Gala*, ran the front page splash, bearing the revelation that the bunting had now been put up for a forthcoming annual fair. On the crime page, petty vandalism and a stolen bike were balanced with the heart-warming headline: *Guinea Pigs Recovered*. Elsewhere, there was an invitation to vote in the Fish and Chip Shop of the Year competition.

But nothing could brighten the fishing pages. Nearly seventy more Scottish vessels were to be destroyed under a government decommissioning scheme. *'A long time to wait for a nail in your own coffin'* wailed the headline, beside thunderous looking mugshots of fishing leaders.

They were all men, yet it hadn't always been this way. Looking at sepia pictures of herring drifters in the Heritage Museum the previous afternoon, I had been struck by the presence of fishwives. There were dozens, hundreds of them, grinning on quaysides and scowling from behind barrels, young lassies and toothless crones alike, gutting and selling fish, baiting lines, mending nets. Traditionally they had even carried their husbands out to their boats on their backs to stop them getting wet feet. Where were the women now?

'Nowadays they think we should be at home, looking after our children, being the loyal wives, dutifully standing by as our husbands' jobs go down,' said Morag Ritchie, smoking angrily as we scanned the paper together. 'They say we should be leaving the politics to the experts.'

In a cheerier week, Morag and her friend Carol would have been in the *Fraserburgh Herald* too, wearing their matching tartan miniskirts and white sweatshirts emblazoned 'Fishing SOS', confronting another Brussels bureaucrat, striking a defensive blow for their beleaguered husbands. They called themselves the Cod Crusaders – ordinary middle-aged wives of trawlermen, whose petitioning and sassy public meetings had caught the imagination of the media in a way the male negotiators had not. They'd blustered their way to a meeting with Franz Fischler, the EU Fisheries commissioner, deposited their petition to 10 Downing Street, even received a good luck message from Sean Connery.

'Sometimes we think we're getting out of our depth, right enough,' said Carol, with a half-smile. 'But at the end of the day we have a duty to our kids.' Her ten-year-old son Aaron sucked patiently at his milkshake through a straw. 'It's our children's future we're bargaining for – so that there's still to be an industry to go into. There's been fishing in Fraserburgh for seven hundred and fifty years. That's an awful lot of heritage to flush away.'

The previous day they had met a delegation from a government strategy unit in London. 'I think we made a lasting impression on them,' said Morag. 'We said if it's all about conservation, why are the foreign fleets waiting to come in?'

'It's politics,' said Carol. 'Politics hiding behind the old story of conservation. The fleet has been sold off in order to make way for the ten countries coming into the EU. There's seven thousand six hundred vessels waiting to come in and fish our waters.'

'It's true!' said Morag. 'And the Spaniards are building a massive new fleet! How does it make sense to scrap our new boats in the name of conservation when they're building new boats to fish our waters?' She stared into her coffee and took a long drag on her cigarette. Morag had grown up in Scotland's mining and steel belt, where her father was paid off as a Ravenscraig welder at fifty. There, too, a wider world undercut the securities of homegrown industries. 'I've seen them close the steelworks, I've seen them close the mines, and now I've moved up here and I'm about to see it all happen again.'

We went for a drive around the docks in Carol's people carrier. 'Welcome to the battle wagon,' she said. 'We've done eighty-one thousand miles in her.' It was a picturesque harbour, still full enough of colourful boats to seem purposeful, though Morag pointed out the condemned boats – one named *Steadfast*. 'There were a hundred and seventy-one applications for sixty-nine decommissionings. Last year it was a hundred and twenty, lots of wooden boats twenty or thirty years old. This time round we're talking *two* years old. Almost new. There's a £3 million boat in Banff that's to be scrapped. What sense does that make?'

The whitefish basin was empty, all the boats away at sea. It was always a tense, difficult time, with their men at the mercy of the elements, and no promise that they'd return. Carol had nearly lost her husband in a force 9 gale. 'A freak wave smashed the wheelhouse windows and took out every piece of electrical equipment on the boat. She was loose on the sea for two hours with no lights or electricity. A lot of people don't understand what these men have to endure to make a fair living. They're under pressure and some of them are going away to sea with depression tablets. Everyone's got their breaking point.'

'The men have to endure the pain,' said Morag. 'Then *we* have to endure *their* pain. They come home and say: *This is it, I've had enough.*'

Aaron looked up, concerned, in the back seat, and Carol reached over and ruffled his hair, her face softening. I thought of the sepia museum photographs, of the fishwives carrying their husbands dutifully to their boats. They were carrying them still.

I had done the rounds of at least a dozen fishing boats that morning, all of them producing the same answer with varying degrees of sarcasm: fishing boats go out to sea and come back to the same place again, full of fish. They're not best suited to hitching from A to B. The best anyone could offer was Peterhead, a few miles south.

'South' had all the wrong connotations just now, thanks to a demoralising discovery I had made about Cormac of the Sea in the public library that afternoon. Ever since visiting his island, I had been wondering what had happened to the seafaring monk. Now it emerged that he had not only given up his search and returned to Durrow as instructed, but – if two folkloric websites were correct – his world had imploded in a quite spectacular manner. He was barely back in his old Irish parish when a fellow cleric had issued a prophesy: that Cormac would be torn to pieces by wolves.

Quite what the homecoming monk was supposed to do with this unhelpful information was not recorded. Terrifed, he erected a strong round stone tower and retreated inside in panic, pulling up his food and drink through a hole or window at the top, hoping to keep the wolves at bay. Yet in the manner of such tales, it was all in vain. 'One day,' ran the fable, 'upon looking out he saw two black snails crawling up the side of the tower, slowly changing shape.' As they slid inside, they morphed back into the form of wolves, chased him out into the fields and – with somewhat wearying inevitability – tore him to pieces.

It had all the usual improbable hallmarks of folklore – the martyr's spilt blood had miraculously become springs of healing holy water – and yet such tales often carried a deeper psychological truth. It seemed to me to be a parable about human weakness, and the potency of fear. How could a man so famed for his sea-going bravery and navigational skill have allowed his life to shrink to such a tiny frame of reference? How did someone who took on the uncertainty of storms and sea monsters and ever-changing horizons become this cowering wretch, walled in by his own private war on terror? He seemed almost another person.

I knew which Cormac I admired, and he had gone north.

It was my B&B owner who eventually gave me the lead I needed. 'You'll have seen *Resolute*?' he said as he shovelled black pudding on to my plate the following morning. 'She's brand new, supposed to have cost between seven and nine *million*. It's her maiden fishing voyage any day now. Now *that'd* be a trip and a half.'

The pelagic fishing boats were docked at the far end of the harbour, vast ships the size of car ferries which dwarfed everything around them. They were the silver lining in the current economic cloud: chasing flourishing shoals of herring and mackerel with the blessing of government scientists, who had actually *raised* acceptable catch quotas that year. Most tantalisingly from my point of view, they often fished the waters round Shetland and sometimes landed their catch in Lerwick, my next target destination.

Resolute was the most impressive of the fleet, a 64-metre virgin with an elegant burgundy hull, gleaming fish chutes and nets of

almost luminous whiteness. The skipper was standing proprietorially on the foredeck, watching his crew loading equipment. His
furrowed brow didn't instantly suggest a man awash with prosper-
ity and confidence, but as I discovered, David West was *downsizing* –
he had halved the family fleet to run a joint operation with his
brother.

'Previously we had a 61-metre and a 51-metre ship,' he
explained, coming ashore to meet me. 'Now we're just working the
single trawler. We've combined two quotas into one to make the
operation more viable. Unfortunately we also had excess crew so
we had to lay off some men.' He looked genuinely regretful at this
contingency. 'We're leaving tonight on the tide with a full crew –
we've got to learn how to fish from her . . .'

He laughed and shook his head when I asked if he'd consider
taking a writer on the maiden voyage. 'I'm not fussy about where
I sleep,' I said pre-emptively. 'I've got a mat and a sleeping bag – any
bit of floor will do.'

He scratched his head, flummoxed by the request. 'You know
there's no guarantee we'll land at Shetland – it depends who's
offering the best prices.' I nodded sympathetically. I had been to
the fish auction the previous morning and noticed that squid had
already halved to barely £100 a box. It was all one big game of
poker.

'That's a risk I'm happy to take.'

David grinned at me. 'You're persistent, aren't you? Well . . .
come back at eleven-thirty tonight and we'll see what we can do.'

28

Jonah and the Shark

Fishing on the *Resolute*

The harbour lights burned holes in a velvety darkness as I crept through the sleeping town. Bleary-eyed, I drank in the intoxicating energy of a busy dockside at night: the electronic bleeping of reversing trucks, the low thunder of generators or engines, the clank of anchor chains. Everything bathed in the sodium weirdness of floodlights. And somewhere beyond the iridescent fringe of tamed water, the dark ocean, waiting.

David greeted me on the gangplank with a sceptical grimace. 'Sure you want to go ahead with this?' He didn't look too sure himself.

'Absolutely.'

He shrugged and led me up to the bridge. It was an open-plan lounge elegantly furnished with red oak desks, vast computer monitors and black leather furniture. Its wooden floor was polished like a ballroom, and the crew were scrunching around in elasticated blue plastic overshoes – a more forensic version of fishermen's slippers. I donned a pair myself, and scanned the 360-degree view through smoked glass over the floodlit decks where young men in fluorescent work gear were readying the nets and securing equip-

ment. We found David's brother George at a computer console —
a man in his fifties, dressed like David in jeans and open-necked
shirt like a company director at work on his day off. He was
frowning at a familiar message on the screen: *Warning: this program has
performed an illegal operation.*

'Good grief,' muttered David. 'What's the matter now?'

George sighed. 'We're on to it . . .'

He looked up with a wry grin, and shook my hand. 'You've got
no idea what you're letting yourself in for, have you?'

Nearby, a younger crewman pointedly failed to return my nod
and smile. 'Are you here to see us get it wrong?' he asked. It seemed
David's decision to allow me to come had been subject to some
debate.

'Er, no, just for the journey . . .'

'Well, it won't be a very long journey the rate we're going.'

I withdrew tactfully to the shadows in my plastic bootees and
read the safety notices while they ironed out the technical glitch.
On the wall a framed crew roster listed a total of nine Wests — not
so much a ship, then, as a floating dynasty.

Another crewman came over to welcome me on his way down to
the aft deck. 'We're all a bit nervous with this being the first time
and all,' explained the man, who I would later pinpoint genealogi-
cally as the son of David's father's cousin Brian. 'We did fishing
and sailing trials and spent the last month in Norway getting her
ready. But now it's the real thing.'

The 6000-horsepower engines caused little more than a light
tremor beneath the feet. On the floodlit decks below, men were
manoeuvring fenders the size of telephone kiosks over the side of
the boat using remote-controlled cranes. It was only when I saw a
lamppost gliding past that I realised we were already under way,
nosing forward through channels barely wide enough for the ship.

'The difficult bit is compensating for the tide,' murmured David, gently manipulating a joystick on a remote control console to nose the vast prow around a tight corner. We hummed quietly out through the harbour entrance into a darkness pricked by a solitary cluster of lights. 'Cargo boat, up ahead,' said George, looking at the radar. 'Crossing our path.' He punched in some numbers, clicked on the mouse a couple of times. 'At current speeds, they'll cross our path with 1.5 miles to spare.' He grinned, pointed at the screen. 'Radar does the calculations for you.'

With the ship locked on a seaward course, David showed me to my room. All the cabins were full on this inaugural trip, so I was to sleep in the ship's small hospital. 'Obviously you'll have to vacate it if we have an emergency,' said David. 'But it's pretty unlikely you'll be disturbed.' It was a generous gesture – I even had my own en-suite bathroom in the shape of the scrubs room. Unrolling my sleeping bag, I clambered on to the operating table.

I woke on the floor with a lozenge of sunlight dancing on the ceiling above me, and my possessions sliding back and forth like flotsam. Bracing myself against the window, I peered out at long, low islands spread along our side. I hurried into the shower and emerged to the unmistakeable smell of frying bacon.

Mess seemed altogether the wrong word for the ship's immaculate wood-panelled dining and recreation area. The West dynasty sat around two long tables, tucking quietly into a full cooked breakfast. A family crest on the wall showing two fish leaping away from an imposing 'W'. A few of the crew members ate their cornflakes sitting in black leather sofas ranged before a vast widescreen television. Most nodded at me, though James, the man who had confronted me the previous night, just frowned. I joined the buffet queue behind Joe, who shook my hand enthusiastically and confirmed that we were passing through the Orkney Isles. There were no plans to stop. 'The fish are a bit soft bellied here. We want them big, ready to spawn but not with the spawn running out of them, like in mid-August. The Shetland ones are best – monsters!'

By the time I made it upstairs to the bridge, the Orkneys were already drifting astern. I hoped to call there on my way back south, but for now there was only the sea ahead, like beaten tin, unbroken by land. The weather forecast churning from the Navtext machine was for strong or near-gale force south-easterly winds in the next twenty-four hours. Nobody seemed too bothered – it was unlikely we'd even feel it up here. George and David sat side by side in magnificent leather pilots' chairs, bouncing slightly on the built-in suspension. An array of buttons in their armrests controlled a vast bank of luminous screens angled in front of them as if they were captaining an intergalactic space cruiser. I ensconced myself in an L-shaped leather sofa and watched the monitors for signs of life.

There was something almost miraculous about herring. Around the east coast they were historically known as silver darlings, rising up from the depths in shimmering columns and clouds, hauled and shaken flapping into the fleet of boats which once followed them from the Northern Isles to Lowestoft or Yarmouth, year after year. At the peak of the industry in the late nineteenth and early twentieth centuries, fishermen converged from across Britain to track the summer shoals down the coast, accompanied by fishwives who set up camp at each port to gut and barrel the catch. It was a vibrant, fishy smelling free-for-all.

'The fish are much more difficult to catch than they used to be,' said George. 'There's two possible explanations: either they've learned how to avoid the nets, or it's a process of selection – we've fished the ones that haven't learned to avoid us, and the others have passed on their genetic make-up to their offspring.'

There was a third option, of course – that there were simply fewer fish. Although the fisheries scientists had raised the limit this year, proclaiming stocks of both fish to be healthy – and perhaps also in compensation for the savage cuts in whitefish quota – were they right? George pulled a face. 'Until recently the herring has been on the rise – but to be honest, in the last six months there's signs that it's tailing off.'

David stared at the empty orange glow of the sonar. 'Fish aren't just commodities,' he said. 'It's like fruit: there are times when it's ripe and there are times when it's not. Sometimes the fish are there but you can't see them. Sometimes they aren't there at all. I'm sceptical about the figures that scientists produce.' He saw no certainty in the future quite the opposite. 'We could easily go the same way as the whitefish boys.'

For the moment, the economics of pelagic fishing were as exhilarating as they were volatile. By combining the licences for their two previous boats, David and George had an annual quota of 2500 tonnes of herring and 5500 of mackerel – with prices around £110 a tonne and £550 a tonne respectively. The fleets of little boats were gone, replaced by a few giants routinely chasing hauls of biblical proportions. 'Values have changed,' said George. 'Back then if you got 20 to 30 tonnes, that was a good night's fishing. Nowadays we need to catch 200 to 300 tonnes just to make it worth landing them.'

We spent much of the afternoon in uneasy suspense, like participants at a séance, waiting for contact from the other side. The monitors showed occasional glowing fingers of red or orange indicating shoals in the 80 fathoms below – though none large enough to convince the skippers to shoot their nets – echoed by the eerie suck and gurgle of the audio feed, like the catheter on a life-support machine. We were 27 miles north-west of Orkney when I noticed a change: the noise was suddenly harder-edged, echoing off something clearly defined below us.

'That's more like it,' said David. A large flame-coloured stalagmite was moving slowly across the screen in front of him. Ahead of the boat, hundreds of fulmars and gannets bobbed or whirled against a blank horizon. 'These birds know better than us what's here. It's a good sign.' We headed into the midst of them and the sonar shape disappeared. David frowned but refused to be put off. 'Sometimes when you go over the top of the fish, they flatten themselves on the bottom.' He clicked on his mouse, which fixed a little fish symbol on the GPS map, then called the men to their stations through an intercom. As they appeared on the aft deck we began a long, slow circle.

The weather, bright if overcast for much of the day, seemed to be on the turn, the wind piling up mounds of water which picked up the bows and plunged them down into dizzying troughs with enormous explosions of foam. The men appeared in coloured oilskins on the afterdeck, bracing themselves against the swell, keeping away from the open stern. George's son Alexander stationed himself at the touch-sensitive computer cockpit overlooking the aft deck. At David's command, he set the giant net rollers in motion.

I recognised crazily inflated versions of the equipment I had seen on Adam's squid boat. The white Kevlar nets unfurled for more than a kilometre, dragged down by weights the size of grain sacks which thundered from welded runners. The stern itself was open at deck level, framing a rectangle of pitching seas like a cinema screen against which the men were silhouettes. The net floats were as big as greenhouses, while the 4-metre-high trawl doors could have sealed a barn. They stood up oddly in our wake for a minute before slowly sinking to spread the 100-metre-wide mouth of the net. The men treated the new equipment with a wary respect. David nodded silent approval from the bridge.

'Now it's just like a game of space invaders,' said David, once the net was fully deployed. The sonar screen showed its devouring curve advancing on luminous fragments, while he steered the boat with a small joystick. 'You just cruise around scooping the bits of fish into your net, then sail home with the result.'

We stared like addicts for two hours, breaking only to have supper. There was a sigh of relief when a flashing panel indicated that the first electronic net sensor had been tripped – meaning the end of the bag was filling up. Then, shortly before 8 p.m., the hauling began: the steel warps rolled on to the drums, dragging the doors rearing from the waves, followed by the floats and weights and long tracts of net. The first fish emerged and broke open with the scissor-like tension, falling to the deck in bloody pieces. The fishermen ignored them, focusing instead on the bulging net end now approaching through the darkening surface water, mobbed by sea birds. From where I stood, up on the mezzanine deck, it seemed a good haul. It would surely have filled Adam Main's little squid boat to the gunwales.

But the men scowled and shook their heads. On the bridge, George gave a grim thumbs down. I watched in puzzlement as one of the men leaned down, unlaced the net bag and pushed it back off the boat. 'We've got maybe half a tonne there,' said George, when I re-entered the bridge. 'Not even worth landing.'

Behind us the gulls went wild as thousands of suffocated fish glittered dead in our wake.

The next morning an air of gloom hung over the breakfast table. 'It's comfort eating,' said an exasperated David, attacking a sausage.

'Cos there's nae fish!' I had mixed feelings about the previous night's disappointment. The fewer fish we caught at this stage, the further north we would go in their pursuit – which suited me fine. Shortly after breakfast a malfunctioning fire alarm raised my hopes still further. 'Looks like we might be going to Shetland,' said David, as George resorted to unscrewing the clanging bell and muffling the mechanism with a T-shirt. 'It may be miles from anywhere, but it's the best place for electronic engineers.' I thought it prudent not to look too pleased about this.

We steamed northwards for the rest of the morning, the emptiness of the screen matched only by the phlegmy snores of the sonar. Below deck I found Joe taking more spiritual measures. When I passed the mess early that afternoon he was ensconced in one of the black leather armchairs listening to 'twenty-four-hour continuous readings from the scriptures' on the Bible Channel.

'Looking for some inspiration,' he said, grinning sheepishly.

Fishermen had always made good disciples. It wasn't hard to understand why. Even with the highest-tech kit, you were essentially reliant on nature's bounty, on the mysterious probabilities of shoaling, on the elements staying on your side. Up on the bridge, I had noticed that Gideon Bibles were kept as handy as tide tables and pilots' guides.

It was dark when the time came to haul again, and the trail of bloody fish pieces seemed more garish in the floodlights. I watched from the mezzanine deck again, feeling more self-conscious than before on account of James, who fired dark looks at me every time I caught his eye. I occupied an uncomfortable niche as redundant, unskilled observer, banned from going near any equipment, with only my notebook to show I had a job to do. So I was glad for the men's sake when the net bag sloshed up against the stern, bulging promisingly with fish. They looked pleased with themselves, and I took a couple of congratulatory photographs of Joe and Matthew posing over their trophy catch.

Then came the news from the bridge: one of the cranes had malfunctioned, making it impossible to get the fish to the storage tanks. They'd have to dump the whole haul. The men slumped visibly, shook their heads. James looked directly at me, poised with my camera, and shouted something. I cupped my ear playfully and went down on to the working deck.

'Jonah!'

It was half-joke, half-accusation. He watched me flush, while others smirked or shifted uneasily. I pretended not to have understood, gesturing them together for a portrait. James responded by dropping his trousers and mooning me.

I slept badly that night, turning James's insult over in my mind. I knew very well the Bible story he was alluding to: Jonah, who brought bad luck on his fellow sailors by trying to flee from God aboard a ship. Jonah, who was thrown overboard when the sailors realised his jinxed status. Jonah, who lived three days in the belly of a whale before it vomited him up on to dry land.

It was probably just an in-house joke, an obvious jibe for an unwanted observer with no obvious function. Yet in the surreally pitching darkness, I found myself pondering mishaps on other boats I had boarded during the trip: the engine failure of *Thistledown*, right at the start; the grounding of *Zeepaard* on an old mattress; the missing bung on the sinking Clyde rowing boat; the travails of the *Colmcille*; the sea rescue on the way to Findhorn. It wasn't the first time I had been blamed for such things. While crossing the Pacific on the reed boat, a Bolivian crewmate had accused me of bringing a storm upon us by failing to observe the taboos of sailors and mentioning it out loud. Was I now being blamed for the poor catches of a twenty-first-century trawler?

It was ludicrous, yet it gnawed at me still. I was as keen as anyone else to see the requisite haul of herring. The sooner we hauled, the sooner we got to Shetland.

'Rise and shine, gentlemen, rise and shine!' crackled the intercom. 'Away tae *shoot!* We've found some fish.'

It was a glorious morning, the early sun glittering through the still air, and in the distance on our rear port quarter the industrial shapes of the Beryl B oilfield were silhouetted against an otherwise flawless sky. Even in the two days we had been out, the crew had honed its routine, and now they were keyed up, impatient. This time everything seemed to happen smoothly, and within minutes of deploying the nets two net sensors had been triggered, indicating a sizeable catch.

The net bag broke surface like a whale showing its bloated white underbelly, a writhing, undulating bubble of fish. Sea birds circled in a frenzy of expectancy. The guys on the fish deck were grinning, glancing back up at David, who nodded. It was time to upload the booty.

'Hit the jackpot?' I was excited.

David looked unconvinced. 'I reckon we've got about 40 tonnes – that's about £3000 – barely enough to cover the cost of the fuel.'

Even so, he began the loading process. The engineers had been at work overnight on the hydraulics problem, and a winch dragged the net forward along beside the boat until it was level with the forward holding tanks, its vast gut bulging just below the surface. A crewman flipped a switch on a remote-control unit around his waist, and a white crane whirred into life. Instead of attempting to drag the nets aboard, the crane lifted the pump over the side. It looked like an enormous silver ammonite from which protruded a rubber tube as thick as a tree trunk. The men secured the net head around the pump and lowered both into the water. Presently, the flat tube fattened and bucked, arching like a devouring sea serpent as water and fish filled its innards.

The connected tube spat water, fattened and vomited fish into the stainless steel box bolted high on the foredeck. Soon they were flowing towards us down a sloping open chute directly below the window of the bridge, silver herring and the occasional bluish fleck of mackerel among them, around a bend and down into the first holding tank, guided by means of a series of steel gates. 'Everything has got a lot easier these days,' said Andrew, putting on his outer jacket to go down to help. 'When I started at sixteen, we used to have to push the fish out of the hold. Now you don't even have to touch them.'

As a landlubber whose ordinary contact with fish began at the supermarket shelf, this wasn't quite the visceral reconnection with nature I had been hoping for. But the men looked happy for the first time in days, channelling this blurred stream of living capital into the chilled brine that would keep them fresh. The quantity was dizzying. Within minutes the first tank was full, and the gate was dropped to divert them into the next tank.

I watched puzzled as the fish, still flowing down from the entry chamber, began to pile up behind the gate which somebody had forgotten to open. They rose towards the rim of the chute with a kind of serene inevitability.

'Open the door!' yelled George, seeing what was happening.

The men looked up blankly from below the chutes. Their expressions changed with remarkable uniformity as the first fish began showering down on their heads. A kind of unchoreographed pantomime ensued. 'Stop the pump!' yelled someone. Fish were falling from every section of the chute now, raining down in their hundreds. The fishermen were already ankle-deep in them as they scrambled to stop the flow. 'Open the chamber!' yelled someone else. And still they came, tumbling slimy and glittering across the deck, flowering outwards towards the gunwales.

'Stop the pump, you idiots!' screamed David.

Somebody waded towards the control panel and the pipe sagged. Agonisingly slowly, the flow ceased. There was no sound but the soggy percussion of fish washing around the deck fixtures as the boat heaved. I thought it tactful to put away my notebook.

'Oh dear, oh dear, oh dear,' said David. 'Not our proudest moment.' George was down on the deck bawling at those responsible, while others slowly began to shovel fish into hods, or hose them out through the scuppers. Someone finally found the right lever to let the backed-up fish flow into the correct hold.

James, inevitably, was scowling at *me*.

'I think there was more fish in that bag than any of us believed,' said David, watching as the net finally emptied itself ten minutes later. 'It's a much bigger bag than we had before. I though we had maybe 40 tonnes, but it looks like we had maybe 150.'

'What a bloody farce that was,' said James, as I came into the mess that night. 'Put on a great show for you, didn't we?' Others sat around him with hangdog expressions. I was aware some kind of statement was expected.

'Come on, guys, that was a great haul — 150 tonnes, they're saying!'

'Shame half of them were on the deck,' persisted James, darkly.

I shrugged. 'But this was supposed to be the trial run, right?' He looked me carefully in the eye then went back to his television. I breathed a quiet sigh of relief.

It didn't seem to stop the bad luck, though. We shot the nets again later that night and hauled another vast catch. The river of fish had been flowing into all the right places for several minutes when the black pipe suddenly sagged, and the motor let out a whine before abruptly cutting out.

Joe peered over the side. 'It's a *shark*,' he reported.

'What?'

'There's a shark in the fish pump.'

And there was. It was 8 feet long and wedged head first in the pump rotors. We all gaped as the crane hoisted the whole sorry mess up into the floodlights.

'Never seen that before,' frowned George, scratching his head.

It took twenty minutes to work out how to extract the larger-than-expected fish from the shiny new equipment. The men tugged at the sandpapery torso, but found it jammed fast. I avoided all eye contact with James.

'Watch yerself,' said Joe nervously, as Matthew tried to ease the beast out of the machinery.

'Don't worry, it's definitely dead,' said Matthew. 'It's got no head.'

Eventually, after lashing ropes to its tail and pulling repeatedly with the remote control crane, the headless corpse sprang suddenly free, showering blood and cartilage into the sea.

David sighed. 'It's been one of those trips, I'm afraid.'

I don't know why I expected my own luck to be any better. Yet it still came as a shock when the truth dawned the following day. Like Jonah's whale, the *Resolute* spat me back out where I began — in *Fraserburgh* — along with 350 tonnes of herring.

It was nothing personal, though I fancy I detected the ghost of a smile from James as we shook hands on the gangplank. 'Remember this, Nick,' he said, as eight tanker lorries queued along the quay to take the regurgitated fish. 'It's all about *economics*.'

Thanking George and David for four days of good food and hospitality and an education in fishing, I shouldered my bag. A more superstitious man might have taken it as a sign that it was time to give up and head south. But as I passed the neighbouring quay I was heartened by the sight of a large cargo boat loading sand. It was a simple craft, just a long black hollowed-out trough overlooked by a boxy black and white wheelhouse, already half filled with builder's sand and bales of timber and barbed wire.

And on its hull were two magical words: *Shetland Trader*.

29

The Man who Loved the Sea

Aboard the *Shetland Trader*

Gratefully adrift on the undulating wastes of the North Sea, the man at the mess table was tucking into his plate of liver and gravy with the gusto of one who knows that each meal might be his last.

'I've got bone cancer, so it's a case of enjoy life while you can,' he said from behind his voluminous beard, sitting opposite me. 'It's spread to my head, my jaw, my lungs, my arms, my fingers.' He smiled sadly and held up the plump stump of his pinkie. 'They took this one off last time I was in hospital. Next time I'll be lucky if that's all I lose.'

There was no bitterness in his Tyneside banter, only a sort of sad resignation. After a working life on the ocean, Merchant Seaman Mike Shipley had ensconced himself in a £25 passenger cabin for a kind of nautical swansong. The *Shetland Trader* suited him perfectly: a no-frills operation, friendly, scruffy, doing exactly what the unpretentious name suggested. In the nicotine-stained mess room, a television quacked fuzzily in the corner, while the wall displayed a cartoon of someone trying to unblock a toilet with dynamite, alongside a faded letter from the RNLI thanking the crew for its contribution of £15.45. Not exactly the *QE2*. But to Mike she was perfect.

'Why would I want to go on a cruise ship? I've worked on them before, and it's all plastic and music and bridge, like a floating Butlins. And this way you don't have to get all dressed up for dinner.' He sprawled cheerfully in T-shirt and shorts, and a knotted red headscarf that put me in mind of a pirate or a hell's angel – though it was probably to hide the effects of chemotherapy. Now too ill for heavy work at sea, he had taken up watercolour painting.

'That's one of Mike's,' chipped in Brian, a white-haired lorry driver from Cheltenham, the only other passenger. He nodded over our heads to a framed watercolour painting of the *Shetland Trader*, smashing her way through a blue-green wave while seabirds danced above her. 'Pretty bloody good, eh?'

Mike grinned modestly. 'I'm crap at perspective, so I have to do them off photos. Did that one on my last trip – came for a week's holiday and ended up staying for six!'

After four days as resident Jonah, I had been looking forward to stowing away in the bedsit anonymity of my cabin until we docked in Lerwick. But my travelling companions had surprised me. 'I never told my friends where I was going on holiday,' chuckled Brian, composing postcards in rhyming couplets over a cooked breakfast. 'They'll never guess!'

This lesser-known vacation option was as curious to me as the sight of grown men writing down locomotive numbers on the end of station platforms – yet I had rarely seen a more contented tourist. Mike too, in spite of his illness, exuded a fierce happiness.

'The one place where barriers don't matter is at sea,' said Mike now, accepting a mug of tea from Rio the chef. 'It doesn't matter what nationality you're working with, everyone rubs along, you're part of a team. When you go to bed tonight you're trusting that someone up there is looking where we're going. You *have* to work together, because otherwise you can't go anywhere! I've never understood why it can't be the same on the land.'

It was indeed a remarkably international ship. I had watched Filipino and Indian crewmen seal the green hold covers, and met the Bangladeshi captain whose company poloshirt bore the logo *Friendly Little Fish in a Very Big Pond*. By the time we slipped out to sea, I was beginning to feel part of the club.

Mike's love affair with the ocean had begun early, kindled by a diligent geography teacher and stories about corsairs. 'It was something about roaming the wide open spaces, like a cowboy, except on water,' he recalled wistfully. 'Unfortunately my dad had me all lined up for A-levels in public school, so I had to be a bit devious about how I was going to do it. In the end I went on a school skiing trip to Norway and just didn't come back.' He grinned impishly at my raised eyebrows. 'I went every day to the shipping pool in Bergen until someone gave me a job, and I signed on as a galley boy on a Norwegian ship. I put myself down as seventeen but actually I was fifteen. The beauty of a cargo boat is that you get on them and you don't really know where you're going to go. I still don't know where I'm going and I'm fifty-nine! So I may not be mentioned on the board of honour at my old school – what were they going to write, *Galley Boy*?'

We all laughed, infected by his enthusiasm. 'I've been all over the world!' he said triumphantly, his eyes wide and wet, his mug quivering in mid-air. 'I've been up the Amazon to Manaus, where you round this corner and there's a magnificent opera house, slap bang in the middle of the jungle! I've been through pack ice – imagine someone running fingers down a blackboard, except a hundred times louder! And the colours of the sea . . .'

The sea had its dark side too. Working on an oil supply boat in 1988, he had witnessed the horror of Britain's worst ever oil rig disaster. 'I had to go to *Piper Alpha* two days after the disaster to pick up bodies. Just bits and pieces, really . . . The seas were still boiling around the rig. The captain had to pull back because otherwise the boat would have lost buoyancy and gone down too. Some of the guys are still traumatised by their memories. I got out soon after that – I had a heart attack – spent a lot more time at home with the wife.'

It was the first time Mike had mentioned a wife. I had assumed he was a roving bachelor. 'I've been married pretty much all the time,' he said, brightening again. 'The secret is to get the right wife – get that wrong and you've got no chance. Mine's pretty tolerant, bless her. You can take leave, but you never get the sea out of your system. You might last six months ashore and then you really miss it.'

He frowned suddenly, poked some tobacco into a chewed old pipe, lit it, took a puff. 'I've got to be home for my daughter's birthday next month. Then they're going to try something called "immuno-therapy" – once they've checked the results of the radio-therapy. It's worth a shot. If it doesn't work, there are no more chances for me.'

He smiled, reading my furrowed forehead, wanting no sympathy. 'I'm very fortunate. I've done what I wanted with my life, had a good crack at it. If I had it again I wouldn't change a thing. How many people can say that?'

Lying in my bunk that night, feeling the strange roll of gravity on my body, I traced the strands that linked me to Mike, to Stumpy the engineer, to the Captain on the bridge, a community bonded by necessity. *When you go to bed tonight you're trusting that some-*

one up there is looking where we're going. The thought warmed me. Suspended above the deep ocean, only an inch of metal from death at any moment, it was easier to remember what we increasingly tried to deny ashore: that human beings need each other.

30

Wild West of Norway

Lerwick

Lerwick was in shock. On the dockside, pale teenagers in baggy clothing sat around squinting as café owners dragged tables into the streets. In the tourist office perspiring Americans zipped off their Gore-Tex trousers at the knee and peered quizzically at pictures of Vikings against thundery skies. Even the basking seals seemed to be curling up at the ends like old sandwiches. Nobody could remember a summer like it. Shetland was good at dark winters and craggy, Nordic romance; unbroken sunshine was more of a conundrum.

'On a hot day you've got less lift, you see,' said Captain Rowan Greenwood, sipping a pint at the dockside pub. As the pilot of *Oscar Charlie*, the islands' air sea rescue helicopter, he much preferred storm-force gales to all this wilting sun. 'We need the air density to be high – wind gives us free air speed for the hover.'

A friend of a friend, Rowan had possibly the world's most glamorous and heroic job. 'It has its moments,' he agreed, modestly. 'But when you're hovering in total darkness in a force 9 gale, trying to drop your mate on to a boat that's pitching in a 40-foot swell, you do sometimes think: why didn't I become a librarian?'

I didn't believe a word of it. Rowan relished the rugged *north-ernness* of his posting as surely as anybody else in this furthest extremity of the United Kingdom. Geographically closer to Bergen and Torshavn than to Edinburgh, the hundred islands of the Shetlands were scattered across the empty blue of the map like the shards of a smashed flagon. Indeed, had King Christian I not pawned them to finance his daughter's marriage to James III of Scotland in 1469, we would have been sitting in the Western Isles of Norway, rather than the Northern Isles of Scotland.

The *Shetland Trader* had dropped me in Lerwick, just in time for the Aith rowing regatta – a ballsy 7-mile head-to-head in which Shetlanders raced their Nordic cousins from Denmark, Sweden and the Faeroe Islands in scaled-down wooden longships known as yoals. The landscape was wild and fertile, with little scatterings of red clapperboard houses overlooking sea lochs called voes. It wasn't clear from records whether the feared Norsemen originally took the islands by force or settled peacefully, but in the good-natured revelry of the previous night, it was obvious they were family now.

Today, after a boat trip out to the gannet colony on neigh-bouring Noss, I had spent a fruitless afternoon trying to blag a lift to Fair Isle, the most southerly of the group. The little ferry *Good Shepherd IV* was booked solid for the next week, and all the yachts in the harbour were bound for Scandinavia. I had wandered the dockside for hours before phoning Rowan for a drink, imagining that the local rescue pilot would have some good maritime con-tacts – if only those he had pulled out of the sea. 'Actually you don't often hear from the people you rescue – they're too embar-rassed,' he said now. 'Though funnily enough, my winchman bumped into one guy just down the road last week – remember Captain Calamity?'

I did. Captain Calamity, an eccentric sailor from Essex, had been the whipping boy of the tabloid silly season in 2001 when he attempted to circumnavigate the British Isles in a rowing boat fitted with a windsurfing sail. Mocked and lectured for weeks for wasting coastguard time and sailing inadvertently through an RAF Tornado bombing range, he had finally overturned in a force 9 gale, 50 miles off Shetland, which was when air sea rescue had first made his acquaintance on the end of a winch.

'You could always ask Captain Calamity to give you a lift,' joked Rowan. 'I hear he's got a new boat.'

31

Captain Calamity

Shetland

Stuart Hill lived above a carpentry workshop in a little village called Cunningsburgh, which straddled the main bus route south of Lerwick. The man who opened the door was not at all what I expected – the tabloid stories had painted him as a kind of hybrid between Captain Haddock and Ken Dodd. Instead, the calm, aqueous eyes and neat silvery beard put me in mind of a monk emerging from his cell.

He had been a little suspicious when I first phoned him, but agreed to meet me when I told him about my own journeyings, past and present. After all, someone who had pushed out into the Pacific on a bundle of reeds clearly had no room to criticise anybody else for recklessness. Even so, I decided not to broach the subject of a lift to Fair Isle until I had got the measure of the man.

'The Captain Calamity thing never bothered me,' he said now, ushering me into a small, wood-panelled flat. 'People pay thousands for that kind of brand recognition – and anybody who knows me knows I'm a good sailor.' He said this without pomposity, but as a statement of simple fact as he put the kettle on.

I glanced around the room. A couple of computers hummed

quietly on a workbench, while abstract prints and a reiki practitioner's certificate hung on the walls above piles of documents and a little balsa model of a sailing boat. It had the friendly, cluttered ambiance of an inventor's studio, with a view across fields and down towards the sea. On the bookshelves were yachting tales of Francis Chichester, *The Celestine Prophecy* and *Cooking in a Bedsitter*. On the computer screen, I noticed, was my own website. My host had been doing his homework.

'You must have come in for a bit of criticism yourself from what I've read,' he said, following my gaze. 'Setting off on a bundle of reeds . . .'

Evidently he saw me as a kindred spirit. 'Absolutely,' I said. 'They thought we were mad – but it was one of the safest vessels I've ever sailed on.'

'Same here,' said Stuart. '*Maximum Exposure* was probably the best equipped small boat of her size in the world – and I took her the length of Great Britain.'

He had first hit on the idea for his odyssey in Essex, where he had enjoyed windsurfing and pottering about in his metal rowing boat. It had been a difficult time. His internet company was looking shaky and he wasn't sure what he was going to do next. Then an idea popped into his head: *Why not sail around Britain?* Others might have been put off by the lack of a suitable boat, but Stuart was not the sort to let go of an idea once conceived, and he got to work with what he had in his garage. What emerged was a sort of hybrid – a technologically equipped, buoyancy enhanced 14-foot metal rowing boat with a windsurfing sail attached to the top.

'There's nothing better than ignorance to help you do something,' he told me cheerfully. 'If you don't know what you can't do then you can do absolutely anything.'

What he hadn't counted on was the effect this improbable little boat would have on a concerned public watching from the shore. When he finally set off, his steady progress along the coast of Norfolk generated a total of nine unsolicited lifeboat callouts and two attempted helicopter rescues. 'People were seeing what they thought was a windsurfer a mile offshore in fairly blowy conditions – and the coastguard must respond to public callouts. My first visitor aboard was a helicopter winchman.'

'That must have been awkward,' I said.

Stuart looked indignant at the memory. 'When he landed on the deck, I said *Hello. I haven't called you, but how are you?* He stayed and chatted and then went away again. And of course the press got hold of the story.'

His close encounter on the bombing range was harder to gloss over. 'I sailed fairly close to what I thought was a navigation marker,' he recalled, irritably. 'I did notice all these aircraft flying around above me but thought nothing of it. Then when I got to the Humber the coastguard said: 'We've been trying to contact you all morning. You've just sailed through the middle of a firing range.' It was on the chart in *tiny* black letters . . .'

Undaunted, he had tacked northwards in the teeth of stubborn headwinds, trying not to be discouraged by the saltwater sores, the vilification of the press and the haemorrhaging patience of his wife and two children. Anchoring each night to sleep beneath his specially designed roller-shelter, he felt the experiment itself was proving a success. The ingenious windsurfing rig was effective and flexible thanks to a system of home-made stays. 'It had three different electronic navigation systems on board. It was self-righting from any position. Unfortunately what I hadn't tested was self-righting from an inverted position with a full load . . .'

It was some months later that *Oscar Charlie* received the call to a stricken vessel 50 miles offshore. Clinging to his upturned boat, alone in mountainous seas, Stuart wrestled inwardly for a few minutes before calling the coastguards. 'Had I known that the next day would dawn bright and clear I could have made myself comfortable with a hammock in the upturned boat. But at the time it was a force 9, about 30-foot waves, it was getting dark and I had to make the decision. Am I going to be a hero or am I going to phone the rescue service?'

As he awaited the helicopter, he brooded over another call he'd received two weeks earlier, from his wife. 'She told me she had sold our flat, bought a flat in France and didn't particularly want me to come with her.'

'She left you?'

He nodded. 'So it was a crossroads in my life. When I arrived on shore I only had thirty pence and the clothes I stood up in. I thought: "Right then, Shetland is where I'm going to be."'

I wasn't sure whether to commiserate with the man, or shake him. He sensed my frustration. 'People asked me why I didn't try and persuade her to stay, but I don't really blame her. She'd put up with a lot. I miss my children, though.'

'You didn't get any money from your flat?'

He shrugged. 'My wife needed it more than me.'

The ensuing silence was interrupted by the doorbell. Stuart disappeared downstairs to answer it, and ushered in a woman in her fifties or sixties. She wore a red checked blouse, floral slacks and a slightly flustered expression as she shook my hand. 'This is Margaret,' said Stuart, throwing me a significant glance. I realised his was not so much a voyage as a life transplant. 'And, Margaret, this is Nick, a writer who likes boats. I've just been telling him how I ended up here.'

Margaret gave a shy smile. 'Stuart's made a lot of new friends here, haven't you? Anybody that comes here gets attached to the place and doesn't want to leave.'

Stuart nodded. 'I feel totally at home here, far more than if I went back to Essex. Up here, people have much more boating awareness. I was being stopped in the street and being shaken by the hand.'

'*I* never shook your hand or congratulated you,' clarified Margaret. 'And *I* never called you Captain Calamity – I called you Stuart.' She looked at me. 'I was never one for sailing.'

'You don't fancy sailing round Britain then?'

She chuckled. 'I don't think I'd even go round Shetland,' she said. 'My grandfathers knew the sea – they built a yoal that's in the museum. But none of us in Cunningsburgh would know how to sail properly now.'

'We've been on camping trips to the islands in *Gazelle* though, haven't we,' persisted Stuart.

'Yes,' nodded Margaret dutifully. 'Very nice.'

'*Gazelle?*' I sensed an opening. 'Is that your new boat?'

Stuart brightened. 'Do you fancy a sail?'

The slightly underinflated tyres of the shopping bike purred soothingly as I followed Stuart down deserted country lanes towards the sea. Margaret had politely declined the offer of a nautical outing and lent me her wheels. The little harbour was almost deserted when we got there, apart from a small boat unloading fish boxes. On the quay were the remains of *Maximum Exposure*; after Stuart's rescue she had been discovered by a Norwegian ship, still afloat in the Gulf Stream off Bergen, and brought back to Shetland, where scavengers systematically stripped her of her fittings. The once simple lines of a rowing boat were just visible below the steroidal bloating of the buoyancy, which had been built up around her to form deck cover. The vibrant red tiger stripes gave her the look of a gaudy cast-off now, her pink and yellow windsurfing rig lying absurdly at her side.

'The coastguard said they wanted a visible colour scheme,' said Stuart, fishing an empty Coke can from the pool of rainwater in her hull. 'I must admit I'm pretty tempted to do her up again. But I don't have the money just now.'

The more I heard, the more intrigued I was by what sustained him. He seemed an ascetic trapped in a suburban life, pushing off in an absurd coracle in search of something indefinable. I couldn't decide if I admired or pitied him.

'I don't mean to sound negative,' I ventured, after taking a few photographs of him in his *Maximum Exposure* baseball cap, 'but didn't you ever think the whole thing had been a complete disaster? I mean, you'd lost your boat, your business, your wife, your family, your home . . .'

He looked slightly offended. 'I've come to believe,' he said firmly, 'that whatever is happening right now is *just perfect*. At the time you may not be able to see the sense of it, but when you look back on it you can see the pattern of what is emerging for the future.' He struck off round the lagoon in the direction of a sleek racing boat lying at anchor, her three pontoons pointing into the wind like the prongs of a fork. '*Gazelle* was a good example. The week I was rescued I got a job in a fish factory, and a trimeran came up for sale in the local paper. I walked past her on the way to work. She'd been an insurance write-off in the round Britain race, and was going for an absurdly low price. I arranged to pay by instalments, two hundred a week – I was earning five hundred. Then I got an allergy to something in the fish factory, so I got a job in the carpentry shop instead. But I got exactly two hundred a week for that. I paid it off by Christmas. She goes like a rocket.'

I followed him, still puzzling over what he'd said. It seemed to me it would have been better if he had not been allergic to the fish factory. 'Ah,' he said, turning to me with a wise smile. 'But we don't always get what we're asking for – we get what we need.'

We squeezed into a little tub of a rowing boat and punted ourselves precariously out to *Gazelle*'s mooring. She had some fibreglass scarring on one of her pontoons, and what looked like a recent touch-up with lemon house paint, but she looked a fast boat. I decided to test out Stuart's theory.

'Think she'd get us to Fair Isle?'

'Easily,' he breezed. 'I've done it before. With a good wind I could probably get us there in a few hours.' He looked out over my shoulder. 'But not when it's foggy.'

Sure enough, a grey wall of mist was peering round the headland, sealing off the outer limits of the wide bay that lay before us, slowly erasing the rocks. He looked almost as disappointed as me. 'You could sleep on my couch tonight, and we could see how things look tomorrow. And in the meantime, there's nothing to stop us taking her out into the bay to catch some supper.'

I sheltered obediently in *Gazelle*'s long thin central cockpit while Stuart got her ready for launching. There was something attractively peaceful about his positive thinking which made me want to believe everything would work out. After all, I needed to get to Fair Isle – and who was to say the universe wouldn't conspire to get me there?

Stuart pulled the starter cord of *Gazelle*'s little outboard motor, and elicited a metallic thud. He tried again, with the same result. 'I hate engines,' he muttered.

'What's wrong?'

'I have absolutely no idea. But it'll certainly make leaving the harbour more interesting.' He pulled the sails up with furious determination.

I opened my mouth to say something, and then didn't. I cast off at the stern, and Stuart vindicated himself with one of the best displays of seamanship I had seen for some time, zigzagging expertly between moored boats under wind power alone, much as he must have done in the teeth of the north wind all those months. I was just beginning to relax when the boat juddered to a halt with a sickening crunch, throwing me chin-first against the rim of the cockpit.

'Shit,' said Stuart. 'I was just thinking it was about time to tack.' He peered over the side to where the daggerboard had hit a rock. He pulled it up slightly to ease us off, while I rubbed my chin. I was feeling suddenly nervous. 'Is the wind blowing in the right direction for getting us back in?' I asked with perhaps a little too much forced gaiety.

'I wouldn't be going out if it wasn't,' he said sharply. 'It's blowing straight back into harbour.'

'Great.' There was a long pause. 'And, er . . . did you say I might be able to borrow a life jacket?'

Once out of the harbour, the exhilaration of sailing took over. It was a speedy boat, slicing ever faster through the water as we trimmed the sails. Skuas wheeled overhead, and, as the bay opened out into charcoal shores and horizons smudged by mist, Captain Calamity gave out a satisfied sigh. 'What a place!' he said, shaking his head with a grin. 'I get up every morning and I think, *Bloody Hell, I live here!* Really, who could ask for more?' He unwound a fishing line from a lump of driftwood and dropped it over the stern.

Failure, I was coming to learn, did not feature in the Hill vocabulary. This was an attractive trait to a habitual worrier like me. Even now, I was choosing to focus on the broken outboard and the sudden grounding and the possibility that we would be engulfed by fog or unable to get back to shore. Stuart, on the other hand, was self-evidently rejoicing in his surroundings, living entirely in the present – while also keeping an eye on the tiller. I envied him.

'I find it strange that people revel in failure,' he agreed, when I admitted this. His own positivity had been instilled by a solitary childhood passion for building model aeroplanes. 'When your plane crashes it really doesn't matter because you can find out *why* it crashed and do it differently next time. If what I'm doing doesn't achieve what I set out to achieve, I can learn from it. So I can never fail.'

His parents had begged to differ, kept him at school till the age of twenty, trying in vain to get the requisite A levels for a university place. Instead, he went to work as a van driver for Victoria Wines. 'What does *qualification* mean?' he said now, as we scythed along. 'Grammatically, a qualification limits the meaning of a sentence. And that's what qualifications seem to do to people. When you become a lawyer it becomes impossible to think of yourself outside that definition. The whole of the education system is designed to fit people into employment, into the system. It's not designed to realise their full creativity.'

Stuart's career path, by contrast, was about as linear as a Jackson Pollock painting. From van driving he had progressed to welding, house conversion, double glazing, and his own shop-fitting business, which he lost when a big customer went bust. Picking himself up, he moved into an old forge in Suffolk and promptly taught himself the trade of village blacksmith. Within a few years his work was winning awards and on display in the Victoria & Albert Museum. 'It made me realise that whatever you do you can be the best in the world at it if you put your mind to it,' he said. 'Generally speaking, standards are not very high.' Yet by 1996 his blacksmith company was also sucked down the pan by a US bankruptcy, and it was time to dabble elsewhere: internet design, a reiki qualification ('I lost interest when it started to fall into a pattern'), a project to build a castle on Cyprus, followed by his foray into solo yachting and another crossroads. 'It's been an interesting experience to land here with nothing and have to find my way. It's totally a matter of attitude. I could have come here and looked at my life as a total disaster. I could have gone down the pub, got into drugs, gone on the streets, been a derelict – but I know it's a choice you make. If you allow yourself to be beaten by failure you'll never do anything.'

His eclectic interests and business plans had, if anything, multiplied since then: after the fish factory and the carpentry work, an entrepreneurial sideline in embroidered pocket handkerchiefs; an art website; and new plans to pioneer a new type of sailing boat using aeronautical principles in a boathouse made of straw bales.

'My complete ignorance enables me to believe that that can be done,' he smiled. 'Everybody knows that if you set your mind on something it will happen. It's got nothing to do with what you do – it's that your mind is acting as a magnet. It's a bit like when you get a new car and suddenly you notice all the other cars like that on the road. But it's more than that. You actually start to send out signals to the universe that start to attract the result you want. I book my car parking space in my head on the way to town and it's always there. I never even question it now. It's just interesting to watch, when you're aware of it . . .'

I pondered this as we goose-winged back through the harbour entrance. It was a kind of amalgam of predestination and chaos theory, exactly the sort of sleight of hand promulgated by certain brands of Christianity: God will answer your prayers, except when He doesn't, in which case it isn't God's will. Stuart didn't believe in God in any conventional religious sense, however, which was why he had adopted a Rolling Stones lyric: *You can't always get what you want, you get what you need.*

It was a sort of reverse paranoia – a conspiracy of goodness. And what was the result? A man who could easily have descended into dysfunctional self-pity had instead tacked through life with exhilarating verve, found new love and a new home on an island far from his starting point. A place of resurrection.

We never did catch any supper. The only thing Stuart reeled in was something called a piltock, which was apparently too bony to eat. But there was some leftover sausage in his fridge, and it was good. I never did get to Fair Isle with Captain Calamity – he'd forgotten about a prior engagement the following day. But that was *just perfect.*

Suddenly, I felt sure there'd be another way.

32

Magnetic Anomalies

Twitching on Fair Isle

The next morning I conducted a simple experiment. Boarding an early bus back to Lerwick, I decided to book my ride on a yacht in much the same way that Captain Calamity reserved his parking spaces. What did I have to lose? By the time I arrived on the quayside, I had convinced myself that somebody was waiting to offer me a lift. I simply had to find them. Striding on to the crowded pontoon with a kind of clenched optimism, I dropped my rucksack and cleared my throat.

'Excuse me – is anyone going to Fair Isle?'

Clearly nautical etiquette didn't accommodate serendipity. Three conversations stopped mid-flow and a Nordic-looking couple froze in their cockpit, breakfast bangers halfway to mouths. Most pennants were Scandinavian, which didn't bode well for a south-bound voyage. The 70 per cent sceptic in me began to flush heavily. Which was when a head popped up from behind a blue awning on one of the outermost yachts in the rafted layers.

'We are,' it said. 'Who's asking?'

Mike, Ken and Adam were on their way home to Moray after a

six-and-a-half-week trip to Iceland on a Bermuda sloop called
Reverie. They were professional men in their fifties with distinguished silvery hair and expensive sunglasses, and they nodded
genially enough as I explained my quest. 'I don't see why not,'
shrugged Mike, who owned the boat. 'We leave tomorrow morning at nine.'

The three men had made contact through a nautical website
after Mike's own mid-life divorce cast him adrift. 'Wife got the
house, I took the boat,' he shrugged, as we motored south the following morning. He had retired from banking some years ago, in
favour of boat repairs and building. 'I got to the point where I
could say *stuff the world, I want to get off.* This way I can move on if I
want. Next year I'm going to New Zealand.'

The two other men were quietly noncommittal on whether they
would be joining Mike in New Zealand. Adam retired below to
read his novel, while Ken gazed placidly out over the water, lost in
his own thoughts. His T-shirt bore the philosophical question: *If
a man speaks in a forest and no woman hears him, is he still wrong?*

Sumburgh Head appeared on our starboard side, its dark cliffs
mottled with yellow lichen, except where scrubby grass took root
on its scalp. We pitched and slid on strange tides as the Atlantic
met the North Sea in switchbacks of dark, foam-flecked water. It
was 21 miles between the tip of Shetland and Fair Isle. Ahead of
us the sea and sky mingled in misty grey, but there was no sign of
the recent fog. 'Visibility is about 10 miles today,' said Mike. 'So
we might just possibly get to see Fair Isle while still seeing
Shetland.'

A little while later he set the autohelm, an electrical device
which was clipped to the tiller and automatically compensated for
the pulling of wind and tide, steering us on a bearing of 200
degrees. That was the theory, anyway.

'Adam, try sitting on the other side for a moment, would you?' yelled Mike, suddenly, staring at the compass. 'We're going all over the place.'

Down in the cabin, Adam stood up without taking his eyes off his book, and deposited himself on the opposite bench. 'There you go!' said Mike presently. 'We're back on course. Every time you sit on that side we deviate! Now sit down there again?' Adam obeyed. 'There you go! We're deviating again! The compass on the locker behind you controls the autohelm. Have you got something metal on you?'

'Only my specs,' said Adam, mildly. He looked as if six and a half weeks at sea had been long enough.

'Must be the steel plate in your head!' quipped Mike.

Presently we put up the sails, and he turned off the autohelm altogether, replacing it with a wind-driven contraption which used a wide spatula of plywood and a finely balanced system of pulleys. We were making good time at 8 knots, though the larger seas gave the impression that most of our movement was up and down.

I tuned in and out of Mike's well-travelled ponderings as we rippled quietly on through a seascape of dark translucent dunes. 'When you see the rest of the world, you realise that this isolationist island mentality is doing a lot of damage . . . If the nationalists wanted to push for independence they should have done it thirty years ago – now they're just going to end up with less say over Britain, less subsidy and the oil reserves running out . . . The trouble is governments never think longer than five years ahead.'

His conversation wandered much like his boat, driven by passionate bursts of purpose only to be pulled sideways into strange detours. But then life was like that sometimes. If there was such a thing as an autopilot of the human heart, it seemed prone to magnetic anomalies which forced you to keep checking your course. Mike could see that New Zealand probably wasn't a long-term solution. 'Money won't last for ever,' he said. 'I'll probably need to do something again before long.'

The problem was identifying that *something* – knowing where to set your helm, what to settle upon. I had met many others like Mike on my trip – a scattered flotilla of secular seafaring hermits. Some, like Captain Calamity, had found a destination of sorts. The danger was that, like souls in limbo, you simply ended up circling forever.

We were not the first arrivals on Fair Isle that day. Small feathered immigrants, blown across angry seas, had reached these gnawed cliffs before us, to be spoken of in the hushed and reverent manner of visiting celebrities. Walking up from the little harbour towards the Bird Observatory – also the island's only hostel – I was hailed by a portly gentleman sitting on the steps.

'Saw a lanceolated warbler this morning!' he said proudly, waving an unlit roll-up in his pudgy fingers. He had a red face, with a scar on the end of his nose, and reminded me of a senior and battle-wounded walrus. I sat down beside him.

'Great!' I said, propping my bag against the steps. 'But I'm afraid I'm not really a bird watcher . . .'

'It's a subspecies of the grasshopper warbler,' he said, kindly, lighting his cigarette. 'The Pallas's grasshopper warbler is here too. Pechora pipits are pretty regular. The great snipe as well. People moan that we don't have beautiful birds like they have in the Caribbean. But have you ever seen a bullfinch? Beautiful bird! The Lancashire warbler here weighs 5.3 grammes. Think of that!'

John was a retired policeman from Sussex, a proud member of the British Ornothological Union. This was his seventh visit. Like the birds, he had flown in, drawn by the anomalous wildlife of this three-and-a-half-mile long speck in the ocean. Unlike them, he relied on the pilot to get him here from Shetland.

'How is it that birds find their way back here?'

'It's a magnetic thing, I think. Nobody knows for sure. I think they navigate by the stars. After a clear night here, a lot of the birds are gone. A cloudy night and they'll stop over. But that doesn't account for the rarities. It's a mystery why they're here and not in Shetland.'

The observatory warden demystified things a little. 'The rare birds that come here are basically blown off course,' he said, checking me in to the visitors' book. 'They're migrating from Scandinavia along the edge of the Continent, blown here by bad weather. They're often very tired, and they stay two or three days to recuperate.' He showed me up to my bunk in the men's dorm. 'How many nights do you think you'll be staying?'

'As long as it takes to catch a lift to Orkney.'

He shook his head. 'You'll not get to Orkney by boat from here. You'd need to go back to Lerwick and get a ferry direct from there.'

'Surely you get small vessels calling in?'

'The one you arrived on is the first we've had in days. Usually they're heading for Norway. You could be waiting a while.'

I went for a walk across the island, following a deserted single-track road through the slanting evening sunshine, enjoying the gentle rustling of reeds in the wind. *Everything that happens is just perfect.* There was nothing I could do about the lack of a boat, so it was a perfect opportunity to surrender to Captain Calamity's vision of life and enjoy the moment. A rabbit scuttered from behind a bush and dashed along the road before me, his white tail flashing. Someone had built long chicken-wire funnels along the roadside ditches, presumably to catch birds flying along them. If you kept things open-ended you never knew what might fly in.

*

Back at the observatory I found two men lurking suspiciously in the entrance hall. With their bushy beards, peaked caps, waxed jackets and chunky telephoto lenses slung over their shoulders like rifles, they could have been Cuban special operatives. They talked in low voices, scrutinising their little notebooks together, and disappeared disdainfully upstairs when I wished them a good evening.

Things got odder as the night wore on. Towards midnight, a scratchy, cackling noise wafted across from the field by the clifftop. On closer investigation, it was coming from a black box about the size of a bedside cabinet which was sitting behind what looked like a volleyball net.

'What you're hearing is a tape recording of a breeding colony of storm petrels,' whispered Alan Bull, the chief ranger, standing in the darkness with a little huddle of guests. 'Any minute now, it'll lure us a catch.' Sure enough, the net suddenly quivered and sagged. Alan retrieved the fluttering shape of the night's first bird — a small black storm petrel with a white tail stripe and a musky smell of fish oil. He brought it into the ringing room in a barn away from the lure, and clipped an identifying ring on its leg.

'Are they rare?'

Alan shook his head. 'I've ringed as many as two hundred and thirty-two in one night before.'

I held the next bird while Alan ringed it. I felt the heart beating between my hands, the tiny warmth. The feet were webbed, for pattering along the tops of waves, and the hooked beak had a tube at its top, where the bird ejected the salt from the seawater, which dripped down the side.

'They convert all their fat to stomach oil so they can regurgitate to feed their young,' said Alan. 'It tastes as horrible as cod liver oil. I should know, I've swallowed some. Since then I've started closing my mouth while taking them out of the net.'

John took a turn holding the bird next, then an Israeli woman and her son. I could see no sign of the Cuban operatives.

Alan smiled. 'They're the serious ones – the twitchers.'

'So is John a twitcher?'

'No, he's a birdwatcher.'

'What's the difference?'

'Well,' said Alan, keeping his voice down. 'A birdwatcher is delighted to see anything that pops up in front of him. He loves being in nature, watching wildlife. A twitcher, on the other hand, is only interested in rare birds. He ticks them off on a list. Whenever the phone rings with a rare sighting, he gives a nervous twitch. A twitcher will drive from here to the Scilly Isles just to tick off a rare bird.'

'And what if the bird leaves half an hour before he arrives?'

Alan smirked. 'That's known as a dip.'

'A dip in his week, I guess.'

'And a dip in his bank balance.'

I woke in bright sunshine to discover that I had missed the dawn walk around the nets. I didn't particularly mind: I aspired to be a watcher rather than a twitcher. John wandered in looking very pleased with himself. They had found a meadow pipit and some wheatears, which had already been brought back in a cotton bag, ringed and released. 'Almost caught a twite today too.'

To help even out the odds a little, the observatory ran a kind of early-warning system for the rarest birds, so that groups of watchers could be rushed by van to different parts of the island before they flew away. That was how I came to be barrelling along the road with Alan later that morning – though I had spotted a different sort of rare breed. At the south end of the island, a red helicopter was shuttling between the lighthouse and a large white ship anchored in the bay.

A few men were standing around wearing luminous orange jumpsuits and Mickey Mouse ears, which turned out, on closer inspection, to be ear mufflers. They flipped them into place whenever the red helicopter flew in, and clipped a bag of old fire extinguishers to the dangling winch. Having made a hurried call to the Northern Lighthouse Board HQ in Edinburgh that morning, I now walked up to the largest orange man, who grinned and thrust a faxed waiver form in front of me: 'You're welcome aboard if you sign this.'

Pharos wasn't quite as rare as a Scops owl, but she wasn't far off. By sheer coincidence, I was on Fair Isle on the only day of the year when she was making her maintenance call and able to offer me a lift to her next destination – which, by still more gratuitous coincidence, was Orkney.

33

The Ladies' Landing

To Orkney

The reflected sun shimmied across the bay as the helicopter wheeled round towards the white ship. For three minutes there was only adrenalin and pale blue air and the sense of weightlessness. We swooped down towards the white 'H' and the word PHAROS inscribed on the helideck, and presently the rotor whine began to tail off. One of the men hurried me out of my headphones and harness and away into a lounge where I watched through a window as men secured the helicopter with straps.

Up on the bridge the captain, Tom Moffat, welcomed me aboard with quiet pride. It was a modern, comfortable ship with a distinguished heritage. A framed display showed a long history of lighthouse tenders, including a number of different *Pharos*es, *Skerryvore*, *Regent*, *Prince of Wales* and an iron paddle steamer called *Terrible*, which lived up to its name by breaking its mooring and beaching itself in 1881. The present incumbent, just under 80 metres long from prow to helideck, balanced its technological modernity with a set of fruit knives once belonging to Sir Walter Scott.

The crew worked four weeks on, four weeks off, twenty-four aboard at any one time, visiting the most remote of the 201 lighthouses controlled by the Northern Lighthouse Board, from the Solway Firth to the Isle of Man. In the old days they rowed lighthouse keepers on and off duty. Nowadays the lighthouses were all automatic, controlled by computer from an office in Edinburgh. *Pharos*'s role was to maintain equipment and administer generator fuel, though even this would soon be unnecessary as the NLB slowly converted them all to solar power.

'Fair Isle South was the last to lose its keeper a few years back,' said Captain Moffat, nodding back over his shoulder towards the squat white tower on the hillside. 'It's sad to think of a whole profession becoming redundant. But the world moves on and it's progress, cost efficiency, technology.' He said this without sarcasm, but a couple of his deputies laughed over their map tables.

'You had what we call a "ladies' landing" today,' he added. 'But when the weather gets up it can be a little trickier.'

'I expect you've got some kind of system to stop the helicopter crashing into the deck when there's a heavy swell?'

'Yes,' said the captain with a half-smile. 'It's called the pilot.'

Over the next few hours, Orkney insinuated itself gently over the horizon, offering first North Ronaldsay, then the north-western tip of Sanday, in pencil-thin wisps of fertile farmland. The charts showed shreds of land torn off the more southerly main island – sixty-seven islands in all, only a third of them inhabited. Unlike the jagged crags of Shetland, they seemed almost flush with the ocean around them, as if the land was plotted to match the two dimensions of the map.

'It can be strange sailing down here,' agreed Tom, peering over the bows. 'You actually see the houses on the horizon before you see what they're standing on.' At the tip of each pancake-flat island a lighthouse rose up to distinguish it, painted in vertical or horizontal stripes like sticks of seaside rock.

The engines quietened to faint vibration as we slowed to take position off Sanday's Start Point. They were quickly replaced by the rising whine of rotors. The helicopter rose from the flight deck, its rounded glass cockpit bulging like the eyes of a dragon-fly. It hovered for a moment, then dipped sideways and away, its shadow sharp on a burnished copper ocean. It wasn't the weather for lighthouses, I thought, remembering the famous photographs of Atlantic outposts buffeted by vast waves. But then it wasn't quite the same without a keeper, either – that wink of human contact across dark seas. I wondered what had become of them all.

'Retired mainly,' said Colin, the bosun, over a mug of tea that afternoon. He evidently preferred the modern helicopter drops to the tricky matter of getting keepers and supplies on to landing stages from a small boat in a huge swell. 'It was quite dangerous really. Years back, we were at the west side landing at the Flanans, we'd just got the relief finished when a great wall of sea came round the corner. I thought: "This is my time. Nobody is going to come out of this lot alive." But with the skill of the coxswain, everybody was okay, even though we took a great wall of water over the top. The captain was that relieved to see us all back that he took us all up to the bridge and gave us a dram.'

Colin was Orcadian, like his friend Jimmy, the ship's carpenter, known affectionately as 'the wood butcher'. Their luminous orange jumpsuits clashed enthusiastically with their sunburned faces as we sat on the aft deck. 'Worst thing about this job is we're away for twenty-eight days at a time,' said Colin. 'I've missed five weddings this year!'

Jimmy was counting the days. 'I'm going to Norway when I get on leave, two weeks on Thursday.' Like Shetlanders, Orcadians considered themselves predominantly Scandinavian, though their land had been pawned to Scotland in the same botched dowry arrangement as Shetland.

'If you ask an Orcadian if he's Scottish, he'll say no, he's Orcadian.' said Jimmy. 'You'll find us very friendly, but a bit reserved. We don't shout a lot about anything – apart from a few Kirkwall folk.'

Kirkwall, I gathered, was too big for its boots. Technically the capital of Orkney, it was looked down upon by lighthouse men in much the same way that Glaswegians viewed Edinburgh. Seamen favoured Stromness, the rival port on the far side of Orkney's main island, an altogether earthier place where adventurers and whalers once set forth for the Arctic.

Later, we watched Kirkwall materialising from the dying evening. The capital lay clustered around a low hill, the spire of its cathedral beckoning beyond a row of austere waterfront buildings. Patchwork fields stretched out around it in rolling greens and browns.

'Where are you planning on going next?' asked Colin, as he got up to take his position for docking.

I knew there was a Kirkwall ferry to Aberdeen at the end of the week, but in the meantime I wanted nothing more than to follow whatever crossed my path. I watched a beacon winking on and off at the end of the dock, and had an idea.

'Colin, where would I find the last lighthouse keeper in Scotland?'

34

The Last Lighthouse Keeper in Scotland

In Stromness

Stromness hunkered on a hillside, its old fishing cottages close enough to the water to get sea spray through their parlour windows. I had taken the bus from Kirkwall that morning, after spending the night in *Pharos'* guest cabin. It was a short journey across the main island, through a treeless landscape of rolling farmland where the corn moved in waves. Two centuries ago the town's narrow lanes would have been full of whalers and agents recruiting for the Hudson's Bay Company. Today it was mainly tourists and the occasional car, edging along the winding streets and forcing pedestrians into doorways.

Angus Hutchison's grey pebbledash house was the antithesis of a lighthouse. Packed in among a maze of identical grey homes on the far side of the bay, it seemed no place for a hermit.

'People think you had to be a loner to be a lighthouse keeper,' said the ruddy, jovial man who opened the door. 'But in fact the opposite is true: you had to mix easily, work out what made your colleagues tick.'

He was a solid, imposing man with a Roman nose and a dry, enveloping handshake. There was nothing retiring about him. After forty years in various lighthouses around Britain – Wester Ross, Sule Skerry, Wick, Stroma, the Isle of Man, finally Fair Isle – he had learned to rub along with almost anybody.

'There were spasmodic blow-ups, but usually they passed over if you gave people a bit of space.' Not always, however. Keepers had served in pairs until a notorious case at Little Ross in Wigtownshire in the sixties, he told me, when relations had got so bad that one had shot the other dead. 'That's when they brought in the minimum staffing level of three.'

His personal low point was a stint on the Isle of Man. 'I had three years with ME in the days before they diagnosed it, and I just couldn't take the mental strain. I had a breakdown and I'd have ended up at the funny farm if it wasn't for my darling wife here.' Yvonne nodded tactfully, coming through from the kitchen with tea. 'I could have stayed on the Isle of Man forever, me,' she said wistfully, remembering one of the few land-based postings on which wives had been allowed to accompany their husbands. 'It was wonderful. There were palm trees!'

On 'rock' stations, Angus had worked one month on, one month off, leaving his family behind as his father, grandfather and great-grandfather had all left theirs. 'Mind you, my wife never had to drive me out of the house with a stick the day I had to go back to the lighthouse. I loved that job. It was like a second family out there. Always something to be getting on with – whitewashing the outside of the towers, keeping the light in working order, playing darts – and always aware of the force of nature.' He grew wistful. 'Aye, you saw it in all its glory out there, in a beautiful sunset or in a raging storm – both impressive in their own way . . .'

He had descended the ninety-three steps of Fair Isle South

Lighthouse for the last time in April 1998. It had been a big deal in the media — a ceremonial unveiling of a plaque by the Princess Royal, ending a two-hundred-year-old tradition of manned lights, many of them built by engineering ancestors of Robert Louis Stevenson.

Beneath the heritage and pomp, it seemed to signal something unsettling. The end of the quintessential man in a Fair Isle jersey tending the beacon as the storm raged outside. A symbol of people looking out for each other.

'It was a very emotional time for me. I fought against it at the time and I still think it was a bad move. Nobody can argue that the technology isn't dependable, but there's no human presence any more — I think that's what most mariners would regret.'

He took a sip of tea. 'I mean, without a pair of human eyes, who's watching Scotland's shores?'

35

Viking Graffiti

To Skara Brae

The following morning I went in search of a bicycle. I followed a signpost down an alley into a deserted backyard, where a note had been pinned to a chair: 'Sorry we have gone away. If you want a bike, just take one and leave money in the envelope.' I almost laughed out loud at this open-spirited and slightly cheeky way of running a business. It was an act of gratuitous trust – and, like most such acts, it made me trust life a little more in return. I chose a reasonable looking road bike from the pile, put my money in the envelope and headed east out of the town. It was a sunny, breezy morning, and the island that opened up before me was gently hilly, bruised purple with heather and pooled with lochs and inlets. As I stood up on the pedals I found myself smiling.

Skara Brae was 'Northern Europe's Best Preserved Neolithic Village', a five-thousand-year-old complex of homes half buried on the edge of the Bay of Skaill. The local laird had discovered it in 1850, when a ferocious winter storm scalped the turf from a sand dune, revealing how families lived in the age before the Pyramids or Stonehenge.

Joining the wind-blasted procession of tourists around the carefully marked paths, I was intrigued to see that each of the little houses was laid out along similar lines, like a Neolithic Barratt Homes estate, complete with matching furniture. A stone dresser stood opposite the doorway like a mantelpiece for displaying family objects; a fireplace was in the middle of the floor, and round the walls were the frames of beds, in some cases with little cabinets built into the walls – all of it hewn from blocks of stones. It made *The Flintstones* look remarkably well researched. There was one communal workshop, but otherwise the concept of family privacy seemed to be surprisingly well developed. At least one of the houses had a sort of built-in safe, a hidden chamber behind the mantelpiece accessible only by crawling underneath. Who were they afraid of: other tribespeople or their own neighbours? It was impossible to know.

The Ring of Brodgar, an hour's cycle further south, was rather more open-access: a vast configuration of stone slabs standing below the stretched sky. Raised a few centuries after the abandonment of Skara Brae for reasons nobody has yet fathomed, it seemed to elevate the eye away from the protected hearth to the stretched horizon. I wandered around the circle, trying to imagine who had come here and for what reason. Astronomical observations? Sacred rites? Community meetings? Or was it, as local legend had it, the remains of ancient giants turned to stone in the midst of a circle dance? There were twenty-seven out of an original sixty still in formation, the rock blotched with lichen and weathered in layers like choux pastry. Had this huge project succeeded in drawing frightened villagers out into the wider community? Or were the stones simply the start of manipulation by powerful religious leaders, evidence of an elite society which had simply worked out how to command the proles?

'We will never know what they mean,' wrote the Orcadian poet

George Mackay Brown. 'I am making marks with a pen and paper that will have no meaning five thousand years from now. A mystery abides . . . We move from silence into silence.'

I ate my lunch with my back to a slab, pondering a couple of etchings in particular: 'Manchester UFC' and 'Gerald 1953'. I pictured Gerald, a fifties geek, standing uncomprehendingly before this five-thousand-year-old mystery, and seizing on the only thing he could think of which might allow him to last as long as the rock.

The Vikings hadn't been much more original. Further down the road, in the middle of a field, the inner walls of the intricate Neolithic burial chamber of Maeshowe were scored with runic graffiti left by a group of eleventh-century Century Nordic vandals. At the end of a narrow entrance tunnel, carefully orientated by the architect to light up with the setting sun of a winter solstice, our guide deciphered such profound messages as 'Thorni fucked, Helgi carved'. Which at least gave some idea how snowbound Danes whiled away their time. 'Ingigerth is the most beautiful of women' seemed almost romantic by contrast, until I noticed the accompanying carving of a slavering dog. You could almost hear the bone-headed guffaws of Vikings echoing in the semi-darkness.

So much had changed, and so little. In five millennia, the earth had shifted on its axis just enough to send the Maeshowe winter solstice sunbeam a few inches across the wall of a tomb. And still we struggled to carve out our significance on this mottled planet. I crawled out into the warm summer's evening and cycled back to Stromness feeling smaller than usual under the scarlet skies.

36

The Man who Told
the Truth

On Scapa Flow

Orcadians had almost as many words for wind as the Inuit have for snow: from the light breath of 'kuil', through a tirl, a gurl, a gushel, a hushle, a skolder, a skuther and a gouster, right up to the wonderfully onomatopoeic howl of the 'skreevar' or 'katrizper'. But even Orkney ran out of words for the gales of 1952 and 1953.

'I've never known anything like it before or since,' said Len Wilson, sitting at the helm of his boat. 'The anemometer broke at 120 mph, so we don't know how high it got.'

We were hugging the southern mainland shore in Len's elegant home-built sailing yoal *Gremsa*, heading east through Orkney's vast natural harbour of Scapa Flow, where dive boats bobbed above the wrecks of battleships. I had needed a lift to catch the night ferry from Kirkwall to Aberdeen, and this white-haired Orcadian was throwing in an island history lesson to boot. Today the elements ruffled only the sunlit water, the wind barely strong enough to fill our terracotta sails. But back in the fifties, whole hen houses had been blown out to sea, where fishermen reported finding them floating like arks, their occupants clucking in terror. The sea walls in both Kirkwall and Stromness were broken, windows shattered and roofing slates tumbled in the streets.

'The great gale of January '52 took part of that roof off, and it's got more broken down ever since,' said Len, pointing to the hollow and desolate shell of a building standing in a field overlooking the foreshore. 'You'd hardly believe it, but that's the Hall of Clestrain, birthplace of John Rae.'

John Rae was Britain's most undervalued Arctic explorer. I had only learned of his existence the previous afternoon at Stromness Museum, and yet his achievements towered above those of many of his more famous Victorian contemporaries. Starting his career as a surgeon with the Hudson's Bay Company, he was the first to identify the final link in the elusive Northwest Passage between Atlantic and Pacific, a fact Amundsen acknowledged after he more famously completed the voyage in 1905.

Unfortunately, Rae's most sensational achievement also ensured his exclusion from Establishment halls of fame. In 1854, he had made the unfortunate career move of discovering the fate of the Franklin expedition, which had set off some years earlier with 134 men in search of the Northwest Passage. After two arduous overland searches, Rae heard eyewitness reports from Inuit trackers who had found both bodies and relics of the expedition. 'From the mutilated state of many of the bodies and the contents of the kettles,' he wrote, 'it is evident that our wretched Countrymen had been driven to the last dread alternative – cannibalism – as a means of prolonging existence.'

The vitriol of the Establishment inevitably sprayed forth. Lady Jane Franklin waged a nineteenth-century media war on the man who had dared to impugn the reputation of her explorer husband, enlisting the help of Charles Dickens who found it unthinkable that the English Navy 'would or could in any extremity of hunger, alleviate that pains of starvation by this horrible means'.

'It was a classic case of shoot the messenger,' said Len, as the ramshackle Hall of Clestrain slipped by. Ironically, it was Rae's particular strengths in the Arctic that proved his Achilles' heel in the profoundly racist colonial world of nineteenth-century London. He had learned his tracking and survival skills from Cree Indians and Inuit, who called him Aglooka ('he who takes long strides') in recognition of his expertise with snowshoes, on which he covered 1200 miles over two months in 1844–5. But his willingness to trust the eyewitness reports of 'Esquimaux savages' ensured he never received the recognition he deserved – though later discoveries confirmed their story. He died in 1893, still wilfully misunderstood by people who were not yet ready to fraternise with those they feared.

'He showed the importance of treating strangers with respect and meeting them with an open mind,' said Len, who was campaigning with fellow Orcadians to restore the family seat as a maritime museum. 'It was not the done thing in Victorian Britain, but it was the key to his success. It's a sad reflection on humanity that people blind themselves to unpalatable truths. I suspect Rae didn't know the effect his words would have – he'd been brought up in Orkney and spent most of his adult life in the Canadian wilderness – but I like to believe that he'd have told the truth anyway. As we all should!'

I found Rae an interesting counterpoint to Cormac of the Sea: one failing in his search for answers, the other harried for bringing answers nobody wanted to hear. It would be heartening to think that John Rae was simply ahead of his time, that, had he travelled now, he would have been fêted as the hero he was, not tamed or crucified. But every age had its unpalatable truths. I suspected we had simply moved on to different certainties.

It was late afternoon by the time we coasted alongside the stone quay at Holm. I thanked Len and dragged my bag towards the bus stop, still pondering the day's discussion. Back in Kirkwall, with time to kill before the ferry to Aberdeen, I wandered into St Magnus' Cathedral. It was a spectacular red sandstone building which seemed almost too portentous for the friendly lanes and houses of the island capital. The air was cool and dimly lit by evening sun falling through stained-glass windows.

I wandered down an aisle in search of someone I felt I almost knew. I had half expected to find him striding forth in snowshoes, but he was reclining – not in death, but with his fur-cuffed sleeves thrown casually behind his head, a rifle at his side, an open book lying on top of a bearskin rug, as if on a Sunday picnic. In his stone memorial, if not in his life, Dr John Rae appeared to have found a contingent sort of peacefulness which a thousand other restless wanderers lacked. His relaxed expression seemed to say: *You may never find the answers you sought – so why not enjoy the journey?*

37

Ban the Beggars

Aberdeen

I woke to the quacking of the ferry tannoy, my mouth like sawdust. Gathering my bedding from the floor of the ship's cinema, I joined herds of dishevelled passengers shuffling towards the off-ramp. *Aberdeen.* Early morning sunlight sliced great swathes of shadow from the cranes and ships, and lit the condensation of my breath. Summer would soon be sliding into autumn.

Oil rig supply vessels dwarfed the wharfside sheds, and fishing boats were double parked around a long, low fish market. It was only just past 7 a.m., but already the sounds of car horns and generators were breaking the stillness of the chilled air. I skirted the docks and went in search of a café where I could slowly resuscitate myself with caffeine.

Aberdeen didn't look like a city that had hit the oil jackpot. Far from exuding the heady whiff of black gold, its austere granite buildings seemed narrow-eyed with suspicion, warning that the good times couldn't last forever. 'BAN THE BEGGARS' ran the front page headline in the local paper. 'We launch bid to clear conmen off our streets'. A fearless investigative reporter was out to end the 'emotional blackmail' after announcing that 70 per cent of beggars had homes. A Tory councillor was quoted in support: 'They give the perception Aberdeen is down at heel,' he said. 'We have to stop it.' No wonder they called it the Granite City.

I spent the morning wandering around perimeter fences trying not to look like a beggar. In one sense, of course, that's exactly what I was. I had been more or less travelling on the generosity of my fellow humans since I left home a few months beforehand. It hadn't occurred to me that this was a demeaning exercise for either party – quite the reverse. But a cloud had passed over the day. Was it a flicker of contempt I saw on the face of the harbour master when I asked permission to leave my bags in his office? I caught my reflection in the window of a dive shop and saw an unshaven drifter with bed hair.

Stay positive. I gave myself an aim – to get nearly 50 miles down the coast to Arbroath for something called Sea Fest by the following evening. Surely it couldn't be that difficult from a major port? I visited the fishing wharves, the tugboat station, the RNLI lifeboat centre. I phoned the navy, customs and fishery protection. No luck. The day filtered quietly away. As a last resort, I found a car parked with a kayak on its roof, and left a note under the windscreen wiper asking if the owners 'fancied coming for a paddle'. Like hell they did.

Sitting on a park bench watching the offices emptying into the pubs at the end of the afternoon, I realised *I* wouldn't have given me a lift either. God knows how real beggars held themselves together day after day. I wondered irritably how Captain Calamity might have coped with the situation, or my Buddhist friend from Findhorn . . .

I was on my ninth inhale, trying to focus on the breath in my nostrils, when the text came through. It was my brother Mark, writing to alert me to the early arrival of a small boy named Samuel Luis Thorpe-Calderon at exactly 4.15 p.m. that afternoon. I was an uncle! The realisation fell on me like a blessing. It made me think of home, and Ali, and how much I wanted to complete my journey. It was something that travel could never rival, this innate belonging to those who knew you best.

I still had no lift. But something would come up. And in the meantime, I was the happiest of beggars, alive and beloved and connected to the world.

38

Mick Jagger's Dungarees

To Arbroath

The following morning was to prove as surreal as the previous one had been static. After a last-minute phone tip-off, I found myself alone on a cliff top on the outskirts of Aberdeen surveying a wrecker's yard full of abandoned orange lifeboats. It looked like the setting for the kind of dream a yachtsman might share with his analyst, and it didn't help my confidence that I was waiting there for a lift from a mysterious organisation called International Rescue. Wasn't that the outfit run by the puppets in *Thunderbirds*? I was beginning to suspect that my local informant had been playing an elaborate practical joke on me when a twin-engined rib roared into the bay below me.

'Actually, it's Maritime Rescue International,' said the chiselled man at the wheel, who looked not unlike Virgil as his two uniformed cohorts helped me aboard. 'Now hold on . . .'

The noise of the engine was too great to permit further conversation, so I just sat and enjoyed the addictive rush of speed as the boat skittered along the surface on its customary Saturday morning training run. The sea was spearmint blue, the towering granite stacks flecked with grass and guano, and the skies brushed with light cirrus clouds. We flew across the surface, spraying pearls. I still had not properly established who these good Samaritans actually *were* when they dropped me in a little fishing village and disappeared with the modest waves of super-heroes.

With 25 miles remaining to Arbroath, the little village of Gourdon looked distinctly unlike a transport hub. I counted two leisure boats at moorings, one of them semi-submerged. My best hope of leaving the place that day – possibly that week – was a fishing boat called *Vivid*, on which a man was quietly filleting lemon sole. He was a rotund, amiable fellow with curly hair and fish-stained dungarees, and he said I could have a lift as far as Montrose – another 10 miles down the coast – if I didn't mind waiting for the skipper to wake up.

'And, um, when will that be?'

'He's only just gone to bed. But you're welcome to come back to my house for a cuppa . . .'

Several hours and cups of tea later, I had met Peter's ninety-three-year-old mother, heard an intricate set of coincidences linking them to the *Titanic*, and pieced together a biography from his prized collection of television clips about fishing. 'That's me aged fifteen now,' he would say, freeze-framing some cine footage of a bobble-hatted youth stacking fish boxes in the corner of the screen. 'And this next one is me on *Weir's Way* in the seventies . . .'

Somehow it was late afternoon by the time we got to the final morsel of TV history, in which my host could be glimpsed aboard a pitching trawler behind a rather green-looking celebrity seafood chef, Nick Nairn. 'He was a bit ill, right enough,' said Peter happily. 'It wasn't the best weather for it. The man skippering is my brother.'

'I wonder,' I said quickly, nudging at my window of opportunity.

'Do you think he might nearly be ready to go to Montrose . . .?'

It was almost 7 p.m. by the time we rumbled level with Montrose pier. Peter's animated conversation had continued for most of the voyage, and I felt I had known him for years, if only from his fleeting appearances at the edge of others' lives. His finale was the story of the time Mick Jagger tried to buy his dungarees.

'I was repainting a boat on the beach, and he just walked up to me,' he said. 'Just like these ones they were – all covered in fish and shite – but he said that made them all the more fashionable.'

'Are you sure it was Mick Jagger?'

'God's honest truth! It was that time in the sixties when dungarees were right fashionable! He was offering good money!'

'So did you sell them?'

A grin spread across his face. 'Course I didn't! I was *wearing* them!'

My next lift was waiting even as I arrived on Montrose dock. The skipper of *Tudor Quest* scrutinised me like a man in a Jag watching his passenger arriving in a dumper truck – but agreed to have me aboard anyway. I had spent all of five minutes ashore. 'Longer coils, please!' he said, starting the engine immediately as I made a hash of gathering his mooring lines. 'Now bring in the fenders!'

Quietly authoritative, with curly ginger hair and a sun-tanned face, Jeremy Taylor was, as it turned out, the rear commodore of Royal Forth Yacht Club, and was in a hurry to get back to his girl-friend. But he seemed to forgive my sloppy nautical habits, and even shared his meatballs and carrots with me as we sailed south under a darkening crimson sky. He wasn't planning to stop in Abroath himself, but seemed to relish the challenge of transferring me to a boat that was, despite the fact that we were half a mile off-shore. By 10.30 I was waving him off into the darkness from the handrail of an obliging yacht called *Braveheart*, feeling dizzy with change as we headed inland towards dancing lights and snatches of ceilidh music. It was the fourth vessel I had boarded since I had woken up this morning in Aberdeen and her skipper assured me that a bed was awaiting me on a fifth when we reached the shore.

I thanked him profusely, feeling my limbs growing pleasantly heavy as the sea walls of Arbroath opened up before us. It was a mystery to me why some days paid off and others didn't. Somehow the trick was to savour them all.

39

The Feeling Wire

Arbroath to Largo

Arbroath was famous for smoked haddock and the most important document in Scottish history. Both were evident at the waterfront fair the following day. Wandering among the candyfloss sellers in the bright sunshine, I met a 6-foot kipper offering samples of Arbroath smokie, followed by a knackered-looking Robert the Bruce. 'I was driving my taxi till four in the morning,' muttered the king, sweating beneath his velvet cloak at the Arbroath Abbey Pageant Society stall. 'Then I had to be back down here at nine . . .'

The real Robert the Bruce had a much bigger headache back in 1320. Having routed the English at the Battle of Bannockburn in 1314, he was still having problems getting his expansionist southern neighbours to recognise him as King of the Scots – which was why he had instructed the Abbot of Arbroath to draft a letter to the Pope. Almost seven centuries later the Declaration of Arbroath, bearing the names of eight earls, thirty-one barons and the 'whole community of the realm of Scotland', remained famous not so much for its rousing support for the king as for its revolutionary caveat:

> Yet if he [Bruce] should give up what he has begun, and agree to make us or our kingdom subject to the King of England or the English, we should exert ourselves at once to drive him out as our enemy and a subverter of his own rights and ours, and make some other man who was well able to defend us our King; for, as long as but a hundred of us remain alive, never will we on any conditions be brought under English rule. It is in truth not for glory, nor riches, nor honours that we are fighting, but for freedom – for that alone, which no honest man gives up but with life itself.

The extraordinary ramifications had been felt down the centuries, inspiring other great political milestones such as the American Declaration of Independence. For in asserting the right to remove their monarch if he sold them out, the Scots were effectively the first in European history formally to question the divine right of kings – and, by implication, the 'divine right' of anyone else to use God as an excuse to violate their freedom. It was a blow against fundamentalism centuries before the Enlightenment.

These days the abbey where the paper had been signed was little more than a peaceful ruin. Ironically, having withstood Viking raids and lightning strikes across the centuries, and guided fishermen home with the beacon in its tower, it was eventually dismantled by parishioners who used it as a quarry for their own building projects. Who knows, perhaps that was a mark of freedom too?

Walking back towards the harbour through the town's narrow streets, I passed a palm reader asking '£5 for 10 minutes' and a rotund fellow doing a brisk trade in inflatable claymores. On the quayside hundreds of spectators were watching a re-enactment of a fisherman's wedding by a local drama group: buxom fishwives in tartan shawls and frilly headgear danced to fiddle music with chimney sweeps and men in top hats. It all ended with the singing of 'Auld Lang Syne' – that riotous, teary, exultant hymn to communal memory. Having taken one set of traditions to pieces, it seemed, the people weren't about to lose their nautical heritage too.

On the far side of the harbour, I kept my eye on an elegant black herring drifter with terracotta sails hung on yards as thick as tree trunks. The *Reaper*, a hundred-year-old floating museum staffed by volunteers in red neckerchiefs and fishing jerseys, was due to sail to Fife that evening – hopefully carrying an itinerant writer with her.

I had slept in her low-beamed hold the previous night, amid fish compartments draped with old nets and lanterns and compasses and fish shovels and sepia photographs of other 'Fifies' racing back to harbour. It felt like another world, centuries away from the vast grey factory boat of progress. My favourite exhibit was a sort of nautical plumb line carrying a lead weight the size of an orange. In the days before you could track shoals on sonar screens, a 'wireman' would lower it over the bows towards the sea bed as a low-tech fish detector, while the skipper navigated slowly through the fishing grounds. A good wireman would sense a shoal, even its size and density, from the thrumming of the line in his palm as a thousand fish brushed past it many fathoms below. Then it was just a matter of turning the boat round and casting the nets. They called it the Feeling Wire.

I thought of it as we navigated south later that night, seemingly guided by ancient male intuition. 'We've got a chart below, but we don't really need to look at it,' explained Tom Gardner, who, at seventy-one, was one of a roster of venerable ex-fishermen equipped to pilot this 20-metre relic to nautical festivals around Britain. 'It just comes back to you from all those years at sea. One year we sailed from Portsoy to Anstruther in the fog with no problem at all.'

We chuntered on through the luminous night, enjoying the unseasonably mild air, crossing the wide Tay estuary, watching Fife Ness looming to starboard. It was past midnight when the lights of Anstruther appeared, signalling our first landfall within the Firth of Forth. I was into the home strait.

'Where is it you're going next?' asked Tom, clambering into the cubbyhole underneath mine, after we had tied up at the quayside.

'Depends what rides I can get. But I'm hoping to get to Largo to learn about Robinson Crusoe.' There was a silence, in which I could hear only quiet plopping and lapping on the outside of the ship.

'Aye, weel,' said Tom, digging out his hearing aid for the night. 'If you play your cards right, we might even give you a lift doon there ourselves.'

The mouth of the Forth Estuary was too wide to see much more than the hint of a far shoreline, but the Isle of May foamed with surf in the middle distance, bathed in morning sunlight. 'If the sea's breaking on the north end of May, we know it's going to be a bit lumpy when we go out,' said Coull happily, scrambling about the deck in a manner not normally associated with an octogenarian. He cast off anyway.

Coull Dees was something of a heritage pin-up in this dignified little fishing village, with its red-roofed shops and houses and cluttered harbour. In the local Fisheries Museum his venerable face grinned from beneath his braided cap on postcards and posters, and he'd been the obvious candidate when the BBC needed an authentic sea dog for a period drama.

Today he was helming *White Wing*, seven years older than he was — a mere 18-foot Fifie, which normally nestled alongside the *Reaper* like a fledgling. 'She's our pride and joy, this boat,' said Tom happily, as Coull steered her towards the harbour entrance. 'There's not many can handle her.'

Outside the sea was choppy and exultant. We passed a bobbing creel buoy flying a Saltire, and steered further away from the rocky shore. Soon church spires drifted across cornfields. The East Neuk of Fife was 'the golden fringe on a beggar's mantle', according to James II. The contrast with the rest of his poverty-stricken kingdom still stood centuries later: the quayside fishing hamlets attracting sleek tourist yachts and rising property prices while the inland mining villages harboured little more than unemployment. Coull pointed out St Monans' village church, where he had found his wife. 'Her father warned her not to marry a fisherman – it's a hard life!'

But Coull's whole lineage lay at sea. He reeled it in for me. 'My mother was a herring gutter . . . My brother went to the fishing, father went to the fishing, grandfather went to the fishing, all my uncles . . . And now I've got two sons at the fishing, and a grandson . . .'

The boat bucked before a wave, and a glittering rainbow of salt spray hung fleetingly in the air, before enveloping us all. Coull chuckled at my flinching reaction, blowing water droplets off the end of his nose. 'We were used to that when we were at sea. We got it all the time out there, full in the face.'

Between us we hauled up the red sail using the old pulleys. The canvas bulged and snapped angrily and the sea foamed around the bow. 'This boat's fleeing, Coull!' chuckled Tom, steering proudly into another faceful of spray as the boat surged forward in the stiff breeze. 'Look at us – two recycled teenagers!'

'Oh aye!' grinned Coull. 'Ye couldnae walk at this speed!'

He handed the tiller to Tom. 'Bilges is needing pumped,' he said suddenly. 'You'll need to take over, unless you want tae see a grown man piss himself.' He scrambled forward to use a bucket wedged in a car tyre by the mast.

Tom laughed and began singing Rod Stewart's 'Sailing'. We bucked through Largo Bay, past a green clam boat, circling slowly, scraping the bottom. 'Ah, she's full of life today!' he said. 'She's enjoying her last sail!'

'Your last sail of the season?'

'Could be our last trip ever. Seems an awful shame – but we're both pretty auld and the museum's no sure they can afford the insurance any more . . .' He gave an apologetic shrug, rheumy-eyed from the wind, or something else. 'I don't know what Coull would do without this boat, right enough. He lives for her.'

Coull scuttled back to the cockpit, peering up at the sails, and Tom fell silent again. Near the shore, oil-coloured shags dipped and dived from the rocks, and in a few minutes we drew level with the village of Lower Largo. We pulled down the sails and motored in to the pier.

'I don't know how our forefathers did this with no engine,' said Tom, shaking his head. 'They must have been great men.'

'Naw, they just threw a barrel in to stop the boat hitting the pier,' said Coull, as we came gently alongside. 'Anstruther harbour was full of broken barrel staves!'

I offered them lunch and a drink at the local pub, but Coull didn't want to risk leaving the boat in choppy seas. I shook each man's hand gratefully, thinking of the Feeling Wire, that instinctive thrumming of life in the palm. How long would it be before the living connection finally broke, and canny old fishermen lived on only in museums?

40

The Real Robinson Crusoe

Lower Largo

I took a room in the Crusoe Hotel overlooking chimney pots and a rectangle of sea. At reception all the keys had carved wooden fobs with themed names: Clipper's Cabin, The Stockade, Cannibals' Cauldron. Mine was The Lonely Castaway.

'It's a marketing person's dream!' said Stuart, the manager, who had just taken over the hotel. 'The original castaway, born here, sailing in this very harbour, right under our noses! And yet we don't know what to do with it! There's barely a road sign! If it was in America we'd have a theme park or something . . .'

I found Largo's reticent local hero in a side street: a life-sized bronze statue of a man dressed in goatskins, staring towards the sea. He carried a flintlock and a sword, and bore the kind of sun-blasted expression that suggests either a visionary or some-one barely holding on to his marbles. A plaque, set below the statue in the alcoved front wall of a private terraced house, read:

In memory of Alexander Selkirk, mariner, the original of
Robinson Crusoe, who lived on the island of Juan Fernandez in
complete solitude for four years and four months. He died 1723
Lieutenant of HMS Weymouth aged 47 years.

It was a sparse sort of epitaph for the birthplace of an international legend, and the date was wrong – he had actually died in
1721. It was probably the least of the discrepancies between the
myth and reality. While Daniel Defoe cast his eponymous eighteenth-century hero as a kind of self-improving survivalist,
Selkirk was cut from rougher cloth. He had run away to sea in
the first place to escape a summons by the church elders for
brawling with his own family, and quickly embraced the life of
a privateer, plundering foreign ships in a kind of legalised
piracy.

While Crusoe's trading ship was torn apart in a storm,
Selkirk actually demanded to be put ashore after an argument
with the captain of his ship. He believed (correctly, as it turned
out) that *Cinque Ports* was riddled with shipworm and would
soon sink, and told Captain Thomas Stradling he would sooner
take his chances on the craggy island than risk another day on
board. The captain took him at his word, and in 1704 had him
dropped on the uninhabited Isla Juan Fernandez with only a
trunk, a musket, a pound of powder and a Bible. An apocryphal
story has it that, as his fellow seamen rowed away from the
beach, he ran flailing into the surf yelling that he had changed
his mind.

'Well, I have not changed mine!' bellowed Stradling. They were
to be the last words he heard from another human for fifty-two
months. It took the stranded mariner eighteen of those to come to
terms with the enormity of his isolation, suffering from depres-

sion, a plague of rats and the haunting calls of sea lions, which he mistook for sea monsters.

Gradually, however, he trained feral cats to keep the rodent population at bay, chased goats for food and recreation and drew inner comfort from his ship's Bible. The British crew of HMS *Duke*, finally coming to his rescue in 1709, found a wild, inarticulate man dressed in goatskins and so athletically fit that he could outrun the ship's bulldog.

Back in London a few months later, he had regained his powers of speech fully enough to romanticise his isolation, telling journalists: 'I am now worth £800, but I shall never be so happy as when I was not worth a farthing.' As if to prove the point, the celebrity castaway returned quickly to his dissolute ways, married two women at once and eventually fled back to sea, where he died horribly from yellow fever.

Defoe, meanwhile, was more reluctant to give up the island idyll. Hearing Selkirk's tale, and weaving in material from various other castaway accounts, he had gone to work on what would become his most enduring fantasy. And it *was* mainly fantasy, as I had discovered a few years previously when I had the chance to visit the true island, 400 miles west of the coast of Chile.

Even from a distance, the renamed Isla Robinson Crusoe hadn't looked quite right. Its peaks were more jagged and menacing than they should have been, the widescreen skies clogged with bruising cloud. It definitely needed more palm trees.

For two queasy days aboard a naval supply ship from Valparaiso, dozens of us had dreamed of a simpler life of solitary footprints in infinite white sand. Pulling into the wide bay, however, we found ourselves gazing across a beach of black volcanic boulders to a line of satellite dishes sprouting on the foreshore. A cluster of low-roofed prefabricated buildings surrounded a muddy square. 'So this is paradise?' asked a Chilean hippie standing next to me at the rail.

The island's police chief seemed to think so. 'We don't have the usual problems of juvenile delinquency, robbery, drugs or alcoholism,' he told us proudly, polishing the chrome on his white four-wheel drive. 'Well, not *much* alcoholism.'

Among the 500 residents there were less positive voices – like the park warden we met while climbing the path to Selkirk's lonely lookout point, 1800 metres above the sea. 'The little vermin are ruining the island,' he said, carrying a gun and four dead rabbits.

With more than one hundred plant species found nowhere else in the world, the four-million-year-old island was protected by Unesco as a Worldwide Reserve of the Biosphere, though nobody seemed to have told the rabbits. Goats and common blackberry bushes were a growing problem too. Not to mention tourists.

'To be honest, life was more beautiful without them,' growled a fisherman. 'Now many people come here in the summer, bringing bad habits, marijuana, other things ...' It was, like most islands, a microcosm of modern society, a kind of crucible in which humanity's virtues and imperfections were magnified and played out.

Most commonly cast as serpent in paradise was the island meteorologist, who, in a fit of altruism, had installed the first televisions. 'Many people say that in the old days there was more solidarity, the people did more sport, and they think that it is the TV which has changed all this,' he said sadly. 'But I don't think that's true. I think what has happened is that the people now have more opportunity to buy things and have therefore become a little more consumerist. They don't need to ask their neighbours for anything because they already have it in their own home.'

Meanwhile, the lobsters on which the island economy virtually depended were growing scarcer by the year, and tourism was the only obvious industry to take its place. But tourism brought change, weakened the links between islanders. There was no going back to the Garden, if it had ever existed.

That was the trouble with the search for simplicity. As Selkirk knew, it was never quite as simple as you thought.

Wandering back through Lower Largo, I checked out the handful of vessels in the harbour, beached at low tide in the shadow of a viaduct spanning the village. I had one thing in common with both Selkirk and Crusoe: I needed a lift home.

The hotel manager didn't rate my chances very highly: Ronnie the creeler wouldn't venture out of the bay, and Robert the fisherman was away on business. The only suitable boat – a gleaming white twin-engined powerboat – was out of action due to her skipper's ankle injury. As the September sun cooled towards autumn, the sea was looking lonelier by the day. Many boats would soon be winched out for winter storage. My options were retreating as surely as the tide.

I slunk back to my room for the night with a borrowed copy of *Robinson Crusoe*. It had been years since I'd read it properly and had forgotten what an infuriatingly pious work it was, shot through with references to biblical runaways like Jonah, and conceived as a kind of modern parable of the Prodigal Son. The traveller as fugitive – running away like most of us were, in one way or another. Crusoe's escape was prefaced with a warning from his bewildered father about the comfortable life he was sacrificing. It read as a sort of middle-class manifesto:

> Temperance, moderation, quietness, health, society, all agreeable
> diversions, and all desirable pleasures, were the blessings attending
> the middle station of life; ... this way men went silently and
> smoothly through the world, and comfortably out of it, not
> embarrassed with the labours of the hands or of the head, not
> sold to a life of slavery for daily bread, nor harassed with perplexed
> circumstances, which rob the soul of peace and the body of rest,
> nor enraged with the passion of envy, or the secret burning lust of
> ambition for great things.

He made it sound as if the whole point of being alive was to have
it hurt as little as possible. But I didn't want to go 'silently and
smoothly through the world'. It seemed less a prescription for happiness than a sort of anaesthetic.

Unsurprisingly, the red-blooded young Crusoe ignored the advice,
and set off on his travels, though dogged by guilt and sudden bouts
of repentance whenever anything went wrong. Once thrown up,
Jonah-like, upon the shore of his island, he lived in fear of attack by
cannibals, and with recurring bouts of illness, until a nightmarish
vision of God terrified him into submission: 'Seeing all these things
have not brought thee to repentance, now thou shalt die.'

Thereafter, he seemed to work diligently to turn his island into
precisely the sort of 'middle station' his father might have approved
of: he put up shelves in his corral, built a 'country house' and a 'sea
coast house' between which he took holidays from his goat rearing
and corn planting.

> I had nothing to covet, for I had all that I was now capable of
> enjoying; I was lord of the whole manor; or, if I pleased, I might
> call myself king or emperor over the whole country which I had
> possession of: there were no rivals.

I knew how it would all end. Now that Crusoe had tamed his own life and landscape, Man Friday would turn up to satisfy that last desire of Victorian colonials — to instruct the natives in how to tame theirs.

Feeling suddenly weary, I shut the book and turned off the light.

41

Marooned in Fife

Largo to Kinghorn

'You could always try walking along the beach,' suggested the wait-ress as I fretted over my breakfast smokie the following morning. 'Maybe you'll get a lift further up the coast.' I pondered this for a moment. It was certainly what Crusoe or Selkirk would have done, pacing out their island in search of a sail. It wasn't going to get me home, but at least I would be moving in the right direction.

It was a long, straight, golden beach, almost deserted apart from a dog walker a mile or so ahead. I walked with the quiet urgency of a castaway, conscious of my solitary footprints behind me, enjoy-ing the crack of razor clam shells underfoot. The dunes blew out little skirmishes of sand.

Fife's golden fringe was getting tatty by the time I reached Leven. Once a thriving linen centre and coal port along with neighbouring Methil, it now poked the gun barrel of its defunct power station chimney accusingly at the heavens. The prom was deserted and the local amusement arcade was blockaded with steel shutters. A sign read *Pleasureland*. There were four cars in the adjoining car park, inside which elderly folk were drinking tea out of Thermos flasks, and staring at the sea. One man stopped chewing his banana in panic as I looked at him. On the other side of the car park, three youths in a Fiesta scowled from beneath their baseball caps, their stereo thudding like a war drum. The engine revved as I walked by, and they squealed out into the road. Rubbish eddied in circles.

What was it that sucked the heart out of such places? I could feel myself shrinking like the pensioner in his car. The beach disappeared into concrete piling and I turned briefly inland, trying to cut past the abandoned power station, where trains sat in nests of long grass threaded through rusty tracks. I walked through pebble-dashed council estates, trying to keep sight of the sea by following the towering scaffold of a half-built oil rig out in the Firth. In truth, I felt more at risk in this urban wasteland than on the water itself. The sea had come to represent safety to me – a place where people pulled together in order to stay afloat. I longed for its enforced community. Instead I hurried past a group of teenagers, caught a snatch of muttered expletives, and spent several nervous moments imagining my own mugging. In reality, when I stopped to listen, they were trying to help me: 'If you shin over the fence there's a short cut, pal!'

Robinson Crusoe would have sympathised. He had spent years in nervous anxiety over a footprint in the sand, building bigger and bigger stockades in front of his camouflaged den, before he actually met one of the 'wretched creatures' he so feared, and discovered he had a friend. That was the problem with fear. It was sometimes hard to tell when it was protecting you and when it was preventing you from moving forward.

I wandered along the coastal path, past fields and abandoned mines, all the time watching the far-off Lothian shore creeping closer in the corner of my eye. I passed straight through the villages of East and West Wemyss, where starched white laundry flapped in the gardens like flags of surrender, and finally discovered a fisherman at Dysart. He laughed when I enquired about a possible lift, pointing to the little harbour: the tide was out. I blushed and kept walking.

The town of Kirkcaldy had the mixed honour of being the birthplace of both Michael Nairn, father of the linoleum floor trade, and Adam Smith, father of market capitalism. On balance it seemed prouder of linoleum, which at least merited a plaque. There was a story going round that the left-wing council had removed all references to Smith, embarrassed that their town could have spawned *Wealth of Nations* and perhaps thereby, eventually, Margaret Thatcher.

Like Fort William, the town had been designed with its arse to the sea, offering only the back entrances of box-like discount stores and four lanes of busy highway to anyone who fancied walking along the esplanade. I was limping by the time I made it to the far end of its long ribbon of beach. I had walked nearly 15 miles and hadn't seen a single suitable boat, only occasional oil tankers gliding past, with smaller white launches ferrying pilots to and fro. I decided to cut my losses, abandon hope of a lift that night and head for Kinghorn. I asked an elderly couple for directions, and basked in their friendly banter. This was what I had loved about the last four months – the excuse to ask people for lifts and favours and directions and experience their pleasure in giving them. The encounter warmed me for the next hour as I walked round the promontory, past a caravan park and on to the deep cut of Kinghorn beach. Finally, at the top of a long flight of steps, I checked into a cliff-top B&B endowed with old books, fogged tropical fish and a glorious sea view.

It was a tantalising place to stop for the night. The darkening sky was streaked with crimson clouds which seemed to point down to the opposite shore like neon signs. The familiar silhouettes of Edinburgh brought a lump to my throat — the lit-up castle rock, the vast tilted lid of Arthur's Seat, the pointed steeples of churches now struggling to break the skyline. The Forth was only 5 miles wide here, and with powerful binoculars I could have looked into the bedroom of our empty new house, perched above Newhaven harbour. I phoned Ali to tell her where I was, and we talked about romantic dinners and a long-overdue homecoming, planned to go to a gig with friends the following night. Home carried such freight after all this weightlessness. It meant a determined rooting, the very opposite of getting up and setting sail. It was a commitment to a certain place, perhaps a particular life — a determination to become a part of a land that wasn't my own. Yet I was almost ready for it now, this meshing of new and old.

All I needed was one last boat.

42

Long Green Tentacles

Kinghorn to Edinburgh

'There's no doubt that we *need* incomers,' said Alastair McIntosh the next morning, sitting in his armchair before a vast wall of books. 'The challenge is how to draw in the right *sort* of incomer.'

I had dropped in on the only person I knew in Kinghorn to ask for some homecoming advice and a lift back across the Forth. So far we were majoring on the advice. Alastair was himself half-English, but grew up on the island of Lewis, where he was waging an environmental battle to prevent a superquarry from scarring the island. He was something of a media figure, travelling all over the world campaigning, yet still saw Scotland unequivocally, passionately, as *home*. I wanted some lessons in how to belong.

'A person belongs in as much as they're willing to cherish and be cherished by a place and the complexity of its people. Are you willing to become part of the community?'

He made it sound like a marriage vow. 'I think so — but how exactly do you cherish a community?'

'You need long, green sensitive tentacles,' he grinned from behind his gingery beard. 'Listen, ask, seek permission, seek blessing, confess where you're coming from, and enquire what the issues are.' Incomer wasn't automatically a dirty word. In fact, he said, there were three sorts of incomer in the Celtic tradition: the intruder, the guest and then the fostered incomer. I liked the idea of being fostered.

'There's a Celtic saying: *The bonds of milk are stronger than the bonds of blood.* You will come to be accepted, but it could take two or three decades, and if that's too long for you then you need to question whether you should be there.'

'Three *decades*?'

The doorbell rang and Alastair's friend Ronnie arrived. 'I don't look at it as an issue of incomers,' he said, throwing in his own contribution to the debate on the doorstep. 'I think there are people who are sensitive and people who aren't. It doesn't matter where they come from.' As if to prove it, he offered me a lift across the Forth in his yacht.

Alastair helped me down the steps with my rucksack. 'In the end it's about being real,' he concluded. 'We're not interested in unreality, posturing. You'll hear Glaswegians say that all the time: "Get real!" Get rid of that stiff upper lip – Scots don't give a damn who you are as long as you're honest about it.'

The shadows of clouds were sweeping across the Forth as I clambered into Ronnie's VW campervan. He looked anxious. 'I'll be honest with you if it's going to be too rough to go – she's only a wee yacht. I'll let you know when we get down to the harbour.'

Kinghorn folk had deep-seated and historic reasons for believing it was better to be safe than sorry. Alexander III, last of the Celtic kings, was so keen to get back from Edinburgh to his new bride in Fife in 1286 that he ignored his boatmen's weather warnings. He survived a stormy trip across the Forth only to be thrown

to his death from his horse in foul weather, at a place now marked
by a dour memorial on the cliff road. His three-year-old daughter
was declared queen, but died a few years later before she'd even set
foot in mainland Scotland, after her own stormy crossing from
Norway to Orkney. All of which severed the royal line, ended the
Scots' golden age and ushered in the wars of independence and all
that followed. It was what you might call a costly mistake, and
Ronnie wasn't about re-enact it.

'I don't like the look of that wind,' he said, peering across the
harbour at his little blue boat pitching on her moorings. Around
her other boats bucked and dipped restlessly, their halyards ping-
ing against the masts like cowbells. 'I think we'd better not chance
it today.'

He looked genuinely disappointed. I grinned reassuringly at
him as I sat in the back of the van, trying to work out what to do
next. It wasn't as if it was the first time I'd had to revise my plans.
Indeed, the whole summer had been a kind of exercise in contingency planning, letting go of one kind of solution in order to
find another. I had blagged, begged and befriended my way
aboard every conceivable sort of boat: barge, yacht, rowing boat,
square rigger, speedboat, narrowboat, fishing trawler, submarine,
cargo boat, ferry, cabin cruiser, inflatable, steamer, catamaran, tri-
maran, lifeboat, lightship, kayak, curragh . . . I had totted them all
up the previous evening, tracing the journey back across my now
crumpled map: nearly 2500 meandering miles full of chance
encounters and impromptu friendships. So what was one more
delay? One more opportunity to practise patience and let go . . .
And yet today it felt wrong to be sitting around waiting, just 5
miles from home.

Further up the Forth I could see a black oil tanker, barely
moving in the swell, while a little white pilot boat sent plumes

of spray into the air. 'Shame you can't get a lift on one of those,' said Ronnie. 'Pilot boats go out in anything.'

I stared at him for a moment, then fished out my mobile. It was probably worth a stab. I called Forth Ports, and got passed around between baffled sounding officials in various departments. After two stony responses about 'passenger insurance problems', I was beginning to think King Alexander's legacy had affected everybody. Finally, however, I dialled a number which got me through to the pilot boats' superintendent. He sounded like he was standing in a wind tunnel.

'Funny you should call,' said the voice, after I explained my predicament. 'But I'm at Brae Head oil terminal just now, about two miles from Burntisland, waiting to be picked up and taken back across . . .' There was a ruffle of wind. '— we'll be with you in half an hour.'

Ronnie laughed, shaking his head at this English chancer. 'That's the fastest taxi I've ever seen.' He ran me round the docks to meet the pilot boat. As it rumbled into the harbour, he put a hand on my shoulder and slipped me a paper bag. 'I was going to share this with you when we got to the other side,' he said. 'Take it with you as a keepsake.'

I was grinning from ear to ear as I clambered aboard the *Panther*. All set for a final sousing in my wet-weather gear, I found the pilot was in a T-shirt. 'Lovely day for a sail,' he breezed. We tore out of the harbour, bouncing on springy leather seats as the sea flung buckets at the windscreen.

And that was it. The final link in a wide and lopsided circle. Not quite a full circle, as it turned out, returning to a new home on Edinburgh's sea-facing side. But don't most worthwhile journeys bring you back to a different place, one way or another?

Looking back at the waving figure on the dockside – last in a chain of generous strangers – I remembered the bag in my water-proof pocket. Feeling inside, I pulled out a bottle of Laphroaig Single Malt.

I smiled and watched the growing blur of home.

Epilogue

Newhaven

'What has religion ever done for us?' says Jack, squinting over the Firth of Forth. 'Wars? Inquisitions? Crusades? And now all these bloody fundamentalists blowing each other up. You want to know how to save the world? Get rid of religion.'

It's a flawless Friday afternoon — amber sunlight, plumped-up clouds, a warm wind rippling the waters — perfect for a spot of philosophising aboard Ernie's wee sloop *Decantae*. It's the second time I've crewed for Jack and Ernie, the one a retired police chief and the other a telephone engineer I met at the local yacht club. So far we've bantered our way through the tribulations of gout, the regional bias of Channel Five newsreaders, the price of the new luxury flats in the docklands. Now, with the ruined abbey on Inchcolm Island growing on the horizon, religion is getting its ritual kicking. It beats staying in and finishing my book.

Ernie grins nervously, in case I'm easily offended. But actually, I don't think Jack's sweeping recommendations go far enough. Sure, if you got rid of religion you'd avoid the Inquisition and the Crusades, not to mention suicide bombers and George Bush, which has to be a bonus. But what about Hitler, Pol Pot, Stalin? Curiously, atheists seemed to slip through Jack's net.

'Surely dogma's the problem, not just religion,' I venture from the cockpit. 'After all, you get some pretty fundamentalist anti-fundamentalists. Maybe it's certainty itself that's ruining the world?'

'Aye, maybe,' growls Jack. 'But keep your eye on the wind. Your jib's backing.'

My outlook has changed since my homecoming. I no longer get my daily glimpse of the canal, with its reassuring strip of mirrored sky, its mathematical waves. Instead, there's the infinitely changing sea, glimmering over red rooftops. Frosted, smooth, serrated, languid, sky-blue or platinum-grey, rain-pocked or dissected by an oily line of arbitrary wind. At times it's as still as glass, sucking gently at the breakwater, the next day wild and jagged-toothed, slavering around the harbour walls. Sometimes the sun lights Fife like the promised land across the Jordan. Sometimes the sea mist rolls silently up the estuary and there's nothing but the blank, ragged edge of the universe.

I had hoped I might have worked out what I believed by now. I've been writing and rewriting this for months, trying to make the bits join up properly, trying to synthesise some grand, ingenious credo from all those philosophies and chewy little aphorisms: *I believe in the mystery of momentum . . . I believe in the buoyancy of the human soul . . .* But more often I find myself thinking fondly of the people I met, back in their ordinary and not-so-ordinary worlds. I looked up George Parsonage recently, still saving lives and winning medals on the Clyde, despite an onslaught of health and safety memos – though he recently managed a two-week break in Sardinia. The last I heard of Captain Calamity he was selling art on the internet and campaigning to have Shetland made semi-autonomous. I've stayed in touch with Machig too, taken her Buddhist meditation class, learning to still the mind. Meanwhile, Mike Shipley's cancer finally got the better of him. His family gave him the sea burial he would

have wanted, attended by his beloved *Shetland Trader*. More unexpected was the recent death of Colin Macleod, Galgael's
boatman of the Clyde, from a suspected heart attack. He was only
39. Several hundred mourners blocked the Govan traffic as they
bore their chieftain through the streets, and sent him back to his
beloved islands in a carved wooden coffin. His abiding strength,
agreed the eulogies, was that he 'dared to believe'.

There was a time, not long after I got home, when I thought my
faith had gone for good. It was more peaceful than I expected –
almost a relief – like looking down on the wet mud of an empty
harbour after the tide had gone out. But then, helping a friend
through a crisis, I found the inexplicable *something* seeping back
again, lifting the boats, lapping at the stonework. I've noticed it
many times since, at unguarded moments: chatting with Ali in the
garden, standing empty-handed in a church service, sitting quietly
in a chair. I'm learning to let go and stop trying to force myself to
believe things, stop trying to understand it all – or at least trying
to stop trying.

Down at Newhaven harbour there's an old church and a little
white lighthouse, each erected in its time to guide storm-tossed
souls back to safety, each looking pretty redundant now. The
church closed years ago, sold as an indoor climbing centre where
adventurous folk learn to trust each other and challenge their fears
(arguably what churches were for in the first place). The lighthouse, once a beacon for herring drifters racing back to market,
now illuminates mainly itself. But there's still one working fishing
boat. I watch the crewmen laying creels sometimes, through the
windows of the new health club in the old docks, where I walk
towards the horizon on an electric treadmill.

It would be easy to turn that into some kind of symbol – the
separation of tradition and modernity, or the rootlessness of

urban life, or something like that. But I'm learning to resist the easy categories, feeling my way into this new life. Even the patron saint of wanderlust turns out to have had a rather more nuanced and leisurely ending than his gothic legend implied. My latest research reveals that the real Cormac of the Sea actually spent his last *twenty years* – 'the happiest period in his stormy life' – ministering to the needy from his tower back home in Ireland. True, he died after being savaged by wolves, probably only after disturbing them on a stroll in the woods – but we've all got to die somehow. The morphing snails, the incessant terror, the prophecy – all were embroidered posthumously, like all great folk myths, to give some sort of answer to the question *why*.

It's our gift and our curse to want to understand things fully, of course. Today it's the tide which has me mesmerised once again, the whole estuary sliding eastwards towards the open sea. For Ernie, it's essentially a maths problem, consulting the tide tables, getting a sense of the flow, aiming off to get where we want to go. He thinks it's high time I stopped relying on other people's navigation skills and learned to work it all out myself. But if any of us stopped to think what is *really* happening when the tide goes out – think of the vast continents of water on opposite sides of the planet bulging outwards under the centrifuge of the spinning earth and the gravitational pull of the moon, both of them hurtling through space – would we not lash ourselves to the mast in awe?

Leonardo da Vinci set out to understand water. It was part scientific quest, part phobia. He had seen the River Arno burst its banks and wanted to pin down this elusive, destructive, creative substance of life. His notebooks were full of sketches of swirling eddies, apocalyptic floods and great storms, along with various devices to control or divert them: canals and lock gates, a street-washing system, plans for draining a marsh. His aim was as all-embracing as you'd expect from Leonardo: 'Describe all the forms taken by water from its greatest to its smallest wave, and their causes.'

More than five centuries later, water remains an enigma. We do, of course, know a little more than Leonardo about its iconic triptych of oxygen flanked by two hydrogen atoms. Under an electron microscope the anarchic moshing of its molecules reveals itself to be a force for transformation – coaxing and fostering reactions from other chemicals, making connections between things. Yet we can't really explain *why*. Scientists admit there is, as yet, no universal theory of water, or even a master equation for all its properties. Despite wave tanks and test labs and all the successors to Leonardo's whorled sketches, we still have no idea why a raindrop will sometimes slalom down a perfectly smooth car window – why whirlpools blort and eddy as erratically as they do. We don't know why our eyes leak tears when we're sad.

As elusive as love, as ordinary and as magical as the boiling of a kettle – that miraculous conversion of agitated molecules taking flight and becoming almost air. Water was the formless chaos from which all creation was brought forth, whether by the Holy Spirit brooding over the watery wastes or *Homo sapiens* evolving from the primeval soup. We think we know water, and yet the deepest oceans of our blue planet are scarcely more familiar to us now than in the age when maps were etched with sea monsters. We know more about the surfaces of Mars and Venus than the bottom of certain Scottish lochs.

The water of life. It protects us in our mothers' wombs, makes up 80 per cent of our bodies, mists us with the aura of its presence in every breath we take. Perhaps that's the best we can say about our quest for a higher meaning, whatever that may be. In the end it's as simple and as complex as water. We yearn for it, we fear it, we *are* it.

*

'Look at that bloody great seal!'

The colossus in question is sunbathing on the tilted platform of the channel buoy. It opens one eye at our passing and slides off into the water with a disgruntled snort. 'You didn't see seals much for years,' says Ernie. 'Now there's plenty of them. The water's getting cleaner, the fish are coming back to the estuary, and the seals are following the fish.'

A big tanker, full of gas pipes like an organ, is turning in a slow circle in front of us, pulled by a tug. I steer away from its wash, and the sail starts flapping. 'Try not to go offwind before you're due to go about,' says Jack. 'Otherwise you'll lose momentum and you won't have enough speed to make the turn, you'll end up being blown off course.'

The tide is strong around the end of Inchcolm Island, and I'm trying to get that sailor's sense of trajectory, that intuition for the bigger picture. Despite all my travellings, it's the first time I've actually had to helm a boat in the complex cross-currents of tidal waters.

'What do you think?' I ask Ernie, setting the tiller with as much confidence as I can muster. 'Is that about right?'

Ernie pours himself another gin. 'What's the tide doing?'

I scan the turbulence ahead, log the little eddies and ripples suggesting underwater rocks, the wind patterns warning me of sudden gusts . . . *As simple and as complex as water.* I check the chart, nudge the tiller for some more clearance, and in that moment I am glowing, alive with adrenalin, entirely present.

'I'm going to steer to starboard of the buoy,' I say, thinking aloud. 'Leave myself room to turn downwind if I need to, use the tide rather than fight it . . . what do you think?'

'You're the skipper,' says Ernie with a gentle smile. 'You decide.'

Acknowledgements

After a journey almost entirely reliant on the generosity of other people, I could write a bookful of acknowledgments. In a sense, I already have. If you recognised yourself in the preceding pages (despite the occasional pseudonym) I'd like to thank you once again for picking up this Sassenach boat-hitcher and sharing stories, passions and sandwiches at the helm. (And if I've chronicled moments you might prefer to have forgotten, I hope you'll take it in the affectionate spirit intended.) But since many who helped me are not mentioned in the narrative, I'm going to attempt the full role call of honour here:

Lowlands: Bill and Sandra Purves, Edith, Tony, Derek, Tom and others at the ECS for those early forays in *Kelvin;* Craig and Kaos in *Armorica* and Norman Foulner at Thistle Hire Boats; Don, Abbie, Carl, Tracey on *Zeepaard,* and those cheery, determined people from British Waterways; Jez, Monisha and Susan for pure Glaswegian hospitality; George Parsonage and Stephanie; 'Jamie' for letting rip on that guitar; Gehan Macleod and the kids for a meal and a bed at short notice — and with profound condolences for the death of Colin, whose memory will always inspire; Gregor Connelly at Seaforce for speed and a lead; HM Naval Base, Faslane; Hoosie, Scott, Wheels and Graeme at the Peace Camp for herbal tea and sympathy; Kenny McNeill and the *Menno* crew; whiteknuckle Darren and his brother Cameron; Nigel and Andrina for an energetic hitch to Crinan.

Western Isles: the Jenkin and Bendell clans for welcoming a gate-crasher on their island holiday; Nick Walker and crew of the *Vic32*; Michael Murray on *Gemini*; Donald, Robin, Peter and all aboard *Colmcille* for so graciously accommodating an apostate; Davie Kirkpatrick aboard the *Iolaire*; Nancy McChesney for befriending a workaholic, and John, Jemma, Shane and Daniel on the *JDL* for cheerfully knocking off his corners; Ken, Pete and Tina at Sea Kayak Scotland for midge initiation.

Highlands and Moray: Don McGregor, Yevgeny and Alexander at the Underwater Centre; Iain MacKay aboard the *Eala Bhan*; Professor Adrian Shine; Caley Cruisers in Inverness; 'Julie' and 'Dave' for that unforgettable day in '*Water Vole*'; Rita, Helga-Marina, Agnes and Machig for adoption into the Findhorn sisterhood; David Byatt and the crew of the Moray Gig; Vernon Carey in Lossiemouth; Colin and Adam Main on *Clarness* and *Shaligar*; Jim Forman; Albert in Fraserburgh harbourmaster's office; Carol Macdonald and Morag Ritchie; David and George West and clan for *Resolute* hospitality amid teething troubles; Captain Ash and the crew of the *Shetland Trader* – and the late Mike Shipley for a lesson in living every minute.

Northern Isles: Andy Steven at Visit Shetland; Aith Rowing Club and the crew of *Sceptre*; Dr Jonathan Wills on the *Dunter III*, Lerwick harbourmaster Archer T Kemp; Captain Rowan Greenwood and the crew of *Oscar Charlie*; Stuart Hill and Margaret for taking risks; Mike, Ken and Adam aboard *Reverie*; Derek and Holly Shaw at the Fair Isle Bird Observatory; Ian and Lise Best for welcoming a stranger; the Northern Lighthouse Board; Captain Tom Moffat and the crew of the *Pharos*; Calum Falconer; Angus and Yvonne Hutchison; Keith Bichan at Roving Eye enterprises; Sarah and John Welburn and Jane Dunn; Len Wilson and Ally and the beautiful *Gremsa*, so resplendent on the front cover.

East Coast: Hamish McDonald and crew at Maritime Rescue. International and Mike Lowson for the timely tip-off, Peter and Steven Morrison on the *Vivid*; the mysterious man in *Montrose* harbour office who put me in touch with Jeremy Taylor on *Tudor Quest*; David Tod on *Braveheart* and Jim Main for setting up my *Reaper* rendezvous; Tom and Coull and their volunteer crewmates for a sail back in time, and Joan Paton for the female perspective; Alastair McIntosh for hospitality, introductions and a lifechanging book; Ronnie Mackay for a parting gift; Ernie, Jack, Willie and others at Forth Corinthian Yacht Club; and Tiso's in Edinburgh for equipping me so generously for a long, watery voyage.

The book itself has had an equally eventful journey to the one it describes. It only happened at all thanks to the enthusiasm of my agent Giles Gordon, whose untimely death meant he never saw the result, and the dedication of his successor, Camilla Hornby. To my patient editor Tim Whiting at Time Warner Books fell the task of taming the leviathan of my first draft and sending it back to me for some radical slimming. Thanks too to Tamsyn Berryman for crucial barnacle-removal. I'm also grateful to Mike Wade, Adrian Turpin and Claire Prentice at the *Sunday Times* in Scotland, who sea-trialed some of my experiences in print, and to Henrik Brandt who gathered the fruits of his excellent photographers. To Robin Connelly, Richard Medrington, Michael Riddell and Marc Marnie I owe a particular debt of thanks for painstaking reading of early drafts and invaluable feedback; and to friends and family bearing timely encouragements: Graham, Janet, Mark, Dan and Han Thorpe; Nick Austin, Phil Buck, Steve and Anne Butler, Angeles Calderon, Paul Chambers, Steve and Alison Goodwin, Stuart Guzinski, Ruth Harvey, Gareth Higgins, Simon Jones, Carole Kinnell, Ken Lawson, Gail McConnell, Will McMillan, Elspeth Murray, Philip and Ali Newell, George and Jan Reiss, Mark

Rickards, Louisa Waugh; Carol, Adam, Ken, and others at CAG. Thanks to the Arvon Foundation and Maralyn McBride for writing retreats with great food, and to Rinchen, Rangjung, Gruva and the others on Holy Isle for inspiration and a good massage during a crucial fortnight. Tom Daly of the Kilcormac Historical Society provided some tantalising new information on the elusive St Cormac, while special thanks are due to Judy Hepburn, Alan Bell and Lisa Clark, Maralyn McBride and Daphne Martin, who shared the trip in an important sense by being there for Ali at a difficult time and making it possible for me to go in the first place.

Finally, my heartfelt gratitude goes to Ali herself: for her patience and passion, for her rigorous close-reading of endless drafts, and for believing in the journey even when she most needed someone reliable to stay at home.

Select Bibliography

St. Adamnan, *Life of St. Columba* trans. Richard Sharpe (Penguin 1995)

Neal Ascherson, *Stone Voices: the Search for Scotland* (Granta 2002)

Philip Ball, *A Biography of Water* (Weidenfeld and Nicolson 1999)

Bella Bathurst, *The Lighthouse Stevensons* (HarperCollins, 1999)

Ian Bradley, *Celtic Christianity: Making Myths and Chasing Dreams* (Edinburgh University Press 1999)

Hamish Brown, *Exploring the Edinburgh to Glasgow Canals* (The Stationery Office, 1997)

George Mackay Brown, *For the Islands I Sing* (John Murray 1997)

Bernard Crick, *George Orwell: A Life* (Penguin 1980)

James D. G. Davidson, *Scots and the Sea* (Mainstream 2003)

Tom Devine, *The Scottish Nation 1700-2000* (Allen Lane 1999)

Owen Dudley Edwards, *Burke and Hare* (Mercat Press 1993)

Ronald Ferguson, *Chasing the Wild Goose: Story of the Iona Community* (Wild Goose Publications 1998)

Hamish Haswell-Smith, *The Scottish Islands* (Canongate 2004)

George Hendry, *Midges in Scotland* (Mercat Press 2003)

Guthrie Hutton, *Scotland's Millennium Canals: the Survival and Revival of the Forth & Clyde and Union Canals* (Stenlake, 2002)

Guthrie Hutton, *The Crinan Canal: Puffers and Paddle Steamers* (Stenlake 1994)

Guthrie Hutton, *Caledonian: the Monster Canal* (Stenlake 1992)

John Keay and Julia Keay, *The Collins Encyclopaedia of Scotland* (HarperCollins 2000)

Brian Lavery, *Historic Scotland: Maritime Scotland* (Historic Scotland 2001)

Dan MacDonald, *The Clyde Puffer* (House of Lochar 1994)

Ken McGoogan, *Fatal Passage* (Bantam 2002)

Alastair McIntosh, *Soil and Soul* (Aurum, 2001)

John Marsden, *Sea-road of the Saints: Celtic Holy Men in the Hebrides* (Floris Books 1995)

Martin Martin, *A Description of the Western Islands of Scotland Circa 1695* (Birlinn 1999)

Alistair Moffat, *The Sea Kingdoms: The History of Celtic Britain and Ireland* (HarperCollins 2002)

Neil Munro, *Para Handy* (Birlinn 1992)

Brian D. Osborne & Ronald Armstrong (ed.), *Echoes of the Sea: Scotland and the Sea* (Canongate, 1998)

George Parsonage, *Rescue His Business, the Clyde his Life* (Glasgow City Libraries 1990)

Denis Rixson, *The West Highland Galley* (Birlinn 1998)

David Rothenberg (ed.), *Writing on Water* (Terra Nova 2001)

June Skinner Sawyers (ed.), *The Road North: 300 years of Classic Scottish Travel Writing* (In Pinn, 2000)

June Skinner Sawyers (ed.), *Dreams of Elsewhere: the Selected Travel Writings of Robert Louis Stevenson* (In Pinn, 2002).

Andrew L Shaw, *The History of Ballyboy, Kilcormac and Killoughy* (Kilcormac Historical Society 1999)

Alex Walker (ed.), *The Kingdom Within: A Guide to the Spiritual Work of the Findhorn Community* (Findhorn Press 1994)

Gordon Wright, *Jura and George Orwell* (1993)